Founders

INNOVATORS IN EDUCATION, 1830–1980

Founders

INNOVATORS IN EDUCATION, 1830–1980

Ernest Stabler

The University of Alberta Press

First published by
The University of Alberta Press
Athabasca Hall
Edmonton, Alberta, Canada
1986

ISBN 0-88864-114-1

Canadian Cataloguing in Publication Data

Stabler, Ernest, 1914–
Founders

Bibliography: p.
ISBN 0-88864-114-1
1. Educators - Biography. 2. Educators - History.
3. Education - Philosophy - History. I. Title.
LA2303.S83 1986 370'.92'2 C86-091443-7

Typesetting by Typeworks, Vancouver, British Columbia, Canada.
Printed by John Deyell Company, Lindsay, Ontario, Canada.

To Ida

CONTENTS

ACKNOWLEDGMENTS

I wish to record my thanks to the Social Sciences and Humanities Research Council of Canada for a two-year research grant which enabled me to make this study. The resulting book has been published with the help of a grant from the Social Science Federation of Canada, using funds provided by the Social Sciences and Humanities Research Council of Canada.

I am deeply grateful to the staffs of the D. B. Weldon Library of the University of Western Ontario, the Main Library of Cambridge University, and to the libraries of St. Francis Xavier University and Mount Holyoke College.

I was graciously received in Denmark by Ebbe Lungaard, Erik Brygmann and Palle Moden, all folk high school principals; by Arne Andresen of the Folk High School Secretariat; and by Vilhelm Nielsen of the Ministry of Education.

My efforts to identify and trace the influence of Kurt Hahn were assisted by Lola Hahn, Peter Carpenter, David Byatt, Freddie Fuller, and David Sutcliffe. Three wardens—Ian Fothergill, Graham Rates, and Wendy Johnson—together with A. R. Johnson of the Outward Bound Trust, brought the Outward Bound movement vividly to life.

At Mount Holyoke College I found the two librarians of the College History Archives, Elaine Trehub and Linda Wendry, extremely cooperative.

Roger Mills was remarkably kind in familiarizing me with Milton Keynes, where the headquarters of the Open University is located.

At St. Francis Xavier University and elsewhere in eastern Nova

Scotia I was assisted by the late George Topshee, former Director of the Extension Department; A. A. MacDonald, Director of the Coady Institute; Daniel MacInnes, of the Sociology Department; Sister Berthold Mackey, Librarian of the Coady Institute; Ellen Arsenault, formerly Dr. Coady's secretary; and two early members of the Co-operative Movement, Peter MacKenzie Campbell and Joseph Laben.

And in Dorothy Knight and the late Henny Vlasman I found those qualities that mark the most able and dedicated secretaries.

I am also indebted to the following publishers for permission to use extracts from the works cited: Allen and Unwin for *Inside the Left* by Fenner Brockway (1942); Basic Books Inc. for *Introduction to Social Movements* by John Wilson (1973); George Braziller Inc. for *Philosophers and Kings* by Dankwort Rustow (1970); Jonathan Cape Ltd. for *My Life with Nye* by Jennie Lee (1980); Danish Institute, Copenhagen, for *The Danish Folk High Schools* by Thomas Rørdam (1980); Harper and Row Publishers Inc. for *Masters of Their Own Destiny* by Moses Coady (1961); Hodder and Stoughton for *The Open University from Within* by John Ferguson (1975) and *Life Is Meeting* by John Hunt (1975); Macmillan for *I'm Radcliffe! Fly Me!: The Seven Sisters and the Failure of Women's Education* by Liva Baker (1976); The Free Press, a Division of Macmillan for *The Theory of Social and Economic Organization* by Max Weber, translated by A. M. Henderson and Talcott Parsons (1947); New York University Press for *Collegiate Women* by Roberta Frankfort (1977); Open University Press for *Open University: A Personal Account* by Walter Perry (1976); Oxford University Press for *The Folk High Schools of Denmark* by Holger Begtrup et al. (1949); Permagon Books Ltd. for *Rural Development and the Changing Countries of the World* by Peter Manniche (1969); Routledge and Kegan Paul for *Kurt Hahn* by Herman Röhrs and H. Turnstall-Behrens (1970); and McMaster University for "Clerics, Fishermen, Farmers and Workers: The Antigonish Movement" by Daniel MacInnes (Ph.D. dissertation, 1978).

INTRODUCTION

This book is a study of six educational innovators, or teams of innovators, whose ideas led to the founding of educational institutions. Their innovations took root, survived, and became a model for institutions in their country of origin. In several instances the institution, with modifications, was transported abroad. Thus my use of the term "innovator in education" is inclusive not only of their ideas but also of the institutions which developed from those ideas. Innovators included in this book are N. F. S. Grundtvig, Mary Lyon, Horace Mann, Moses Coady and James Tompkins, Kurt Hahn, and the group that founded the British Open University.

N. F. S. Grundtvig started the Danish folk high schools, privately owned residential schools which gave a liberal education to young farmers. In Massachusetts, Mary Lyon opened a seminary for young women which became Mount Holyoke College and influenced the development of independent women's colleges. Horace Mann, also of Massachusetts, recognized that the common schools had fallen into moral and physical disrepair and that his state in a period of industrial revolution and immigration needed a well-managed system of public elementary schools. Moses Coady and James Tompkins organized study circles and co-operatives in Nova Scotia among fishermen and farmers through the Extension Department of St. Francis Xavier University. Kurt Hahn founded Salem in Germany and Gordonstoun in Scotland, two secondary schools in which community service, adventure, and physical challenge were part of the curriculum, and from those beginnings came Outward Bound, Atlantic College, and the

Duke of Edinburgh Award schemes. And the British Open University—open in the sense that anyone over the age of twenty-one could apply and earn a quality degree through correspondence—needed the political intelligence of Harold Wilson and Jennie Lee, the administrative skill of Walter Perry, and the sound judgment of Peter Venables in order to become a reality.

Influential as these leaders were, new educational institutions such as those described do not arise solely from the visions of individuals. "Pure" innovation is seldom found in education, and the innovations discussed here were influenced by earlier developments. The Open University did not invent distance education (degree courses through correspondence had been available in Britain for many years), but an open admissions policy, development of a national learning system through correspondence, radio, television, and the tutorial, together with the production of course materials of high quality, resulted in unique combinations of teaching and learning. And Tompkins and Coady were not the first to ignite a self-help movement through adult education. In other words, I have stressed the need to consider forerunners and contemporaries.

Each founder worked in a period of stress in his country, state, or province. A problem demanded attention and a new educational development was seen as part of the solution. A standard of education for young women comparable to that of young men in American colleges, together with strong religious conviction, inspired Mary Lyon; Kurt Hahn wanted education to offer physical challenge, adventure, and service so that youth could escape from "the misery of unimportance" in an industrial society. These stresses, concerns, and problems ranged from social unease to economic crises and are explored in each chapter.

Each chapter deals with a particular innovator or team of innovators, their economic and social environment, and the history of the institutions founded. The innovators themselves helped achieve adoption of their ideas by becoming expert in what we now call public relations. Consequently, their unique personalities cannot be overlooked. As well, they all had an intensity and vitality through which they pursued their mission or "calling." A passion for service, and often religious conviction expressed through great bursts of energy and, frequently, deep depression, colored their lives. All had a profound belief in the power of education to change individual lives and the social and economic structure. These men and women had a charisma that inspired followers with devotion and enthusiasm.

I have chosen these founders largely because they worked in five countries and at different levels of education. Horace Mann was primarily concerned with elementary schools; Kurt Hahn was committed to the adolescent; Mary Lyon was drawn to middle-class women of college age; and Grundtvig, Tompkins and Coady, and the Open University group were involved in the formal and informal education of adults. There are, of course, innovators I have not included. Friedrich Froebel, father of the kindergarten, Maria Montessori, and Rudolf Steiner come to mind. Their ideas and the institutions they founded could be the subject of another study.

ONE

N. F. S. Grundtvig
1783–1872

N. F. S. Grundtvig: The Danish Folk High School

N. F. S. Grundtvig, contemporary drawing by P. C. Skovgaard, 1947, courtesy of the Frederiksborg Museum Copenhagen, Denmark.

N. F. S. Grundtvig's Ideas and Influence

Throughout much of the nineteenth century, Denmark was in a ferment of change. By 1800 Copenhagen had become the centre of a thriving mercantile trade, but this was destroyed when Britain, angry over Denmark's refusal to join it against Napoleon, shelled Copenhagen and in 1807 forced the surrender of the Danish fleet. Denmark's humiliation was complete when it was forced to declare a state of national bankruptcy in 1813 and a year later to cede Norway, which had been a part of Denmark for 400 years, to the King of Sweden. A half-century later Denmark was again humiliated through a military defeat by a Prussian-Austrian army and the transfer to Bismarck of the duchies of Schleswig and Holstein, a loss of two-fifths of Denmark's territory and a third of her population.

Despite these military and political disasters, a fall in agricultural prices, and virtual collapse of the economy after 1815, Denmark adopted a substantial body of liberal legislation. In the last quarter of the eighteenth century a group of landowners influenced by the French Enlightenment introduced a series of reforms which released the Danish peasant from a system of feudal tenure. The peasants gradually became freeholders who changed the face of rural Denmark to a landscape of small farms. In 1814, during the period of national bankruptcy, primary education from the ages of seven to fourteen was made compulsory. Later in the century, local advisory councils drawing their numbers from the nobility, clergy, town dwellers, and the peasantry were established to advise the king. And at mid-century Denmark changed from an absolute to a constitutional monarchy with a bicameral parliament. In moving toward political democracy the Danes spilled no blood, their towns were scarcely touched by the blemishes of the Industrial Revolution, the population remained remarkably homogeneous, and in the second half of the nineteenth century a literate and liberated peasantry was emerging. In short, Denmark was developing the instruments needed to restore self-confidence and recover from a series of humiliating defeats.

The leader of this national regeneration was N. F. S. Grundtvig, who lived from 1783 to 1872. During those nine decades he was of enormous influence in the life of Denmark as a poet and historian, theologian and preacher, politician and philosopher. At university he studied theology but his mind turned more toward history. His *Nordic Mythology* was published in 1808. From original manuscripts in Latin, Old Norse, and Anglo-Saxon he translated ancient myths and sagas and wrote some 1,500 hymns, many of which are still sung in Danish churches. He created the patriotic song as a genre and, as a poet, recited the glories of Danish history. As a politician he was independent of political parties but joined the struggle to preserve Danish culture in the face of strong influences from Germany. As a lecturer and preacher Grundtvig inspired artisans, farmers, scholars, and students. On one occasion when he spoke for an hour and a quarter to an audience of several thousand at an open air meeting in South Jutland, a newspaper report remarked on "the immediate understanding and audible resonance with which every innuendo, even the slightest, was received by the large crowd."[1] Grundtvig helped frame the Danish constitution, adopted in 1849, and in parliamentary debate spoke freely with both wit and strong feeling. In private conversation he was a good listener and in his old age his home was filled wih friends and visitors—farmers, politicians, scholars, and theologians—who sought his advice.

Throughout his life he was attracted to women. As a young man he fell in love with the mother of the children he tutored. During a visit to England an evening's conversation with a doctor's wife influenced him for years afterward. He married three times; his first two wives predeceased him and in 1858 at the age of seventy-five he married again and became a father.

His official memorial is Grundtvig's Kirke in northwest Copenhagen, a modern cathedral modelled on a Danish village church, paid for by national subscriptions and a state subsidy, and constructed between 1921 and 1940. But in Danish hearts Grundtvig's memorials lie in "Grundtvigianism," a movement of liberal Christianity within the Danish Church, and in the folk high schools, which are Scandinavia's most significant contribution to adult education.

Grundtvig's ideas for a residential school for young adults stemmed from his reaction to the two years he spent at a dreary Latin grammar school in Arhus, his experience at university in Copenhagen when his cousin Henrik Steffens inspired him with lectures on the romantic movement, his visits to England—Cambridge in particular—and from his long inner journey from Lutheran orthodoxy to a more liberal Christianity. At his boyhood home in a vicarage in South Zealand, his mother told him stories from the Old Norse sagas and taught him to read. By the age of eight he was reading a *Life of Luther* and throughout his youth accepted his father's Lutheran Christianity, a form of pietism that regarded man as a pilgrim on a penitential journey at the end of which, liberated by death, he could be admitted to the Kingdom. The conflict between this version of Christianity and a more poetic-historical view of the course of human life troubled Grundtvig for many years and contributed to severe emotional and mental breakdowns.

He left home at nine to be tutored in Latin in a parsonage in Jutland and for two years attended the grammar school. This preparation for university was probably the most unhappy period in his life. Grundtvig never lost his hostility to the "black school," where he had felt imprisoned by mathematics, Latin, and Greek. Similarly, his years at Copenhagen University were a period of apathy and cynicism during which he was, in his own phrase, "without spirit and without faith." However, one event during his university years became a turning point in his life. In 1802–3 his Norwegian-German cousin Henrik Steffens delivered two series of lectures which introduced Grundtvig to the leading figures of the German Romantic movement. Steffens spoke with great enthusiasm in crowded lecture halls, and in a university climate of dry rationalism students found him a new and inspiring voice. He aroused Grundtvig and his fellow students in a way Grundtvig later believed the folk high schools could awaken all Danish youth.

On leaving university, Grundtvig became a tutor in a manor house on the island of Langeland. There he fell hopelessly in love with Constance Leth, mistress of the house, lively and beautiful and bored with her marriage. "Now the hour had come!" said Grundtvig. "I saw a woman and I, the coldest and bitterest mocker of love, loved at first sight as deeply, as glowingly, as it is possible for a mortal to do."[2] But he soon realized that the conventions were an insurmountable barrier and took the only rescue path he knew: scholarly work. He found nourishment in Schiller, Goethe, Schelling, and Fichte. His work on the northern myths began at this time, first as a solace ("It is their glory alone which helps me to bear the burden of life"), and later as a means of expressing his patriotism and affection for Denmark. The suffering of his people after the bombardment of Copenhagen in 1807, which he had seen at first hand, and the capture of the Danish fleet moved him deeply. Through the northern myths and legends he felt he could appeal to "the hero-days of old" and rally the Danes from apathy and despair. In an early book, *Masquerade Ball in Denmark* (1808), he urged his countrymen to show themselves worthy of their ancestors, and for nearly a decade he translated the ancient chronicles into modern Danish that ordinary people could read and appreciate.

Throughout Grundtvig's life Scandinavian mythology was one of the richest sources of his inspiration ("In the ancient North alone I have my home," he says in one poem), and through the myths and his own poetry he tried to awaken the Danes to a new national consciousness. This sense of mission remained with him throughout his life and the combination of the religious and patriotic strands in his thought gave his writings and sermons an apocalyptic tone and led to the title his countrymen gave him, "Prophet of the North." He could be both critical and hopeful, but for him the Danes were a chosen people and his faith in Denmark's future seldom wavered. In one poem he gives a glowing prophesy of "the realm of little Denmark . . . with peace and freedom, heroic courage, folk-song and gladness, [and] wisdom clad in childlike garb . . . outshining the glory of the Great Powers and yet not arousing grudging envy."

By the 1830s, however, Grundtvig had become convinced that exhortation was not enough, nor was poetry, mythology, or even the Church. If the Danish people were to be fully awakened a new kind of institution was needed—a free school for young adults. In an introduction to the revised edition of his *Northern Mythology* (1832), he outlined for the first time his proposals for a folk high school. His ideas for a residential school for adults drawn from all sectors of society with major emphasis on history and the mother tongue were new and original. The foundation of his thought is his belief in the power of the "living word," a principle essentially related to his view of man's nature.

When he moved away from his father's Lutheranism he gained a decidedly more positive and optimistic view of the human condition. In place of the penitential pilgrim, man was "a matchless and wonderful creature in whom divine power will proclaim, develop and manifest itself for a thousand generations; a divine experiment revealing how spirit and dust can impregnate one another and be glorified in united, divine consciousness."[3] When this potential for becoming fully human is awakened and unfolded, man is better prepared to become a Christian. This belief is summarized in a well-known line from a poem Grundtvig wrote in 1837 and returned to in his old age: "First a man and then a Christian." The essence of Christianity—here again Grundtvig has moved away from his earlier beliefs—is not to be found in the Bible but rather in the sacraments of the Church and the Apostles' Creed, which have come down through the ages as the Word. In embracing the Word man can be reborn. Similarly, in education, man can be reborn, but here "the word" is the mother tongue, which for Grundtvig was the expression of the unique character of a people. History becomes "the recollection of the fathers," which has come down through the generations as a living narrative.

By setting books aside and emphasizing the spoken word through lecture, discussion, lively conversation, anecdote, indignant comment, or joke a teacher can awaken his pupils spiritually and help them realize their full humanity. But, said Grundtvig, "Something of the flame of the prophet and the bard must fire the tongue of him who would kindle youth to action. The living word has its source in lofty idealism, in a deep belief in nation and humanity. It cannot draw its power from books alone."[4]

This new kind of school that would not only awaken the individual but also strengthen national spirit and rouse a sense of pride in being Danish would be very different from the schools Grundtvig himself had attended. He rejected the secondary grammar school with its deadly grind of Latin, competitive examinations, and deepening of class divisions. Such a school had few foundations in the life of the people; its language was not the mother tongue and instead of giving pupils a love of country it isolated them from the common tasks of daily life. Grundtvig was vehemently opposed to imprisoning the adolescent by pen and books and once said that if the question arose of closing all the grammar schools in the kingdom he would vote for it. Boys should leave school at fourteen and enter "the workshops of good artisans and the farms of clever farmers" where they could develop a genuine interest in the calling they would follow. Then at eighteen when they had some experience in life they should return to school with questions to be answered and enthusiasm to be shared, a school with a lively communal life and open to all sons and daughters. It would be "as free and democratic as possible" and a part of the Nordic tradition:

> That these, the root and trunk of the nation, tenants and freeholders, both great and small, artisans of every class, sailors and traders, should have no other knowledge and education than they get behind the plough, in the workshop, aloft on the mast, or in the general store, only barbarians and tyrants can accept. But it has never, either in King or Nation, been the Nordic way of thinking, and never could be, for it is true that the rule applies here if anywhere, that we are all of "one blood," and so the same receptivity to culture is to be found in cottages and stately halls.[5]

For Grundtvig the cardinal objective of the folk school was to awaken, nourish, and enlighten human life. He distinguishes clearly between a human and a Christian education, and declared that the school should not proselytize. As democratic as the proposal appears, it had, as so many reforms in education, both a radical and a conservative purpose. As a first step toward democratic government the king had introduced provincial advisory councils. If the peasants were to participate in them, they needed more education, particularly a deeper understanding of Denmark itself, its past and present. But Grundtvig feared that with the trend toward greater participation, particularly in 1848, there was the danger of excess. He saw the need to save his country from revolution and to make the transition from an absolutist monarchy to a parliamentary democracy as tranquil as possible. "The sign of the times," he wrote,

> and the events of the day show all too clearly that without such natural, gentle and salutary enlightenment, which has been shamefully neglected everywhere, the hour will strike in all countries when the

masses of the people who have been treated unnaturally and debased to the life of cattle, will and must, sooner or later, rise like wild beasts and render asunder all that is human.[6]

In developing his ideas on education and on the future of Denmark politically and economically, Grundtvig found much to reflect on following three visits to England in the summer months between 1829 and 1831. Using a travelling scholarship granted by King Frederik VI, he studied Anglo-Saxon manuscripts at the British Museum, Exeter, and Oxford, but it was the bold enterprise of England's industrial development, her vigorous civic life, and the corporate life of Oxford and Cambridge colleges that interested him most. On walks through London streets and during his visits to docks and machine shops he felt a pulsating energy, an "heroic spirit" that he contrasted with Denmark's quiet apathy. But Grundtvig's feelings about industrialization were mixed: "To be sure, there was something dismal about it, especially the sight of thousands of men made mere cogs in a machine, indeed, unthinking serfs for the factory lord."[7] He was equally critical of the enclosure movement which had severed people from the land and which was, he thought, "the inner sore of England, which one easily overlooks, dazzled by her outward splendour." This, to him, tragic mistake in the life of English agriculture convinced him still further of the need to press forward with an adult education movement in Denmark.

What impressed Grundtvig most about the English were their creative energy and their practicality, which together gave them what he called a "masterly grasp of the useful." On his first visit Grundtvig was critical of English materialism, but his new friends countered his criticism by asking, "What do you do in Denmark, then?" He later recalled that if he lived to be a hundred he would never forget that "What do you do?" His visits to England thus persuaded Grundtvig to lay more emphasis on actuality rather than on appearance or theory, and when he returned to Denmark it was to the practical proposal for a high school sponsored by the king that he turned his attention, a proposal specifically influenced by his English experience. He had stayed for a fortnight in Cambridge, which, surprisingly, he described as "the ugly town at the gutter of the Cam," and had lived in Trinity College, where he was treated, not as a stranger, but "like a good old Fellow coming back to visit the place he came from." In formulating his proposals for a high school he recalled living in two colleges, Valkendorf's Kollegium in Copenhagen, and Trinity, where the common life was an "unsurpassed feast" enjoyed daily by tutors and students. He wanted to create a similar kind of communal and corporate life in the new Danish high schools. Grundtvig's enmity toward England following the shelling of Copenhagen had become a warm yet critical respect which led him to say, "Were I not a Dane, I should prefer above all to be an Englishman."

From 1832 onward Grundtvig never ceased to press, through books and pamphlets, correspondence, public lectures, and parliamentary addresses, for acceptance of his folk high school proposal. His immediate objective was a royal high school at Sorö, fifty miles west of Copenhagen, an old Cistercian monastery that for 200 years had been a boys' academy. Grundtvig knew that the only way the academy could be converted to a folk school was through state action, and he persuaded King Christian VIII to issue a royal decree under which Sorö Real-Hojskole was to be established. Although the decree stipulated that the school would provide "an opportunity to acquire a thorough knowledge of the language of our country, of history, statistics, and the constitution," it was not quite the model Grundtvig had in mind. Before the decree could be implemented, however, King Christian died and the new king, Frederik VII, suspended all deliberations on the recommendation of his minister of culture.

As a member of the Constitutional Assembly, Grundtvig made a passionate appeal to the minister to carry out the late king's wishes. In this address Grundtvig admitted that he was speaking with great anxiety because the school had been his cherished idea for a generation. He reminded the assembly that the king had promised a school that would be open to all regardless of station in life or occupation and that would have no entrance examination. The aim of the school would be to awaken national consciousness and nourish a love of country. Furthermore, Grundtvig cautioned, the king had given his royal word that "I should be given the opportunity at Sorö, in my advancing years [he was then sixty-five] freely to prove whether the idea of the school was, as many believed, a brainstorm, a poet's dream, or whether it was in the people's best interest that such a school be established."[8] The minister of culture remained unmoved, and the school at Sorö never opened.

Meanwhile, however, through the initiative of two of Grundtvig's supporters, the high school movement had begun. In 1844 Christian

Flor, a professor at the University of Kiel, founded the first folk high school in Rødding in South Jutland, and in 1851 Kristen Kold opened his school at Ryslinge on the island of Fyn. As other schools followed they adopted Grundtvig's ideas. He had not drawn up a detailed syllabus but, as reflected in the king's decree, he had given history first place in the curriculum: "History as the experience of life on a large scale, is not only the best, but the only thing by means of which one can rightly enlighten young people."[9] The other subject to which Grundtvig assigned pre-eminence in his "school for life" was the mother tongue, which "has its home neither in the brain of scholars nor even in the pen of the best writers, but in the mouth of the people, and it is here, and not there, that the mother tongue must live and move and work, express and extend Danish patriotism, enlightenment, joy, and gladness."[10] Danish literature would include myths and legends of the heroic past and poets whose work could be read aloud. Language training should be largely oral and conversational with a view to preparing pupils for later participation in public life. Ballads, proverbs, and maxims, "with all their Danish imagery, their wisdom and innocent jest,"[11] should be dusted off, revived, and promoted.

The third subject should be song, not the serious study of music or solo singing, but hearty, natural community singing led by a teacher who knew and loved the songs of the people. For many years each class in the folk schools began and ended with a song selected from the *Danish Folk High School Song Book,* in which Grundtvig's hymns and poems outnumber those of any other writer. In place of the king's "national statistics" Grundtvig preferred a course in current affairs that he called the "mirror of Denmark," reflecting the life and economic activities of contemporary Denmark. Students should also become familiar with a well-managed farm and a variety of workshops which could surround the school and be associated with it. He did not, however, propose any vocational training, and as the schools spread throughout rural Denmark they did not teach technical or vocational subjects.

For Grundtvig, late youth was the proper time for enlightenment. This is the age of mental awakening when the great questions about life are asked and when feelings for poetry and fatherland are awakened. An appropriate age of entry would be eighteen and attendance would, of course, be voluntary. There would be no examinations, diplomas, or certificates. Grundtvig originally expected that young people from towns and rural areas would attend, but in this he was disappointed. For many years the schools drew their pupils almost entirely from farm families. The schools themselves were all residential, some in former manor houses, others in much more spartan settings, and all privately owned and managed. Grundtvig never wanted the new schools to become part of the state system of education; in education, as in political economy, he believed strongly in free enterprise and thought that private management would give the schools an independent vitality and healthy diversity. Each principal would appoint his staff and establish his syllabus.

Grundtvig's contribution to the folk high school movement lies more in establishing ends than means. In mid-nineteenth-century Europe his proposals were audacious. He wanted an "open" school that would inspire and awaken rather than train and instruct, offer a liberal education rather than practical training, give no paper rewards, and prepare young people for a full life on the land rather than help them escape from it. To modern ears Grundtvig's emphasis on Danishness sounds too nationalistic, and modern educators would have less confidence in the power of the living word to inspire young people's pride in their past. Nevertheless, Grundtvig's ideas were instrumental in turning the Romantic revival in Denmark into a "romance of hard work," which in the late nineteenth century was translated into an agricultural revival and development of a new rural culture. In this the folk high schools were both directly and indirectly involved, as we shall presently see. Meanwhile, it is time to turn to men who gave shape and reality to Grundtvig's ideas, since Grundtvig himself was never directly involved in founding or administering a school.

FLOR, KOLD, SCHRØDER, AND THE EARLY HIGH SCHOOLS, 1845-1900

The first practical application of Grundtvig's ideas took place in 1844 at Rødding in northern Schlesvig, where German and Danish culture were in conflict. The majority of the population were Danes, but German was the official language used both in the courts and in secondary schools. Christian Flor (1792–1874), for many years a friend of Grundtvig, thought that something must be done to resist further Germanization. He managed to raise sufficient money to buy a farmhouse near the village of Rødding. In November 1844, twenty young men all dressed in homespun arrived from nearby farms for a winter course planned on Grundtvigian lines that would be taught in Danish. The following July, Grundtvig gave his blessing to the school in the course of an address to some 10,000 Danes at Skamlingsbanken, also in north Schlesvig. Rødding was not only the first school to open, but it also established two important precedents. In 1852 it received a direct grant from the state, and several years later the principal successfully resisted attempts of the Ministry of Education to introduce examinations. His defence of existing practice is a definitive statement of the high school attitude toward examinations:

> The aim of the school is to awaken and nourish the sense for spiritual life by means of free lectures, and to promote the love of the fatherland by throwing light on its language and literature, its nature and history, its conditions in the past and present.... Our learning is for life and not for the school. We wish our students to leave us with the desire to devote themselves to the tasks of life and to use with understanding the means which life offers.... For such an education a conclusion like the Preliminary Examination is by no means fitted... [as we emphasize] teaching matter of a very different kind from that required by the examination.[12]

Christen Kold (1816–1870) opened his school in a house he had built with the help of peasants of the Ryslinge district, using funds raised by Grundtvig and his friends. Throughout the first winter Kold and ten of his fifteen students slept in the attic of this thatched cottage. In many ways Kold was an "original," a rustic Socrates who could rivet an audience with stories from the Bible, Norse myths, or recollections from his own experience. For some years he had lived in the Middle East. He returned by ship to Trieste and from there travelled on foot to Denmark. He was strongly attached to Grundtvig and visited him in Copenhagen at least once a year, literally sitting at the sage's feet and asking him questions. At his school he was like a father to his pupils, attempting through the living word "to speak to their very souls." His contribution to the early high school movement was the atmosphere of warmth and sympathy he created, together with a communal feeling closely resembling the family life his pupils came from. He lived with his students, shared their meals, and as the patriarch inspired them with national and Christian ideals. Kold also established the five-month winter term from November to March, which was when young men could most easily be spared from the farms, and he introduced a summer course for girls from May to the end of July. But his major contribution was in setting the example of a school with a family atmosphere in which rural youth were comfortable.

Ludvig Schrøder (1836–1908) was the leader of the second generation of high school principals in Denmark. While at university he had become a member of a small group of theology students (the Little Theologicum) who had come under Grundtvig's influence and who later joined the high school movement. Schrøder became principal at Rødding in 1862 but was forced to close the school when North Schleswig became German territory after 1864. With help from Christian Flor, who appears to have been tireless in his efforts to raise funds, Schrøder and his wife began a new school at Askov, three kilometers north of the new border. Under the Schrøders, Askov was an "extended high school" open to students who had previously attended one of the other schools or spent a term at Askov. In fact, it became the focal point of the high school movement and later it became the custom for leaders of schools in other parts of Scandinavia to make the pilgrimage to Askov. Schrøder was a man of many activities: as headmaster, lecturer, member of parliament, writer, publisher of the *High School Song Book,* and one of three directors of the Society for the Reclamation of the Jutland Heaths. He lectured on Scandinavian mythology, but one of his best-known books was *The Natural Resources and Industries of Denmark.* He operated a farm and was proud to own the prize milking cow in Jutland.

With these many interests, Schrøder found Grundtvig's proposals for a farm and craft community in the vicinity of the school entirely congenial. Slöjd (manual training) and weaving schools made their appearance at Askov, as did a new type of windmill and an experimental plant station. Schrøder initiated a series of public meetings for residents of the district at which he and his staff spoke on topics ranging from Germanism in Denmark to spavin in horses. Also at Askov, the "autumn meeting" began, at which farm people gathered after the harvest for several days of lectures, singing, and entertainment. Behind activities of this kind and in the schools themselves Schrøder and his fellow principals were acutely aware of the need to rekindle a national spirit after the 1864 loss in territory and population. With resounding understatement Schrøder said: "It is an age when something can be done." As new high schools were founded it was as if principals had a campaign to carry the newly coined national aphorism on their shields: "What is lost outwardly shall be won inwardly."

With the legacy of Grundtvig's vision, Flor's indefatigable zeal for organizing support, Kold's capacity to inspire the young, and Schrøder's talent for leadership, the folk high school movement began. As it gathered momentum, highly capable and dedicated men became principals and in turn attracted able staff. Thus the schools were, without doubt, the product of the men who made them. There were few women principals and staff in the early schools, although Charlotte Schrøder began the tradition of the active and influential principal's wife who joined her husband in creating the intellectual and spiritual climate of the schools. But important as the founders were, other influences also shaped the schools, among which was the liberation and rise of the Danish peasantry.

Under an absolute monarchy dating from 1660, agricultural land was held by members of the nobility in the form of large feudal estates. The free and independent yeoman disappeared after 1733, when peasants were tied from the age of fourteen to thirty-six to the estate on which they were born. Peasants worked two, three, sometimes four days a week on their lord's estate and on other days in the enclosed fields around the village or on the commons beyond their fields. This system, which required a good deal of negotiation and compromise, together with the low level of initiative among the peasants, resulted in meagre production—probably less than a fifth of present yields. Beginning in the last quarter of the eighteenth century as a result of the "enlightened absolutism" of the Danish monarchy and the efforts of liberal-minded members of the nobility, a series of reforms continued into the next century broke the peasant's bondage to the large estate, freed him from joint cultivation, consolidated his holdings from scattered strips of land into a compact unit, and allowed him to become a freeholder. Through these measures Denmark avoided the evils that followed England's policy of land reform, which created a powerful class of landed proprietors and a poor country proletariat.

The reforms in agricultural production were made for the sake of the peasant but not initiated by him. The National Committee for Agricultural Reform in its initial efforts had no peasant representatives, the first agricultural societies being started by government officials and the owners of the then large estates. Experiments with new methods of cultivation, land drainage, and cattle breeding were also the work of large landowners. Gradually, however, as a result of other reforms, peasants began to take matters into their own hands. Under the Compulsory Education Act of 1814 both boys and girls between the ages of seven and fourteen were to be given an education. This act did not imply that there was to be compulsory schooling in state schools; parents could choose to send their children to "free" or private schools, or teach them at home. The act also provided that primary school teachers should keep in touch with young people after they were confirmed at fourteen or fifteen, not only to give them occasional instruction but also to acquaint them with "the duties which their riper age and changed circumstances carry with them." This section of the act was not effectively enforced, but it did establish the principle of further teaching. In 1834 the provincial advisory councils met for the first time and several years later new forms of local government were introduced in rural communities. The major political development was the adoption of a new constitution in 1849. For its time this was one of the most liberal constitutions in Europe, providing for two houses of Parliament elected by all men over thirty. Because Denmark was predominantly rural, two-thirds of the eligible voters were peasants but in the first years of the new Constitution only some 10 per cent took advantage of their right to vote. Gradually a Farmers' party was formed which by the end of the century elected half the members of the Lower House and in 1901 formed a government.

These educational and political developments were among the factors which gave rise to the folk high schools, and at the same time the schools had an effect on the rise of a peasant party. Grundtvig, the high school principals, and the peasants themselves saw clearly that participation in local government and in parliamentary democracy made an enlightened peasantry a necessity. There was now something to be awakened for, and political developments were closely related to the growth of the folk high schools. It was the Peasants' party in the Lower House which supported increasingly larger state grants for the schools and resisted right-wing attempts to introduce examinations and impose a form of state control and supervision. On the other side of the coin is the influence of the schools on political development. High school principals joined the Peasants' party and although the schools avoided direct participation in political affairs, high school graduates did become politically active. In 1903 over 35 per cent of the members of the Danish Parliament had attended a folk high school. The schools were not politically or religiously neutral. Although they received state support they were not state schools and from the beginning enjoyed a substantial degree of autonomy.

After 1864 some schools were openly anti-German while others which belonged to the "Inner Mission" group taught a pietistic form of Christianity. In the second half of the nineteenth century, however, the schools were in the main Grundtvigian in tone and thus committed to an "awakening" and "enlightening" process that was not overtly political. But few Danes would deny the "cross-fertilization" that took place between the rise of the peasantry and the growth of the schools.

This blurring of cause and effect can also be seen in the agricultural crisis of the 1870s. Before it, Denmark was primarily concerned with growing and exporting grain, but in the seventies grain from Russia, Argentina, and the United States began to pour into western Europe. Because it was produced by large-scale methods it was cheaper, and small-scale Danish farmers faced bankruptcy. The alternative was to change the face of Danish agriculture radically and quickly, to make it primarily dairy-oriented. Farmers accepted this alternative and bought cheap foreign grain for fodder. Butter and bacon became the chief exports and production in each case rose twelvefold between 1870 and 1900. A crisis was thus averted without resort to protective tariffs and without government edict.

It was a voluntary effort that employed an instrument also new to Denmark, the co-operative. The first consumers' society was formed in Jutland in 1866, and the first co-operative dairy opened in 1882. As dairy production increased and co-operatives needed larger processing plants, members who had become freeholders and held the deeds of their farms were regarded as good security risks for loans. This guarantee of security was reinforced when the co-operative movement adopted the principle of the "unlimited joint and several liability" of its members. Co-operative dairies and bacon factories were followed by consumer co-operatives of many kinds through which a farmer could buy seed, fertilizer, cement, and electricity, and still others at which he could secure credit or bank his savings. This comprehensive system of co-operation with its concern for efficient production, improvement of products through research, and aggressive marketing has allowed Denmark to compete in world markets. Small farmers created the co-operative movement, and in turn the movement made it possible for small farmers both to survive and to prosper.

It is widely believed in Denmark that the folk high schools exerted a powerful influence on the co-operative movement. Studies have shown that half or more of the managers of co-operative dairies and chairmen of the boards of co-operative dairy associations were former high school students.[13] But the more pervasive influence is indirect and intangible:

> The schools tend to awaken in young people a sense of what the individual owes to the community, a feeling of confidence in others, and a willingness to make sacrifices for the common good. . . . The folk high school's ideal of freedom with responsibility has become an ethical force in the co-operatives.[14]

If the schools gave the people of rural Denmark the initiative they needed to create the co-operative movement and thus cope with the agricultural crisis, the co-operatives in return brought to Danish farmers a prosperity that enabled them to found new high schools for their sons and daughters.

It may be excessive to speak of a "rural renaissance," but clearly life in the Danish countryside changed during the nineteenth century. Village associations were formed and village halls were built in which youth organizations, gymnastic clubs, choral societies, and lecture unions held their meetings. Leading figures in these groups were frequently former high school students, and staff from nearby high schools gave public lectures. The youth associations were self-governing groups of rural youth aged fourteen to twenty-five who organized lectures and sang and acted in amateur theatre groups. When the Ling system of gymnastics was imported from Sweden, the high schools adopted it and abandoned the earlier system, which closely resembled military drill. From the schools the new system found its way into village gymnastic societies. Through this network of organizations, the autumn meetings, or the residential agricultural schools which gave direct vocational training but adopted the tone and spirit of the folk schools, almost all farm families at some time came into direct or indirect contact with the folk high schools.

It is possible to idealize the schools and overestimate their influence. There were other factors which cannot be ignored, particularly with regard to the agricultural crisis and the growth of the co-operative movement. One is that Denmark found markets for its dairy products, notably in Britain, which imposed no import duties. In the second half of the nineteenth century the price of Danish butter increased by 70 per cent and bacon by 40 per cent. Denmark had an internal network of railways and the growth of the Danish shipping industry paralleled the increase of production for export. The invention of the mechanical cream separator in 1880 by L. C. Nielsen, a Danish engineer, enabled small-scale co-operative dairies to produce butter that could meet the demands of the English market in both quality and quantity. The Royal Agricultural College, the agricultural schools, and the milk recording societies trained farmers in modern methods and carried out research, particularly in animal husbandry.

In the last quarter of the nineteenth century Danish farmers, on average, had the inestimable advantage of basic literacy. The majority had attended primary schools for several years, normally to the age of fourteen, and could read and write comfortably and keep accounts. As is so frequently the case among literate farmers, they were prepared to learn more. It may be too much to say that they welcomed change; on the other hand they did not fear it. Furthermore, the few class distinctions among farmers made it possible for them to mix socially and come together comfortably in co-operatives. They had little choice: either they changed direction or perished. Fortunately they had the necessary skill and flexibility to change course and a sufficient trust in each other to co-operate.

The transformation of the schools into strongholds of "Danishness" after the loss of North Schlesvig in 1864 and the prosperity following the agricultural crisis led to a marked growth in the number of schools. The period after 1864 has been called the "Golden Age" of the high schools, a time when fifty high schools were established in five years and the number of students increased almost tenfold between 1864 and 1876. The closing years of the century were not, however, a golden age for parliamentary democracy in Denmark or for the freedom of the high schools. The National Liberal party, representing the urban middle class, was blamed for the defeat of 1864 and as its excuse took the view that the 1849 Constitution had been too liberal. Henceforth, Denmark should leave government in the hands of "the intelligent, the cultured and the wealthy." In a coalition with the large landowner party the Liberals passed a bill in 1866 which confined the franchise in the Upper House of Parliament (Landsting) to the privileged class. Grundtvig and the Farmers' party, led by two folk high school teachers, protested vigorously and were soon joined by high school leaders, including Schrøder. Another dispute arose ten years later when the prime minister, then leader of the Right party, failing to secure passage of a finance bill in the Lower House (Folketing) dissolved Parliament and issued a Provisional Finance Law. In protest, Schrøder and other principals of the Little Theologicum group refused to apply for state grants for their schools and thirty-two other principals followed their example. The government then temporarily struck Askov and other schools from the list for grants and accused the principals of subversive activity. Only through gifts from former students and friends were these schools kept open. Grants were issued again in 1892 when the High School Act of that year granted the schools complete freedom of speech.

Meanwhile, the Farmers' party was demanding that the king call on the majority in the democratically elected Lower House to form a government. This he was obliged to do in 1901. Previously, in 1894, the schools had celebrated the fiftieth anniversary of the founding of Rødding and attendance had reached 5,100, the largest enrolment thus far recorded. The struggle for parliamentary democracy and the need to cope with the disaster of 1864 and the agricultural crisis confirmed the usefulness of the folk high schools and in turn gave the graduates of the schools a role to play in Denmark:

> The Danish peasantry at the beginning of the nineteenth century was an underclass. In sullen resignation it spent its life in dependence on estate owners and government officials. It was without culture and technical skill, and was seldom able to rise above the level of a bare existence. . . . In the course of a century this underclass has been changed into a well-to-do middle class which potentially and socially now takes the lead among the Danish people.[15]

THE SECOND PHASE, 1900-45

For over fifty years (1864–1920) the Danes in North Schlesvig lived under German rule. In the struggle to save their language and culture the high schools were a decisive influence. Soon after Denmark's defeat in 1864 the new rulers of North Schlesvig began a comprehensive move to Germanize all institutions, including churches and schools, and teaching of the Danish language was prohibited. Private schools were not permitted and parents could not send school-age children across the border to Danish schools. As counter-measures, residential continuation schools (Efterskoler) were set up north of the border for children who had reached the age of fourteen and had completed their German schooling. These schools were mainly established by former high school students, and in a six-month term gave instruction in Danish language and history. They were similar to the folk high schools in spirit and tone. Toward the end of the nineteenth century a substantial number of young people from North Schlesvig enrolled in the Danish high schools with the help of bursaries made available through a national Danish association. From 1892 to 1914 this assistance made it possible for some 6,000 young people to attend a high school or continuation school north of the border. Danish high school leaders and former students supported the building of village halls in North Schlesvig and, from 1907 onward, the formation of youth associations. By 1914 these had a membership of nearly 5,000.

Political leaders among the Danes in Schlesvig during this period were former high school students who had been elected members of the German Reichstag and the Prussian Diet. In the fall of 1918, a few weeks before the armistice, one of these Danish leaders had raised the question in the Reichstag of the reunion of Southern Jutland (North Schlesvig) with the mother country and a group of prominent Danes had issued an appeal that "the population that speaks Danish, feels Danish, and wishes to be Danish shall return to Denmark." A small delegation of North Schlesvigian Danes, all former high school students, attended the peace conference in Paris and in the plebiscite of 1920, conducted under the terms of the Versailles Treaty, three-quarters of the population voted for a return to Denmark. In June that year King Christian X rode across the old frontier and, symbolically, finished his tour of the area with a visit to Askov.

During the first half of the century Askov continued to hold a special place among the schools. Jacob Appel succeeded Schrøder in 1906 and as principal held three cabinet portfolios, one of which was that of minister of education. He had studied mathematics and physics at Copenhagen University and the Polytechnic Institute, also in Copenhagen, and during his regime at Askov more emphasis was given to the natural sciences, actually, the history of the sciences. The two-year course enrolled both men and women but most subjects were taught to each group separately. In the mid-twenties when enrolment was 300 and residence facilities were crowded, twelve students were normally assigned to live in each of the married teachers' homes. Fru Appel was active in the life of the school, particularly in her husband's absence when she became principal. She set forth the "house rules" clearly and firmly at the beginning of a term and presided over the dining room. She and her husband entertained students each week, and both taught part-time. In spite of a large enrolment everything possible was done to preserve the home and family atmosphere Kold had established in his school decades earlier.

Students lived simply and accepted regulations which included prohibition of liquor and confined smoking to one's own room. Men and women could not visit each other's rooms at any time and quiet settled over the school each night at 10:30. So strong was the belief in the "Living Word" that no writing of notes was allowed in the lecture rooms. A party of Americans visited Askov for several weeks in the early twenties and was surprised, if not astonished, at the atmosphere:

> Studying these young people, we never cease to wonder at their apparent capacity to absorb and their orderly compliance with the rules. We did hear later that one student . . . had been asked to leave. Doubtless there are occasionally such cases though we saw nothing that could be remotely interpreted as disorder. The work is not compulsory, yet no one seems to wish to miss what is offered. Hour after hour, day after day, we watched them hurrying to lectures, sitting quietly, good-humored, unwearied, to receive the flow of new thoughts. They seem to us less restless than our American young folk, less demanding in the way of change and recreation. Perhaps they have the inheritance of a small and ancient nation, and with fewer economic opportunities to pursue, more limited spaces to explore, have learned to suck pleasure and profit out of the simple things of every day. Or does the secret lie in the kind of teaching, in the natural relationship of faculty and students, the lack of any element of compulsion or competition? One must remember too, that they come to this hungry after a number of years of practical work in field, creamery, shop, and home. Certainly no one could make the mistake of calling them unintelligent. They are too thoroughly interested in what they are hearing.[16]

The time table of classes for first-year students at Askov on a typical day in 1922–23 is shown below:[17]

8:00–9:00	all students	geography
9:00–10:00	men	Danish
	women	gymnastics
10:10–10:25	all students	coffee and *smörrebröd*
10:30–11:30	all students	historical physics
11:30–12:30	men	arithmetic
	women	history
12:30–2:00	men	gymnastics
	women	handwork and drawing
2:00	all students	dinner
4:00–5:00	all students	Bible
5:00–6:00	men	hygiene
	women	Danish
6:00–7:00	all students	world history

Classes followed this schedule, with minor variations, six days a week throughout the six-month term. Each class began and ended with a song, and an hour and a half of gymnastics each day broke the pattern of incessant instruction. Because these students had attended at least one term in a high school prior to enrolling at Askov, they were familiar with student life. Nevertheless, a diet of fifty classes a week is heavy fare and one wonders whether the living word was still alive at week's end.

In the years following the First World War some schools lost their vitality and spiritual depth, others became introspective and parochial. The days of national causes seemed over and the former peasants had become freehold farmers who had achieved economic and social equality with other classes. The co-operative movement ran into financial trouble in the early twenties but soon recovered, parliamentary democracy was achieved, women won the franchise in 1915, and the return of North Schlesvig was no longer an issue. Holger Begtrup, a highly respected principal and an historian of the high school movement, spoke at the sixtieth anniversary of Askov in 1925. In his address he recalled rather wistfully the challenges of days past and the narrowing of the schools' vision in recent years:

> The Folk High School has narrowed down its spiritual activity all too much to enlightenment for life in the individual soul and home circles. It has become, so to speak, too private, and has no living relationship to the country at large nor to the great questions of mankind's world around us, as the old High Schools had in relation to the opportunities of their times.[18]

Another long-standing criticism of the schools was their inability to attract young people from the towns. In 1920 only 5–6 per cent of pupils came from the towns and while this proportion increased to 10–15 per cent in the 1940s, it was the enrolment of unemployed urban youth that largely accounted for the increase. There were several attempts to create labor high schools for young people working in towns, regardless of class, but a five- or six-month term in a residential setting was impractical for young people working in towns. Nor did isolation in the country appeal to them, particularly if they were young socialists or trade unionists who were skeptical of national and religious revivalism. A number of schools attempted to counteract these attitudes by arranging one-week summer courses for townspeople, and annual attendance climbed to over 1,000 for several years.

The most successful town school was Johan Borup's school in Copenhagen. Borup was a theology student influenced by Grundtvig, but he realized that an urban high school could not be built on traditional lines. In 1891 he attracted 140 pupils for "advanced education for non-university ladies and gentlemen" in general subjects. Classes were in the evening and Borup met his students where they were. "General subjects" frequently meant the three R's, but through discussion and conversation, not lectures, he introduced history, literature, and sociology. "The young people of Copenhagen," Borup wrote, "are born sceptics, and little can be done with them unless they feel confident that they will not be drilled along the lines of certain doctrines." By the 1920s enrolment had reached 700, day courses had begun, and the school (still known as Borup's High School) became a part of the cultural life of Copenhagen through public lectures, concerts, and readings. It was not, however, until after the Second World War that traditional high schools began to attract a substantial proportion of students from the towns.

High school enrolment remained relatively stable during the first half of the century, but the number of schools decreased, as shown in Table 1.[19]

Table 1

	1900–1	1910–11	1920–21	1930–31	1940–41	1950–51
Number of schools	74	79	58	59	54	58
Number of pupils	5,362	6,707	7,006	6,407	6,023	5,866

The schools may have lost some of their earlier crusading zeal, but they had the resilience and flexibility to make a number of significant changes in the syllabus and methods of teaching. Scandinavian myths gave way to modern literature, more respect was given to historical fact and less to a romantic, nationalistic, and poetic view of history, and twentieth-century social problems were introduced. The principal and his staff continued to lecture to the whole student body, but increasingly students became involved in group discussion, read more, and listened less. Danish history and literature continued to be the principal subjects, accounting for ten to twelve of the weekly lessons which, surprisingly, in total remained at about fifty. High school staff were a mixed group who came from universities, teachers' colleges, agricultural schools, the teachers' course at Askov, or gymnastic schools. The number of theology graduates who used the high school as a station on the way to a parsonage became smaller. A Swiss teacher, Fritz Wartenweiler, who knew the Danish schools well in the twenties and thirties, has given his impressions of high school staff:

> I came to know many different types of High School and also came into contact with principals and teachers of the most dissimilar character: highly educated theologians and natural scientists, plain men and women, enthusiastic, energetic politicians and leaders in the agricultural field, orthodox Grundtvigians and free thinkers—and in spite of all the differences I noticed a unity which could only be the result of a deep stir. I saw with astonishment that some of the best men in the country had engaged themselves in the service of this cause. Here was one who had given up a brilliant university

> career in order to serve the people direct. There was another who had worked his way up from beneath, through all the farm worker's difficulties, and had overcome the irregular form of his development in order to be able to help folk of his own category better.[20]

At the turn of the century one-third of the schools were teaching technical or practical courses such as carpentry or domestic science. These were optional subjects and only a minority of students chose them. In time, however, schools with a special function appeared: these included gymnastic schools, and schools for nurses, child welfare workers, co-operative store managers, and shop clerks. By a 1943 Ministry of Education order a specialized school was eligible for government grants if no more than half its classes were devoted to a special field. Specialization did not necessarily take on a vocational character. The gymnastic schools, for example, began when Niels Bukh built his school at Ollerup in 1920, and between the wars his team of gymnasts travelled all over the world. Bukh's aim was to combine physical education with other high school subjects and prepare students to teach gymnastics in their leisure time to youth groups in villages. Supporters of the "pure" high school who were dubious of any degree of specialization criticized Bukh's program as the triumph of "the external over the internal" and derided Danish youth who "stretched and bent under the shades of Fujiyama." A further variation of the Grundtvigian high school were the ten "Inner Mission" schools.

Another school with a special function, known around the world, is the International People's College founded by Peter Manniche in an old manor house at Elsinore in 1921. The twenty-four students in the first class came from seven countries and Manniche recruited English, German, and American teachers. During the thirty-four years that he was principal, enrolment grew to well over 400 students, who were divided among regular winter and summer courses and shorter vacation courses. New buildings have gradually been added and the original house renovated, with students doing much of the work, but the college has retained its atmosphere of simplicity and has kept its fees low. Folk high school traditions have been followed in a curriculum that stresses the study and discussion of international questions and the teaching of several languages. The principal of Askov began a summer course for teachers from the Nordic countries in 1932, and a Nordic folk high school was founded in Geneva about the same time to give participants from Denmark, Norway, Finland, and Sweden access to the resources of the international agencies based in Switzerland. This international emphasis was, indirectly, a refutation of Holger Begtrup's allegation of a "narrowing down."

Diversity and specialization among the schools were made possible, as we have seen, through the assistance of state grants. The Act of 1892, the first of several to deal with government subsidies, awarded direct grants to cover one-third of the cost of teachers' salaries and teaching materials. In later years these grants were as shown in Table 2.

Table 2

Year of Legislation	Percentage of teachers' salaries paid by grant	Percentage of teaching materials paid by grant
1913	50	35
1942	70	50
1970	85	85

The state has also given direct grants on the basis of student enrolment, and as a means of protecting the small schools these subsidies have varied inversely with the number of students enrolled. Such protection was needed when small schools were forced to close in the early twenties and again during the Depression of the thirties. The basic subsidy was doubled in 1942, but some high school leaders feared that larger grants would bring greater government influence and control. If the government guaranteed the schools economic security the responsibility of the principal would be undermined and the quality of a school's work would be diminished.

Discussion on this matter also included the topic of ownership of the schools. When the first high schools were founded, practically every school was owned by its principal. By 1910 a quarter of the schools had changed from individual to corporate ownership through a board, trust, or association, and by the mid-thirties principals owned roughly half the schools. The proprietor-principal was a man of awesome authority. (The number of women principals remained minimal, four or six at most.) The only official qualifications he needed were evidence of seven years of schooling and a medical certificate stating he was not suffering from tuberculosis. Normally, however, he had taught in a high school. To the public and the government a school was not an institution in its own right, it was the school of its principal. He was a patriarch who made all staff appointments, drew up the syllabus, lectured several times a week to the full student body, and negotiated with the Ministry of Education. State grants were made to the principal in person, and for years, the principal, on his retirement, discharged the entire staff to give his successor a free hand.

At its worst, the system of individual ownership allowed a principal to dominate his school and reduce his staff to poorly paid hired hands. But the young adults who enrolled voluntarily quickly learned which schools were to be avoided, and when enrolment dropped bankruptcy soon followed. Between 1894 and 1910 over forty schools closed and thirty-six were established. In the early twenties, twenty more schools disappeared. In later years boards of management as owners gave the schools greater stability but did not destroy the authority of the principal. Once a board had ratified a principal's appointment he had the freedom and authority to imprint his personality on the school. To a considerable degree it was *his* school, and he could still play the role of patriarch, but he was ultimately responsible to his board.

The discreet celebrations of the 100th anniversary of the founding of Rødding in the war-time atmosphere of 1944 marked the closing of the second phase of the movement. The schools could point to an impressive accomplishment: their 400,000 former students had made no small impact on the political, economic, and social life of rural Denmark. Direct influence on national issues had declined by 1944, but the schools were still important in the lives of young people, as the messages received by the schools at the anniversary celebrations testified. But the messages revealed a difference: those from older former students spoke of the inspiration and creative experience they had gained in the schools; the younger generation referred to their training in independent thinking and mutual understanding. The schools themselves no longer formed a movement with a high degree of unity; a marked diversity had been created through specialized departments and the founding of specialized schools.

Thus the schools spoke more to the needs and interests of individuals and small groups and did not play a significant role in the two world wars or the Depression. During the First World War Denmark remained neutral and relatively uninvolved; in the Second World War the Danes were in the path of Germany's occupation of Norway and could offer no more than token resistance. Winston Churchill recognized this difficulty when he said, "I could not reproach Denmark if she surrendered to a Nazi attack. The two other Scandinavian countries, Norway and Sweden, have at least a ditch over which they can feed the tiger, but Denmark is so terribly near Germany that it would be impossible to bring help. Personally, I would not in any case undertake to guarantee Denmark." Following the occupation in April 1940, there was an outburst of national emotion and the king's birthday in the fall of 1940 called forth a celebration not matched since the reunion with North Schlesvig twenty years before. Professor Hal Koch gave a series of lectures on Grundtvig to a packed auditorium at Copenhagen University and in 1941–42 high school enrolment rose to 7,200, the highest figure since 1920.

Later in the war, however, attendance dropped when some schools were requisitioned by the Germans and when the resistance movement escalated in 1943. But no unified voice came from the schools, no stimulus to the national life as had been the case after 1864. An assessment, if not an indictment of the schools during the interwar and wartime years, was made in 1944 by Thorkil Kristensen, later Secretary-General of the Organization for Economic Cooperation and Development (O.E.C.D.).

> At a private party, conversation turned to the High School, and various opinions were voiced. One which met with general approval was that "nearly everybody who had attended a High School had liked it, whether they had been noticeably influenced by it or not." Surely this is true of the High Schools of the last generation. Those who have gone to High School, and even the greater number who had attended some of the series of meetings influenced by the High School spirit were, most of them, quite happy about it. In fact, nearly the whole nation regards the High School with feelings of good will and a certain pride. But what is its influence? The friends of the High School have to admit that it has not, in the interwar years, been the stimulus they had hoped for, and which we so badly needed. Further, in the national regeneration, which was not lacking under German oppression, the High School and the farmer class (which supplied most of its students) were not in the front rank. . . . [21]

DENMARK AFTER THE SECOND WORLD WAR

Denmark did not suffer major losses in either life or property during the war, but its economy was severely damaged. With Marshall Plan aid it achieved economic reconstruction through the development of industry and the expansion of farm production. During the fifties and sixties Denmark had a second economic transformation, not as in the nineteenth century from one form of agriculture to another, but from agriculture to industry. In the post-war years Danish farmers ran into heavy competition and protectionist policies from other European countries and were obliged to mechanize their holdings and concentrate on single products. Small holders found it difficult to compete and many gave up, moved to the nearest town, and found jobs in the new factories. Danish agriculture continued to be known for its uniformly high quality, and through specialization and mechanization a smaller work force was able to maintain and increase production. But for export purposes, the value of industrial production grew more rapidly and it was during the decade 1953–63 that industrial exports for the first time exceeded export revenue from agriculture. This was a transformation based on a complex set of causes, some of which were similar to those that transformed agriculture nearly a century earlier: a capacity for ingenuity and flexibility in creating new products of high quality through small work units, and imagination and efficiency in marketing. Now, however, the folk high schools were more acted upon than acting, and instead of being a decisive factor in assisting the transition, it was the schools that were affected by the industrialization that transformed Danish society in the sixties and seventies.

Industrial plants, large and small, existed long before the 1960s but one characteristic of Danish industrial development has been the emergence of many small and medium-sized firms. In 1980 the average number of employees in Danish industry is sixty, and three-quarters of all companies had fewer than fifty employees. The Danes are not reluctant to point out the advantages: "In firms of this size there are not so many doors to knock on, and fewer layers of prestige to break through. A good idea can be discussed the day it arrives, perhaps be tested the following week and then offered on export markets within a month."[22] Danish industry has developed in spite of a dearth of oil (although North Sea deposits have been found), coal, iron, and other metals. Instead, agriculture has provided the raw material and the Danes not only process the meat, make grain into beer and milk into chocolate, but take the next step by designing and building the plant and machinery for abbatoirs, meat-canning factories, dairies, and breweries. An exporting nation needs ships and in the wake of a shipbuilding tradition, the Danes geared their industrial production to the needs of a mercantile fleet—from hawsers to radar, engines to refrigeration units.

Danish industry is in two main fields, food and engineering, but another of its most distinctive features is industrial art and design in glass, textiles, porcelain, silver and, above all, furniture. As with so many movements in art, this too began as a protest led by a group of young artists, critics, and teachers against the banality of so much European design in the mid-twenties. In 1924 the Royal Academy of Fine Arts established a lectureship in furniture design and appointed Kaare Klint to what later became known as the "furniture school." (Klint and his father were the chief architects of Grundtvig's Kirke in Copenhagen.) In creating a new school of furniture design Klint never wavered from his emphasis that furniture above all must be designed and tailored for the user. Young cabinet-makers accepted the ideas of Klint and his students, and for forty years (1927–66) the Copenhagen Cabinet-makers' Guild held an annual exhibition of members' work. This union of designers and producers appealed not only to the Danes but, by 1950, to a world market that now spends well over $200 million on Danish furniture each year. The permanent Exhibition of Danish Arts and Crafts (Den Permanente) is a handsome showcase in Copenhagen for many craftsmen whose work has been judged to be of high quality by an impartial jury and is then made available for sale. Thus through the teamwork of designers, craftsmen, and small industry and through ingenious and vigorous marketing techniques, the Danes have created a highly successful enterprise.

The industrial revolution of the post-war years (the value of Danish industrial exports increased sevenfold in the fifteen years from 1958 to 1973) brought with it a new wealth that the Danes used in two ways: they adopted a higher standard of living and extended their social legislation to establish one of the most comprehensive welfare networks in the world. By the mid-seventies the Danish average per capita disposable income ranked among the world's ten highest, and along with other industrial countries Denmark had plunged into making a consumer society. As one Danish writer has said: "The Danes are no more content than other people. They do not think so much of what they have as what they want."[23] As keen as their appetite for material goods may be they have also wanted, and believed they could afford, social legislation of many kinds. The first welfare legislation was incorporated in the Constitution of 1849 and established the right of anyone who was unable to maintain himself to secure assistance from public funds. Toward the end of the nineteenth century local authorities were made responsible for the care of the destitute and the sick, and legislation gave every Danish citizen over sixty a legal right to receive support if he were unable to maintain himself.

Further legislation followed, based on the principle that the standard of civilization in a society is determined by how it treats its weakest members. Modern Danes have gone further by accepting a state security system under which they are automatically insured and for which they pay "premiums" in the form of taxes according to their capacity. In return, a number of security nets of varying mesh are suspended beneath them. Eligibility for this security is residence in Denmark; Danish citizenship is not necessary. The cost of social welfare services explains why Denmark has one of the highest tax rates in the world. It also explains why social services account for more than 45 per cent of the national budget. During the recession of the mid-seventies following the 1973–74 oil crisis, Denmark was obliged to borrow heavily from foreign sources to meet social welfare costs. By the early eighties its budget deficit had risen fivefold since 1975 and was of the order of $4 billion per year. So serious were Denmark's affairs that *The Times* of London described her condition as "economic chaos" and asked if the Danish dream was about to end:

> Mr. Hansen, the archetypal Danish equivalent to Britain's John Bull, is not quite himself these days. Waves of economic woe in recent years have broken over this latter-day Viking, this most extrovert and friendly of Scandinavians. Could the end of the "Danish dream" symbolized by the super welfare state be in sight? he asks himself, as with a sigh, he orders another (heavily-taxed) lager.[24]

Protests about the cost of social welfare and the high level of taxation became louder in the seventies and from the right wing appeared the Progress party led by Mogens Glistrup. With a manifesto promising to abolish income tax and make drastic cuts in government spending, the party won 15 per cent of the votes in the 1977 election and elected twenty members to Parliament in 1979. But in spite of mounting criticism there is little evidence of a major change of policy affecting social legislation. The commitment is too deep and popular expectations too high for any government to attempt radical change and survive. Meanwhile, although the economic crisis persists and Denmark suffers from inflation and unemployment, the Danes continue to enjoy one of the highest standards of living in the European Economic Community.

Denmark has become, predominantly, an urban and industrial society; only 7 per cent of the total working population is now involved in farming, but the family farms, now somewhat enlarged on average to sixty acres, produce enough butter, bacon, and other animal foodstuffs to meet the needs of some 15 million people—three times as many as the population of Denmark. This agricultural miracle stems largely from 1973, when Denmark joined the E.E.C. and won entry to larger markets with favorable price support policies. But high taxation, inflation, and increasing production costs have eroded farm income and driven many livestock farmers into debt. In 1980 the government stepped in by providing state-guaranteed loans. These proved to be insufficient and by mid-1981 the more radical wing of the farm lobby was threatening to spill milk in the streets if more government aid was not forthcoming. Thus very few aspects of the Danish economy are escaping recession, if not crisis.

Another aspect of Danish society that has changed irreversibly since the Second World War lies in the field of education. By any standard of comparison, Denmark gives its children and young people a remarkable range of options; indeed, O.E.C.D. placed Denmark ahead of all other member countries in the variety of choices available in youth education. The unique feature of the education system is the variety and scope of what the acts of 1972, 1974, and 1975 designate as "leisure-time education." The plethora of schools, courses, clubs, and interest groups for which this legislation provides are legacies of two traditions: the folk high schools and extensive social legislation. The continuation schools for pupils aged fourteen to eighteen are descendants of those that flourished in Jutland after 1864. They are private, self-governing institutions and, like the folk high schools, are residential. They enrol approximately 10,000 students each year for a ten-month course. Another option for the 14–18 year-olds are the youth schools, supported and operated by local authorities and offering both general and vocational education. They supplement the primary/secondary schools with afternoon and evening classes or accept students as boarders. In recent years the youth schools have expanded explosively and some 160,000 youth are now enrolled.

Leisure-time education for adults includes evening high schools and study circles which, in effect, are part-time, non-residential folk high schools. They offer general education in the humanities, social sciences, and natural sciences, and teachers' salaries are paid in whole or largely by the state. Such is the case also for courses of lectures on humanistic, social, and scientific topics for a minimum of twenty-five adults. The Ministry of Education encourages, supports, and supervises many other leisure-time activities for young people and adults—interest groups, clubs, vocational courses, correspondence schools—which are informal and voluntary but nevertheless a vital part of the national and municipal system of education. So vital, in fact, that in 1980 over 600,000 Danes of all ages were enrolled. In commenting on the many choices in formal and informal education a Danish journalist has said: "Danes like to consider themselves as intelligent, well-educated, industrious and artistically-gifted people; perhaps to preserve their belief in the country's future. The people are Denmark's only raw material, and everything depends upon how we develop ourselves and the coming generations."[25] This belief in education is widespread: in 1980 one-third of the total population was enrolled in formal or leisure-time courses.

THE FOLK HIGH SCHOOLS IN THE LATE TWENTIETH CENTURY

*Conversations with a High School Principal**

Skaelskor is located in southeastern Sealand in rolling countryside overlooking Skaelskor Inner Fjord. The setting is quite magnificent. Both the school and staff houses are set on a hillside; swans and sailboats give life to the water, and among trees on the far side of the fjord are the ruins of a medieval castle. The school opened in 1973 and still has the feel of a new building. It is well equipped, with an auditorium and gymnasium, several seminar rooms, specialized rooms for music, film, weaving, a pottery, a library,

*In 1960 and 1981 I visited several folk high schools. On 17 and 18 June 1981, I had three conversations with Ebbe Lundgaard, principal of Skaelskor Folk High School.

and a dining room that can comfortably seat 100 people. The corridors are hung with photographs and posters, and a large tapestry rivets one's attention in the auditorium. Elsewhere, in the kitchen, dining room, residences, and courtyard, Danish design is evident in metal, china, wood, and textiles.

Ebbe Lundgaard became principal in 1977 and one of his first tasks was to save the school from bankruptcy. The community of Skaelskor had given the site, valued at 1.6 million kroner, the state had loaned 5 million kroner (about $300,000 in 1973), interest only was to be paid, and a further loan of 6 million kroner, which the principal referred to as a "real estate loan," was secured from private companies. This, of course, had to be repaid and it was the yearly payments that were causing the threat of bankruptcy. By scheduling a series of short summer courses, improving the existing fall and winter courses, and mounting a vigorous recruiting drive, enrolments were increased and financial disaster avoided. The principal gained a reputation for astute financial management which he disclaims. His success, essentially, lies in the program he created.

When he reflects on the high schools during the past twenty years he is critical of principals who did not demonstrate their ability because they were overawed by the leaders of the movement in earlier years. Furthermore, in the sixties and seventies the student body changed to a predominantly urban group and they, particularly those who had joined the new counter-culture, brought a different set of values, attitudes, and problems to the schools that older schoolmen were not prepared to cope with. Rather than make changes in their programs they waited to see what the future would bring. Lundgaard is a new breed of principal who has no desire to be a patriarch. He is a university graduate who has travelled and lived abroad; he recognizes that his students are better educated, more vocal, and less passive than those of earlier generations and are prepared to accept a good measure of freedom and responsibility. He treats them as adults and involves them in developing programs and governing the school.

In the winter course (October to May) students are eighteen to forty years old, the number of men and women is similar, and the average age is twenty-four. The previous winter some 65 per cent were unemployed and either continued to receive unemployment benefits or were granted bursaries. The others were young people who came directly from school or had worked for some time and decided to change jobs. Apparently no firms send their employees or give them leave of absence. Students participate actively in theatre, music, the visual arts, and several crafts. This experience is valuable in itself but is also a means of learning one's heritage. From weaving and pottery, for example, a student learns something of the role of these crafs in the history of Denmark. Students also become involved in social, political, and environmental problems and frequently do practical work. A recent project was the installation of a solar heating unit on the school roof that now heats all the school's water during the summer months.

The school involves itself in the Skaelskor community in a variety of ways. It is a critical voice in the community—its conscience, so to speak—and both staff and students attend public meetings and speak on controversial issues. In Lundgaard's view the folk high schools should be "the soul of the nation." There is, however, no town-gown tension in terms, say, of conflict between students and town youth, but there may be wide differences of opinion between the school community and older and more conservative members of the community on such issues as pollution control. Community groups use the school without charge and members of the community are always invited to public lectures and social events. Students interview the mayor and local politicians as part of their courses, and community leaders come to the school to speak on local history and community issues.

The principal and his staff cling to the tradition of awakening and enlightening the individual while at the same time raising his awareness of major problems in Denmark, Europe, and the Third World. The staff may attempt to politicize students by arousing interest in political issues, but they do not consciously transmit a particular dogma. While most high school teachers tend to be left of centre, among the staff at Skaelskor there are several shades of political thought. One gets the impression that the principal has a deep faith that through a term at his school students can change as much today as they did a century ago. "In my experience," he says, "the change is always from passive to active, never the other way." There are eleven full-time staff members, four of whom are women, for a maximum enrolment of 100. On average they teach sixteen hours a week and lead evening programs. The majority live in staff houses on campus.

There would appear to be no difficulty filling vacancies; for a recent opening there were sixty applications, the majority of which were of high quality. The principal teaches literature, philosophy, and psychology and recognizes that the traditional role of a folk high school principal is that of a public figure. He appears to enjoy what is expected of him—speaking to local adult education classes and giving lectures in village halls in various parts of the country and talks on radio. He is expected to take a stand on public issues and to serve on committees and commissions. His status is equal to, and possibly above, that of a secondary school headmaster or university professor. He has no illusions that he will stay in his present job for the rest of his life; most principals of his age group are, he believes, quite satisfied to accept five-to eight-year terms.

The winter term curriculum is based on history, psychology, Danish folk culture, ecology, crafts, and theatre. There is also a wide selection of optional courses. Generally speaking, the school emphasizes the humanities, social sciences, and arts; little attention is given to the natural sciences. Students work on individual and group projects using the school library or the community as a source of information, but the staff do not assume that students will read widely or deeply on specific topics. One ongoing project is the collection of songs, stories, and legends from elderly people who live in the vicinity, and recording these on tape or in print. There is a good deal of singing; in fact there is a return to song after a period of disaffection in which students were reluctant to sing. (The latest edition of the *Folk High School Song Book,* the sixteenth, includes 500 hymns, patriotic songs, historic poems set to music, and an appendix of English and American folk songs.) In the evenings and on weekends, students and staff jointly organize an extracurricular program of films, lectures, discussion, and dances. The principal feels quite strongly that if a term at high school is to be memorable it should be a happy time during which students enjoy themselves through singing and dancing. It is all to easy for young people to become depressed about problems of the world and of their own.

Skaelskor is occupied throughout the year except for two weeks at Christmas and a period in September when it is available for conferences. In the summer months there are short one- or two-week courses for pensioners, parents and their children, and for women only. The principal was delighted with the response to these courses and frankly admitted that they helped pay off the mortgage. Some courses are broad and general, others have a theme, such as Danish society in the future. There are also craft courses with a week devoted to each of five crafts. Permanent staff teach these summer courses on a rotating basis and at the time of these conversations with the principal, his wife, a full-time member of staff, was directing a course for pensioners.

Finally, we discussed how the school is managed and administered. The board of governors is elected in an unusual way. Each high school has a "constituency" of a given size stipulated in its constitution. The constituency is made up of men and women who have indicated an interest in the life of the school, frequently local people and former students or staff. In the case of Skaelskor the constituency numbers 170 and meets once a year, mainly to elect members of the board of governors. The board is responsible for the finances of the school, sees that it is operated within the high school law, and chooses the principal. It does not become involved in selection of staff, determination of program, or administration of the school. Those are the responsibilities of the principal and his staff. (The law stipulates that the principal and the teachers of a school constitute a teachers' council, but the extent of the council's function is not defined.) The board meets only four times a year but its executive committee meets with the principal once a month, and it is through the committee that the board and the principal work together and share decisions.

In law it would appear that Ebbe Lundgaard has several masters. The minister of education must approve his appointment, the school curriculum, and the board's by-laws. An inspector of the ministry supervises all the high schools. In fact, the ministry has seldom refused to approve a principal's appointment, a curriculum, or a board's by-laws. The inspector is more a liaison officer between the high schools and the ministry and is helpful to both. The law stipulates that the school must be a private, self-governing institution and the only definition of what a folk high school should be is as "a residential school which provides general education to adult students." In reality, Skaelskor has a high degree of autonomy. It is free to devise its program, appoint its staff, select its students, and operate as the principal and staff decide. It is neither a creature of the state nor of the board but a private school managed by the principal, who can delegate authority as he so decides.

Well over 50 per cent of all recurrent costs are paid for by the state, including 85 per cent of staff salaries. The principal is emphatic that the high schools are unique institutions. Because students attend voluntarily, write no examinations, and are not competing for selection to a higher place on the educational ladder, they can be relaxed, dig in to issues and values, and not be confined to intellectual performance. They can be critical of teachers and courses. This kind of freedom is, Lundgaard thinks, remarkable, particularly when it is supported by state grants to the schools and bursaries to students, and neither are judged by examination results. This freedom puts considerable moral responsibility on the school and its students.

Recent Developments

In the 1980s there are more high schools than ever before: some ninety schools with 9,500 students, 500 of whom come from other countries. Most are like Skaelskor and follow the Grundtvig/Kold tradition, but an increasing number are either sponsored by special groups or emphasize a particular kind of instruction. At least five political parties have begun high schools and three others are sponsored by trade unions; there are schools for pensioners and for women, one that emphasizes health, and a travelling high school which is part of the Tvind complex, which is organized on communal lines and consists of several schools, a teachers' college, and various business enterprises. There are schools that are avowedly Marxist, and others that stress an evangelical, pietistic form of Christianity.

This diversity is, in part, a result of the "troubles" of the early seventies which, in turn, reflected the staff and student protest movement that swept across North America and western Europe. At Askov, for example, a serious disagreement as to how the school should function developed among the staff in the fall of 1970. A minority of the staff, with support from the principal, argued that traditional teaching methods were outmoded and that teachers should reveal their political beliefs and encourage students to engage in direct political and social action. The debate at Askov received extensive press coverage and the controversy spread to other schools. In 1971 the Askov board of governors dismissed the principal, and eight teachers in the minority group agreed to resign. They have since built their own school, Kolding, which is dedicated to reforming society and promoting change in the conditions which distort and repress human life."The social intercourse at a folk high school and the work we do there must not be a goal in themselves. . . . The essence is not the small community at Kolding Folk High School but the large one outside it. That is where the changes have to be made. That is where evaluations are needed. That is the ultimate aim of the enterprise."[26]

Askov and other schools are now sailing in less troubled waters, and the trend appears to be to reduce the sovereignty of the principal, to give more responsibility to a council composed of both staff and students, and to decrease the number of lectures and class meetings. In the Askov curriculum there are no required subjects. Students choose from a rich *smörrebröd* of electives, and a full course load usually consists of twenty classes a week. Time for independent study and group projects has increased markedly. Relatively few schools have become politicized and the great majority share the objectives of Skaelskor, not Kolding. The schools are more European and international and less Danish in outlook and there is among many staff and students a genuine concern for Third World problems. No longer do the schools have a direct or indirect impact on a large segment of Danish society. They do, however, influence individuals within a much broader age range than formerly and groups with special interests.

Since the Second World War—with the development of industry and decline in the numbers employed in agriculture; the move to the towns and growth of a consumer society; a wealth of social legislation; and problems related to unemployment, inflation, and high taxation—in the midst of all these factors the high schools continue to flourish and the idea of a liberal and general education for young adults is still generally accepted. But if Danish society seriously falters, can the schools remain healthy?

Folk High Schools in Other Countries

Norway

Within twenty-five years of the founding of Rødding, folk high schools had opened in Norway and Sweden. Because of Russian oppression Finland had to wait until 1889. Grundtvig, Kold, Schrøder, and members of the Little Theologicum were influential. In 1837, when Grundtvig was mounting his campaign in Denmark, he wrote a pamphlet called *To the Norwegians, Concerning a Norwegian High School,* in which he exhorted them to start a school where the genuine mother tongue of the Norwegians would be revived. The two Norwegian theologians, Olaus Arvesen and Herman Anker, who established the first school in Norway in 1864 had belonged to Schrøder's circle in Copenhagen and had attended Grundtvig's lectures three years earlier. Anker's aims for his new school could have been written by Kold or one of the other Danish principals:

> The object of the school is, on the foundation laid by the elementary schools, to provide for the farmers' sons a more advanced general education which may be of service to them as a source of inspiration for life, giving them the ability and the desire to develop and further the evolution of their country. . . . There will be no classes devoted to the Christian religion, but we shall endeavour to see all subjects in the light of Christianity.

The home and family atmosphere Kold created was also part of the early Norwegian schools. Initially, because it feared a political awakening of the peasants, the Norwegian government opposed the high schools and tried to end them by refusing to give them state grants. Only by agreeing to a measure of control by the county councils were the schools able to secure grants in 1875. Later the schools gained support from the organizations of young farmers, gave strong backing to the peasant language movement, and became part of the national current which broke Norway's link with Sweden. (For four centuries ending in 1814 Norway was part of the Danish-Norwegian monarchy; Copenhagen was Norway's capital and Danish was the official language. From 1814 to 1905 Norway was united with Sweden.) The schools flourished in the twentieth century, rising in number from ten in 1900–1 to eighty-eight in 1976. Their students have made an impact on Norwegian society through founding youth organizations and co-operatives and giving leadership in country districts. In 1966 nearly half the members of the Norwegian Parliament were former students of folk high schools.

Sweden

Grundtvig was known and respected in Sweden and his major works were translated into Swedish, but his influence was never as great there as in Norway. When the first high school opened in 1868, Sweden was not in the midst of a national crisis or struggling for survival. She had adopted a parliamentary constitution and the peasantry had acquired equal suffrage in 1866. The schools were not, however, confined to rural youth nor did they develop a religious emphasis or a political objective. It has been said that the reason the Danish and Swedish schools were so different was that the first Danish principal was a theologian and the first principal in Sweden was a geologist. One of the first Swedish schools issued this down-to-earth statement of its purpose: "A school in which a youth may be given instruction for the improvement of his mind as well as for the practical affairs of life, a school in which he may acquire general knowledge, decide what occupation he is best fitted for. Learn to respect work and to take pleasure in working himself. . . . "

The first schools catered to young peasants, largely because only a small minority of Swedes then lived in towns. Recently, however, the proportion of young people from industrial families is larger in Swedish high schools than in the other Scandinavian countries. A two- or three-year course is common and there has always been an emphasis on independent study, the use of books, and the transfer of knowledge. University men were closely identified with the early schools and there was more formality in the atmosphere than in the Danish and Norwegian schools. History and literature were not stressed to the same degree as in the other countries because the schools were not concerned with a national purpose. As a result, the natural sciences were given greater emphasis. The state supported the schools almost from the beginning and no friction developed later, largely because the schools were prepared to accept a certain degree of state control. There is now a highly diversified group of schools (108 in 1976), including schools operated by local authorities and those owned by labour organizations, the temperance movement, the Swedish Church, and other private bodies. Objectives and methods to suit the Swedish national character were decided soon after the schools were founded:

> A nation as predominantly sober and practical as the Swedes is not to be won by words alone. It will never be content with just listening and having its emotions awakened. . . . The best representatives of our youth are too hard-working, too energetic to be able to sit for five months on a bench, merely to look and listen passively, while the teacher uses all his physical and mental strength to collect and present all the best he knows, understands, and can do. The young want themselves to lend a hand to the work, and demand the means and assistance necessary for such cooperation.[27]

Finland

Grundtvigian ideas took root in Finland when a former Askov student, Sofia Hagman, started the first high school in 1889. In the nineteenth century Finland and Denmark were both struggling to counteract the dominance of a neighboring power. In 1809 Finland was separated from Sweden to become a grand duchy under the Russian czar. Finnish university leaders soon began a movement to create a national cultural awakening through collecting and publishing ancient lays and legends. Attempts to found a folk high school, however, did not succeed until late in the century when the foundations of an elementary school system had been set down. A powerful incentive was the threat of increasing russification and by the turn of the century there were twenty-one high schools. Five were Finno-Swedish, founded by the Swedish minority in their determination to preserve their language and culture. After the Great Strike in Finland in 1905, Russia became more oppressive and, predictably, new schools continued to open. After 1917, when Finland declared its independence, the schools achieved greater stability with the assurance of state grants. The schools were and still are, mainly owned by private societies, foundations, and organizations which include churches, trade unions, and the Temperance League. While founded on Grundtvigian lines, they have developed their own traditions, including a combination of humanistic subjects, handicraft training, and a stress on religious instruction. People's academies, the first of which was modelled on Askov, offer courses to students who have previously attended a high school course. In 1976 there were eighty-six high schools, all residential, with winter courses of at least thirty weeks and short courses in the summer term. Over almost a century of operation the enrolments have been largely young people from agriculture and forestry.

Among the Scandinavian countries Finland has had to struggle most to retain its culture and establish its independence. In a little over two decades after achieving independence it was involved against Russia in the "Winter War" of 1939–40. After the surrender of a large part of southeastern Karelia, six of the high schools and their students were moved into Finland and continued their work. This close connection between national aspiration, indeed national survival, and the folk school movement is evident in Denmark, Norway, and Finland, but less marked in Sweden. The high schools of Sweden have not influenced the nation's history as the Danish schools have done. They have had, nevertheless, a national objective: one law governing the high schools has stipulated that students "learn to know their neighbourhood and their country, its historical development and present social structure, its moral and material resources."[28]

Attempts to establish folk high schools outside Scandinavia have met with only modest success. Fircroft College in England, Coleg Harlech in Wales, and Newbattle Abbey in Scotland were founded by British educators who had visited Danish schools, but a network or movement of residential colleges did not develop. Beginning in 1878, Danish immigrants to the United States and Canada transplanted the high schools to at least six communities but none has survived. Variations of the Nordic high school have appeared in The Netherlands, Germany, Austria, Switzerland, and Japan, and a small number have taken permanent root. Following the Second World War there was a burst of enthusiasm in Denmark for exporting the folk high school idea to the developing countries. In 1947 the first vidyapeeth, or people's college, was set up in Mysore on the Danish pattern but with careful attention to Indian tradition. Some years later an evaluation report was not encouraging on the results of the agricultural training of former students. In Ghana a residential college with Danes on the staff and assistance provided by the Danish Association for International Co-operation opened in 1954. For political reasons it closed in 1966.

In the belief that Denmark could be used as a laboratory to study the interaction among adult education, co-operatives, and agriculture, the Danes set up a rural development college in Holte in 1964. Civil servants came from countries south of the Sahara for in-service training. For nearly ten years the Danish government supported this college, and several hundred Africans in adult education, agricultural extension, and community development took the course. Testimony from participants was clearly favorable, but the Danish government came to think that this kind of training could more profitably take place in the developing countries themselves.

Transplanting an educational institution to a different culture raises the question of whether or not a unique set of circumstances must be present before an innovation can take root and flourish. In Denmark, national figures of the stature of Grundtvig and Schröder combined their energies to hasten the liberation of peasants and to awaken them spiritually; political and military defeats gave an impetus to national regeneration; and an agricultural crisis called forth the flexibility and acumen of small holders to change farming methods and engage in co-operation. The result was economic prosperity and the achievement of political power. When these events follow each other relatively quickly or indeed occur simultaneously in an ethnically and religiously homogeneous society not rocked by internal violence, a new kind of school closely related to these events is likely to succeed. But Denmark's experience is not going to be repeated elsewhere, and we must ask whether attempts to transplant the folk high school will fail when circumstances are markedly different. Probably yes, if the aim is to build a replica of the Danish model.

TWO

Horace Mann
1796–1859

Horace Mann: The American Public School System

Horace Mann, reprinted from *Horace Mann: A Biography* by Jonathan Messerli with permission from Alfred A. Knopf, Inc. and Jonathan Messerli.

The Great Circuit

One morning in late August 1837 Horace Mann saddled his dark bay mare and rode out of Boston headed for Worcester, where he would deliver his first address as secretary of the Massachusetts Board of Education. At forty-one and president of the state Senate, Mann had surprised his friends by accepting this new post and abandoning a promising career in politics and the law. For the better part of two months he had wrestled with the decision; the state legislature had just created the Board of Education and Governor Edward Everett had appointed Mann as one of its eight members. Edmund Dwight, a manufacturer and philanthropist, had privately assured Mann that he would nominate him as secretary, but in the early summer Mann had wavered. Could a man with no experience in public education adequately carry out the duties of this high and responsible office? In spite of his zeal as a reformer for the cause of the common schools, would the opposition and irritations be too great?

> Whoever shall undertake that task must encounter privation, labor and an infinite annoyance from an infinite number of schemers. He must condense the steam of enthusiasts and soften the rock of the incredulous. What toil in arriving at a true system himself! What toil in infusing that system into the minds of others![1]

But, on the other hand, the law establishing the board was "the first great movement toward an organized system of common education, which shall at once be thorough and universal."[2] And what a thought it was to have the minds of multitudes of children "dependent in any perceptible degree upon one's own exertions!"[3]

Finally, the day before the board met to discuss the appointment and after further consultation with Dwight, who volunteered to add $500 from his own resources to the board's meagre $1,000 annual salary (from which travel expenses and the cost of maintaining an office would be deducted), Horace Mann decided to let his nomination stand. And when the board confirmed his appointment he rejoiced in the privacy of his journal in the spirit of a true reformer:

> I have received the offer. The path of usefulness is opened before me. . . . God grant me an annihilation of selfishness, a mind of wisdom, a heart of benevolence! . . . There is but one spirit in which . . . impediments can be met with success: it is the spirit of self-abandonment, the spirit of martyrdom.[4]

After meeting with the board in his new capacity he wrote: "Henceforth, so long as I hold this office, I devote myself to the supremest welfare of mankind upon earth. . . . I have faith in the improvability of the race—in their accelerating improvability."[5] As later events would prove, in accepting his new position, whatever his motives may have been, he was responding to a call to shape the system of public schools in the United States.

In July, Mann returned to his family home in the town of Franklin to read in his "new subject" of education and to prepare an address he planned to give at conventions of school committee members throughout the state. The first one was in Worcester and Mann held the attention of his large audience for an hour and a half with a presentation that a local newspaper reported as "a performance of a superior order, and listened to with an intensity of attention." Knowing the strength of the tradition in Massachusetts for local control of schools, Mann began his address, "Means and Objects of Common School Education,"[6] by reassuring his audience that the newly appointed state Board of Education had no real powers, either to direct or to restrain, no authority to impose new modes of education, and no funds at its disposal. Its only strengths were its powers of persuasion. Through its secretary it was, however, obliged to collect information on the efficiency and condition of the common schools and distribute this, together with information on new and enlightened teaching methods, throughout the Commonwealth. Once he had established that the board was essentially an organ of information and the secretary its agent, Mann revealed his view of the local or district schools:

> In this Commonwealth there are about three thousand public schools, in all of which the rudiments of knowledge are taught. These schools, at the present time, are so many distinct, independent communities; each being governed by its own habits, traditions, and local customs. There is no common, superintending power over them; there is no bond of brotherhood or family between them. They are strangers and aliens to each other.[7]

Flowery rhetoric, colorful analogies, and the seeds of Mann's educational thought can be found in this, his first formal address as secretary. He scorns the teacher who strikes fear into pupils' hearts, and he vividly pictures a child in the act of learning:

> Mark a child when a clear, well-defined, vivid conception seizes it. The whole nervous tissue vibrates. Every muscle leaps. Every joint plays. The face becomes auroral. The spirit flashes through the body, like lightning through a cloud.[8]

With irony, Mann describes the appalling condition of Massachusetts schoolhouses, which he regarded as "a very general calamity." Eminent physicians had assured him that because of the poor construction of schoolhouses there was, annually, loss of life, destruction of health, and "such anatomical distortion as renders life hardly worth possessing." One school he had seen had such a large hole in its roof that it operated like a funnel to catch all the rain and pour it into the classroom. On inquiry, the teacher reassured Mann that she and her little ones were in no danger of drowning because the floor leaked as badly as the roof and drained off the water. A further "mischief" lay in the surfeit of school texts which publishers had sold to Massachusetts district schools, 300 different titles, in fact.

By contrast, there was little equipment for teaching science and geography. And so Mann's litany of malpractice continued: the prevalence of rote learning, the mindless use of corporal punishment, the encouragement of competition within the classroom, and the statewide neglect of instruction in care of the body. More generally, he emphasized that the responsibility for education rested "upon the people" of Massachusetts, not the legislature or the Board of Education; that education must be universal because a literate electorate was essential to a republican form of government; and that the ultimate aim of education was to develop character and create a higher level of individual and public morality. When he concluded, Mann was given a warm ovation and men rose from all sections of the hall to present resolutions supporting his proposals, including one to form then and there the Worcester County Association for the Improvement of the Common Schools.

For the next three months Mann travelled to every county in the state but one, holding similar conventions for school committee members and others interested in common schools. Not all were well-attended or enthusiastic. At Salem, for example, attendance was minimal and Mann commented sadly, "Things had not been arranged beforehand, and everything dragged and stuck,—one of the poorest conventions I have had."[9] By late October, Mann was back in Boston, having travelled over 500 miles on horseback and stage coach. "My great circuit," he wrote in his journal, "is now completed."

The Rugged Nursing of Toil

In spite of his disclaimers Horace Mann had, through experience and training, unusual qualifications for his new career. At the age of seven he was helping on the family farm in the town of Franklin, and a few years later enrolled in a dilapidated district school for the six-week winter term. Memories of his boyhood were largely of unrelenting work, and in an autobiographical sketch he wrote:

> I believe in the rugged nursing of Toil; but she nursed me too much. . . . I have derived one compensation, however, from the rigor of my early lot. Industry, or diligence, became my second nature. . . . Owing to these ingrained habits, work has always been to me what water is to a fish. I have wondered a thousand times to hear people say, "I don't like this business"; or, "I wish I could ex-

change for that"; for with me whenever I have had anything to do, I do not remember ever to have demurred, but have always set about it like a fatalist; and it was as sure to be done as the sun is to set.[10]

Mann's childhood and youth were blighted not only by toil but by Calvinist theology as preached by Dr. Nathaniel Emmons, who ruled the Franklin community for more than fifty years and expounded the doctrines of depravity, reprobation, and the eternal torments of hell. When Horace was fourteen his brother Stephen was drowned one Sunday in a nearby pond where he had gone to fish or swim. To Dr. Emmons this was was a clear case of profaning the Sabbath and at the funeral service, instead of consoling the Mann family, he seized the opportunity to remind the young people present that Stephen had wilfully sinned and had died unconverted. His after-life would be one of eternal punishment. This scene left an indelible scar on Horace and although later in life he became a Unitarian, the legacy of a Calvinist boyhood remained with him. Whether from the influence of Dr. Emmons or the austerity of his family life, Mann ended his autobiographical sketch with the candid statement that whatever may have been his shortcomings he had always been exempt from the common vices. He was never in his life intoxicated, he never swore, and never used the "vile weed" in any form. Yet his friends in later years testified to his fund of humor and sparkling wit.[11]

By the time he was eighteen Mann had decided that he had to escape from the family farm. His older brother, Stanley, had left Franklin to become a textile entrepreneur, but Horace was not attracted to a career in business. He was much more attached to books and had read all the works on history in the town library. But the young Mann had only a very modest education and by the age of sixteen had never attended school for more than ten weeks a year. If he were going to follow some of his boyhood friends to university and a career in one of the professions he needed to pass entrance examinations in Latin, Greek, and mathematics. He began to study these subjects alone, but within a year realized he needed help. Happily, an itinerant tutor, Samuel Barrett, appeared in Franklin and, when sober, proved to be a brilliant classicist. For instruction in mathematics Horace walked four miles to Wrentham, where the Reverend William Williams coached local boys to qualify for his alma mater, Brown. Throughout the winter, spring, and summer of 1816 this intense tutoring continued and by mid-September Horace, now in his twentieth year, set off by stage-coach for Providence. At Brown he was examined by President Asa Messer and two professors of classics. He performed so well that he was admitted to the sophomore year.

In Mann's day Brown was not as distinguished a university as it later became. There were few outstanding men on its faculty and their method of teaching was the traditional recitation during which students regurgitated the contents of a textbook. There was, however, a recent innovation which particularly appealed to Mann: the appointment of a professor of oratory and belles-lettres. Through delivering highly ornamented declamations, strong in style and weak in substance, for Professor Tristram Burges' benefit, and through active involvement in a literary and debating society known as the United Brothers, Mann learned the art and technique of platform rhetoric and parliamentary debate. At Brown he also deepened his intellectual interests, particularly in history and politics, though his essays were often blatantly chauvinistic.

He had little use for literature, particularly the novel. "Perhaps few kinds of amusement are more prejudicial to the attainment of solid sciences, or productive of more permanent injury to the mind than the excessive perusal of that species of fictitious history embraced in novels and romances," he wrote in an undergraduate essay. From the beginning of his years at Brown, Mann nurtured a twin ambition: to lead his class and to be its valedictorian. Again he showed his capacity for diligence and toil and at the commencement exercises of September 1819 he received both honors. In his valedictory on the topic "The Gradual Advancement of the Human Species in Dignity and Happiness," he expressed his belief that man was involved in a gradual and inevitable process of perfectibility. Outwardly at least he appeared to have repudiated Dr. Emmons.

President Messer persuaded Mann to return to Brown for two years as a tutor, but his heavy-handed attempts to win the respect of his freshmen students were no more acceptable than his outspoken criticism of several faculty members. His second departure from Brown had none of the glory of the first, but Mann now was convinced that his future lay not in teaching but in law.

From former Brown classmates Mann learned that the most direct route to success in law was by way of Tapping Reeve's law school in Litchfield, Connecticut. Judge Reeve was no longer in charge, but under the direction of James Gould the school continued to flourish and its alumni could be found on the bench of the Supreme Court, in the federal Cabinet, and in the United States Senate. Gould was a brilliant lecturer and, while the school work was demanding, Mann found its atmosphere more congenial and relaxed than that of Brown. Litchfield also presented the considerable advantage of Miss Pierce's seminary for young ladies, and social life, chaperoned of course, flourished between the two institutions. Litchfield gave Mann an excellent professional education and an introduction to the customs and pleasures of genteel society.

Following a year of apprenticeship he was called to the bar and began to practise in Dedham, Massachusetts, then a quiet town of 2,500 but soon to attract cotton and woollen mills and a shoe factory. Even during his legal apprenticeship Mann caught the attention of the town fathers and was asked to deliver the 1823 4th of July oration. In the early nineteenth century New England towns commemorated independence with a happy and noisy enthusiasm that lasted most of the day. It was between the parade and the banquet that Mann, dressed in a black cloak draped like a Roman toga, spoke to a crowded audience in the Unitarian Church. He had labored long on his oration and put to use all the rhetorical skill he had learned at Brown and in Gould's moot court in Litchfield. With nationalist fervor he blasted the monarchs and despots of Europe and praised those American patriots who had given the republic the blessings of representative government. It was they who had bequeathed to future generations "one of the most transcendently important and glorious events in history."

Again, three years later, Mann was called on to give a public address to the people of Dedham. Fifty years to the day after they had signed the Declaration of Independence, Thomas Jefferson and John Adams both died on 4 July 1826. Sombrely, the towns of New England marked the occasion and the weighty leaders of Dedham chose Mann, still the town's youngest attorney, to deliver the eulogy. This he did with a style and hyperbole that fitted the occasion and the expectations of his listeners. One of these was the president of the United States, John Quincy Adams who, before returning to his home in nearby Quincy, made a point of meeting the young speaker and thanking him for his inspiring address. Later he wrote that Mann's eulogy was "of splendid composition and lofty eloquence. . . . "

POLITICIAN AND REFORMER

Mann was now not only a rising lawyer and a proven public speaker but an entrepreneur who in partnership with his brother Stanley had acquired, almost entirely through promissory notes, two near-bankrupt mills. One further prospect attracted him: politics. Starting with the Dedham town meeting, and soon becoming its moderator, he graduated in 1827 to the state House of Representatives or General Court, taking his seat with 300 others. His first major speech in the House was in support of railroads and his opening lines were, "Machinery is the enlargement of human power. . . . Here strength of mind makes up for the weakness of the body." For the next several years he spoke on the railroad issue many times, was appointed to a committee on railways and canals, and insisted that a railroad from Boston to the Hudson was essential to the growth of commercial and manufacturing interests. His support of industrialization and urbanization was part of his general faith in science and technology, revealed earlier in his valedictory at Brown: "Science," he declaimed, had "amassed invention upon invention and crowned discovery with discovery, until it . . . scaled the very Olympus . . . and brought down the fire from heaven."

In the midst of his considerable success as a lawyer and legislator and the rapid increase in both his income and status, Mann did not lose his sense of a social mission. Indeed, in his own characteristic idiom he said, after reflecting on the progressive legislation passed by the General Court in 1830, "I feel my desire for human and benevolent effort invigorated."[12] As a humanitarian reformer he addressed himself first to the issues of intemperance and the treatment of the insane. In the legislature Mann proposed that a study be made of the extent to which crime and pauperism were caused by "the intemperate use of ardent spirits." Not surprisingly, a committee was struck and he was named its chairman. Concern about the drinking habits of the lower classes was widespread and temperance societies were appearing throughout New England. Mann and a group of friends formed such a society in Dedham, of which he became president in 1829. The leading families of Dedham were moderate in their views, did not counsel prohibition or total abstinence, and believed that moral suasion and the distribution of information on the evils of drink would persuade men to change their habits.

As a legislator Mann went one step further: he proposed a change in licensing laws. The most recent census revealed that in Boston there was one person licensed to sell spirits for every fifty adult males in the city. The bill Mann introduced would sharply reduce the number of licensed outlets; it was opposed not only by liquor retailers but with equal vigor by one of the state-wide temperance societies, which believed that intervention through legal restraints was a less effective remedy than a campaign under the auspices of the churches to encourage total voluntary abstinence. Mann's bill was passed, but only after he led a six-hour battle in the legislature. The temperance issue revealed two features of Mann's social philosophy: a belief that intemperance was the cause, not the symptom of poverty; and that in the eradication of social evils and the reform of society voluntary bodies and sectarian groups may have a role to play, but it was also necessary to invoke the power and authority of the state.

The same year that Mann took his seat in the legislature a House committee reported on the appalling conditions under which the insane were incarcerated in jails and houses of correction. A voluntary organization, the Prison Discipline Society, also issued a report in 1827 which documented cases of the mentally ill clothed in rags, living in unheated cells, and sleeping on straw. One inmate had been allowed to leave his cell only twice in eight years. Mann soon took up the appeal for action, and made his own position clear: the insane should become wards of the state. When the matter was referred to a committee of which he was already chairman, he initiated a further survey of provisions for the insane which revealed that some "lunatics and persons furiously mad" had been confined for as long as forty-five years without therapeutic treatment.

In a moving speech to the House, Mann described the suffering of the insane, of whom he estimated there were at least 500 in Massachusetts. He reported that he had visited a mental hospital in Connecticut and had studied the reports of doctors in Europe. These investigations had persuaded him that with proper treatment there could be a larger proportion of recoveries from insanity than from most other diseases. His recommendations, which appeared later in the form of a bill, called on the state to select and purchase a site and erect a hospital to accommodate 120 persons. The legislature accepted his recommendations, passed the bill, and appropriated $30,000 for a "Lunatic Hospital" in Worcester, for which Governor Levi Lincoln appointed a commission of three to supervise construction and devise "a system of discipline and government." As chairman of this commission, Horace Mann, then thirty-four, directed the founding of the first state mental hospital in the United States.

During his undergraduate and teaching days at Brown, Mann had often visited the president's home and first met Charlotte Messer when she was a child. He continued these visits during his years in Litchfield and Dedham and was deeply attracted by Charlotte's delicate beauty. For several years he admired her in secret but by July 1829 he could wait no longer to declare his intentions. Regardless of his ability with the spoken word he felt more comfortable in this instance with the pen, and in his first sentence he came immediately to the point:

> Miss Charlotte Messer
>
> In obedience to feelings whose utterance I can no longer repress, I take the liberty of this mode to request permission to visit you hereafter in the character of an *avowed*, as I have hitherto done, in that of a *secret* admirer.[13]

The courtship that followed was passionate, but it too was conducted through the mails. In September 1830, they were married and made their first home in Dedham. In the early months of the marriage Mann was piloting the legislation for the mental hospital through the House and was burdened with other affairs of state. These responsibilities forced him to remain in Boston for days at a time and Charlotte, lonely, homesick, and often unwell (she probably had tuberculosis), frequently returned to her parents' home in Providence. For nearly a year and a half these intermittent separations continued and Charlotte was seldom in good health. In the late spring of 1832 she improved noticeably and Mann was free of responsibility in Boston. May and June were the happiest months of their marriage, but their joy was short-lived. By late July her doctor visited Charlotte daily and as she grew weaker Mann gave her constant attention. As her delirium increased it became, as Mann later recalled, "a scene of anxiety, of dismay, of struggling, of death."[14] She was only twenty-three.

Charlotte's death had a profound affect on Mann. In his grief he wrote that his world had changed. "I seem to stand in a world of shadows. That which gave light and beauty and reality to all is gone. But it is within, that desolation has done its perfect work."[15] His friends attempted to comfort him but with little success; they did, however, persuade him to leave his house in Dedham and take lodgings in Mrs. Clarke's boarding house in Boston. Then in 1834 another blow struck Mann. His brother Stanley was so hopelessly in debt that he abandoned his wife and children, moved to Kentucky, and left Horace to pay the promissory notes held by his creditors. This Mann was legally obliged to do and for the next three years he lived in his office, slept on a horsehair sofa, and restricted his expenses in every possible way. During one six-month period he was frequently unable to buy dinner, and fell ill from hunger and overwork. It was only in November 1837 that he was sufficiently free of debt to move to rooms at the corner of Tremont and School streets.

Both Charlotte's death and Stanley's defection may help to explain why Horace Mann took the surprising step of becoming secretary of the Board of Education. In his grief for Charlotte and his disillusion over Stanley, Mann convinced himself that his values and ideals needed to be reordered. If he were to be genuinely a humanitarian reformer he thought he should be motivated more by a desire to serve others and less by personal ambition. At the same time, however, his ambition prompted him to be sure that he was attaching himself to a great cause: "The bar is no longer my forum," he wrote. "My jurisdiction is changed. I have abandoned jurisprudence, and betaken myself to the larger sphere of mind and morals."[16] His belief that a change in career would be a form of release from his grief was to some degree vindicated, as he explained to his sister Lydia when he returned to Boston after his circuit ride to the county conventions: "I confess I feel, now, more as though life had a value, and as though I had a specific work to do, than I have done before for these last five years."[17] And as he wound up his last cases in court he did not underestimate, or understate, the magnitude of his new position: "The interests of a client are small, compared with the interests of the next generation. Let the next generation, then, be my client. . . . "[18] Like all people, Mann was driven by a mixture of motives.

Secretary of the Board

On New Year's Day, 1838, Horace Mann read the first of his annual reports to the Board of Education. Since his appointment six months earlier he had collected much information: 294 of the 305 towns (townships) had responded to his request for statistics; during his travels to county conventions he had either personally examined or otherwise obtained specific information on the size, construction, and condition of some 800 schoolhouses; and through correspondence he had secured knowledge of at least 1,000 more.[19] In examining this wealth of evidence he was able to assure the Board of the "vast preponderance" of the excellencies of the system over its defects, but, having said that, he then in more than forty pages of fine print revealed the shortcomings.

These were similar to those delineated in his address to the county conventions on the great circuit, but now he had firmer evidence. Behind the short terms and irregular attendance, incompetent and underpaid teachers, decrepit and unsanitary school buildings were the apathy and irresponsibility of school committees. By law these committees were required to secure from teachers evidence of their moral character, literary qualifications, and capacity for the government of schools, but Mann found that two-thirds of the towns had failed to collect such evidence.[20] School committees were also responsible for visitation and inspection, but in only fifty or sixty towns did committee members visit their schools, an oversight which led Mann to observe that the teachers of Massachusetts "have not one-thousandth part of the supervision which watches the same number of persons, having the care of cattle or spindles, or of the retail of shop-goods."[21] In one town with forty school districts, the school committee had not examined a teacher or visited a school for the past eight years.[22]

This neglect of duty by school committees reflected the extent of public apathy toward the common schools. "It is generally believed," said Mann, "that there is an increasing class of people amongst us, who are losing sight of the necessity of securing ample opportunities for the education of their children. And thus, on one side, the institution of common schools is losing its natural support, if it be not incurring actual opposition."[23] But on the "other side" there was a class of parents who were so deeply interested in the education of their children that they were turning away from the common schools and establishing private schools. When parents in a village or town took this step, Mann observed, the results aggravated each other: such parents no longer served on the school committee, had no motive for voting for an increase in the annual appropriation, and as their children deserted the common schools the quality of those schools was damaged. As this happened still other parents turned toward the private schools, and the common school was left to the management of those "who have not the desire or the power either to improve it or to command a better."[24]

Mann reserved his final criticism for the common school teachers, but here he had to avoid antagonizing the teachers and at the same time speak with candor. He used the device of referring to conversations he had had with intelligent men throughout the state, among whom there was a unanimous conviction of "an extensive want of competent teachers for the common schools." But then, he hastened to add, this judgment should not be regarded as a reproach to teachers; the fault lay more with the public: "The teachers," he said, with conspicuous ambiguity, "are as good as public opinion has demanded."[25] His analysis of school committee reports revealed that teachers were grossly underpaid. Throughout Massachusetts the average monthly salary for males was $15.45 and for females $5.38. Few taught regularly. In Boston, for example, only 100 men and a slightly larger number of women were career teachers devoting themselves to teaching as a regular and continuous form of employment. And few of these had any special training.

Such was Mann's indictment of Massachusetts schools. The decline of the common schools was the result of decentralization of control. In the seventeenth century the General Court of Massachusetts Bay Colony had legislated primary and grammar schools for towns of specified populations and from these laws, the earliest recognition of the need for public education in America, there grew the tradition of town or township schools, usually free and supervised by selectmen and ministers who carried out the wishes and instructions of the town meeting. Originally a town was a collection of families clustered around the meeting house, but as the population increased and settlers moved into the wilderness, the town became a population scattered over a township. A central school was no longer sufficient and the travelling or moving school made its appearance. Again as the population grew, this kind of school gave way to permanent district schools located throughout the township. Increasingly, districts achieved greater autonomy and by the early nineteenth century were selecting their own teachers and using their own discretion in spending the grant apportioned to them by the town school committees. The district school was a creature of the school district and it was not uncommon, even in Mann's day, for districts to spend less than $10.00 a year for a child's schooling. Teachers were "boarded round" from one family to another and paid little.

Mann was, of course, well aware of the practice of creating smaller and smaller districts which, he said in his lecture to the second round of county conventions, yielded "the calamitous consequences of stinted means . . . cheap schoolhouses, cheap teachers and short schools." Never at a loss to invoke a vivid image, he added: "Under this weakening process, many of our children have fared like southern fruits in a northern clime, where, owing to the coldness of the soil and shortness of the season, they never more than half ripen."[26] In the State House he successfully lobbied for new school legislation, including compensation for members of school committees (one dollar per day) and a clearer definition of their duties. These were to embrace the selection of books to be used in all town schools, the visitation of schools once each month (this, Mann explained, must involve more than fastening a horse at the schoolhouse door and going in for a few minutes to rest or get warm), and the selection of teachers which, if a town so decided, would no longer be a district responsibility. The school committee would be obliged to keep a permanent record of its proceedings and to submit annually a detailed report of the condition of the schools, including specific recommendations for their improvement.

Furthermore, the new legislation allowed two or more school districts to form a union or central school and while this was permissive rather than compulsory, it was the first step toward consolidation of schools. (In his report on schoolhouses, a supplement of his first report, Mann proposed that children under eight could walk one mile to school and should continue to attend district schools, while older children could walk two miles or more to union schools.) By the end of the 1838 spring session of the legislature Mann was able to say that every recommendation and suggestion made in his reports had been turned into law. In the judgment of one of his biographers, he had accomplished "as much in legislation as had been done in the previous twenty years."[27] And he had set Massachusetts in the direction of a coherent system of public education.

There were many lectures during that first year. Mann followed William Ellery Channing and Ralph Waldo Emerson on Boston's most prestigious platform, with three weekly lectures on education to the

Society for the Diffusion of Useful Knowledge. He gave a series of talks to the primary teachers of Boston and, by invitation, addressed the House of Representatives on what he now regarded as one of his central interests—the need for better teachers. In spite of limited time for preparation—one day—he was not dissatisfied with his performance in the legislature: "A pretty full house, though the weather was unpleasant: held them one hour and a half, stiller and stiller to the end."[28] And late in the year he launched the semi-monthly *Common School Journal.* The first issue noted that the editorial department would be under the care of the Honorable Horace Mann, that each of the twenty-four issues would be sixteen pages, and that the annual subscription would be one dollar.

> The great object of the work will be the improvement of Common Schools and other means of Popular Education. It is also intended to make it a depository of the Laws of the Commonwealth in relation to Schools, and of Reports, Proceedings, etc., of the Massachusetts Board of Education. As the documents of that Board will have a general interest, they ought to be widely diffused and permanently preserved. . . .
>
> The Paper will be kept entirely aloof from partisanship in politics, and sectarianism in religion, vindicating, and commending to practice, only the great and fundamental truths of civil and social obligation, of moral and religious duty.

As a publicist Mann had few peers. The *Journal* gave him a platform on which to discuss educational issues and an organ through which to disseminate widely his annual reports, new school legislation, and a broad range of opinion by authors at home and abroad.

Teachers at School

The idea of a special institution to train schoolmasters did not originate with Horace Mann. Teachers' seminaries were established in Germany and normal schools in France in the eighteenth century, and two of Mann's contemporaries, James G. Carter and the Reverend Charles Brooks, had campaigned for teacher training in Massachusetts prior to Mann's appointment as secretary. Brooks had visited the Prussian seminaries and on his return addressed meetings throughout New England in what became a crusade for normal schools. Carter, a member of both the House of Representatives and the Board of Education, had put forth several new ideas in an essay entitled "Outlines for an Institution for the Education of Teachers." Carter was, in fact, an influential figure in the inner group of educational reformers and it was a surprise to many that he was not appointed as the board's first secretary. Instead, he served as Horace Mann's John the Baptist.

There was, then, a growing consensus among Mann's friends that the founding of schools or seminaries for teachers was the most direct and effective means of improving the quality of the common schools. To Mann's delight, Edward Dwight again offered to contribute $10,000 to promote the improvement of teachers, provided the legislature would allocate a similar amount. Mann communicated word of this private munificence to the House and in little over a month a resolution to match Dwight's gift had swept through both House and Senate with only one dissenting vote. The chief reason for such little opposition probably lay in Mann's political acumen both in rallying support and in keeping the wording of the resolution vague. There was no specific designation of the nature, name, curriculum, or location of the institution the promoters had in mind, simply a recommendation to allocate $10,000 to be used under the direction of the Board of Education "in qualifying teachers for the Common Schools in Massachusetts." If the wording sounded innocuous the intent was specific and startling. A new institution supported by state funds and under state control would educate teachers for the common schools. It was a break with Massachusetts tradition. Hitherto, whatever training teachers received had been in schools, seminaries, or academies controlled by either school committees or private bodies.

In "Normal Schools," the lead article in the third issue of the *Common School Journal,* Mann gave full details of the Dwight bequest, the action taken by the legislature, and the subsequent decision of the Board of Education to establish three normal schools for an experimental period of three years. The term "normal school" was borrowed from Europe, the word "normal" being derived from "norm" or "norma" meaning a rule, pattern, or model. A normal school would fix the norms and establish the principles of teaching. Furthermore, said Mann, "The name is short, descriptive of its etymology, and in no danger of being misunderstood or misapplied." The Board of Education, acting on Mann's recommendation, had determined the admission requirements for the new schools: a minimum age of sixteen for young women, seventeen for young men; an examination in the basic subjects taught in common schools, and evidence of high moral character. The minimum term of study was fixed at one year, but students could remain longer and thus increase their qualifications. Each school would have an experimental or model school attached to it where students would apply theory to practice, and the total institution would be supervised and inspected by a committee of "visiters" appointed by the board. Mann ended the article by observing that "For aught that can be now forseen, the first system of Normal Schools, properly so called, to be founded in this country, will be established in Massachusetts." Six weeks later, and also in the *Common School Journal,*[29] the Board of Education announced that the first of the normal schools would be established in Lexington. The four visiters were listed—three members of the Board of Education and its secretary. Lexington and Barre normal schools opened in 1839 and Bridgewater in 1840. By the latter date the normal schools and the Board of Education itself had weathered a crisis that threatened their existence.

The first state normal school in the United States opened on 3 July 1839, with three students in a building facing Lexington Green. With uncharacteristic understatement Mann admitted that "in point of numbers, this is not a promising commencement." By the end of the first year twenty-five had enrolled. As the agent of the Board of Education, Mann had considerable authority: he chose the first three principals and proposed a curriculum. There were no American precedents to guide him, no other normal schools he could raid for ideas or faculty, and as a result the first principals came from very different backgrounds: one was a high school principal, one a college professor, and one a retired army officer. The budget of each school was sufficient to pay the salaries only of the principal and an assistant with little left for anything else. When Cyrus Peirce, the first principal at Lexington, submitted his bills for equipment Mann could pay them only by selling his own law library. There were few certainties in these early days but there was consensus on one: the normal schools would not match the standards of the colleges and, therefore, would not grant degrees. Otherwise Mann and the board groped their way: "As we have none of the lights of experience," Mann wrote to Thomas Robbins, a member of the board, "we must throw the light of judgment and common sense forward as far as we can."

Through county conventions, recent legislation, circulation of annual reports, and new normal schools Mann and his board had succeeded quickly and well. But too quickly and well for some members of the House of Representatives who were fearful of allowing power to be centralized in the Board of Education. Early in 1840 this group attempted to abolish both the board and the normal schools. A new governor, Marcus Morton, opened the attack in his inaugural address by stressing the importance of keeping the control of schools within the town and district meetings, "those little pure democracies," and by denigrating the value of seminaries for teachers. Both in the tone and substance of his address he made it clear that he saw no need for the Board of Education or its secretary. Members of the General Court with similar views were instrumental in directing the House Committee on Education "to consider the expediency of abolishing the Board of Education and the Normal Schools."[30] Moving with unseemly haste, four days after its appointment the committee presented a majority report which attempted to discredit the board by attacking it from two directions: "If, then, the Board has any actival power, it is a dangerous power, trenching directly upon the rights and duties of the Legislature; if it has no power, why continue its existence, at an annual expense to the Commonwealth?"[31] Furthermore, the report argued, the board was introducing into Massachusetts a centralized system of education modelled on the French and Prussian systems and placing "a monopoly of power in a few hands, contrary, in every respect, to the true spirit of our democratical institutions."[32] As for the normal schools, the committee was not persuaded that "keeping school" should become a separate and distinct profession, an idea that would take root if the normal schools continued.

Mann, of course, fought back but organized his counter-attack privately. He wrote a long letter to John Shaw, a member of the education committee friendly to the board, and Shaw used it in preparing a minority report that eloquently countered the accusations. With Mann's help Shaw showed, for example, that the secretary in his annual reports had not recommended the Prussian system of schools as a model for Massachusetts. The House ordered the printing of 2,000 copies of both the majority and minority reports and on 18 March

1840 devoted a full day of debate to the issues. The next day it voted 245 to 182 to reject the majority report and in so doing reaffirmed Mann's work as secretary. The board was now safe from harassment by the legislature, and the normal schools were secure. Their enrolment grew slowly and both private philanthropy and the General Court supported their expansion although Mann found it necessary to borrow $2,000 privately and use his own railroad shares as security when the bills to complete one of the new schools fell due. Mann nurtured them with a remarkable passion; and with the support and influence of education reformers such as James Carter, the preparation of teachers for elementary schools became a state responsibility and was assigned to a separate institution. Gradually the normal schools became state colleges for teachers and in many parts of the United States kept their separate identity for over a century.

The Common School Movement

In 1842 Mann travelled by train and stagecoach to attend a state convention of school superintendents in Utica, New York. On the first morning of the convention a resolution was brought forward by one delegate:

> *Resolved,* That the best police for our cities, the lowest insurance of our houses, the firmest security for our banks, the most effective means of preventing pauperism, vice and crime, and the only sure defense of our country, are our common schools; and woe to us, if their means of education be not commensurate with the wants and the powers of the people.[33]

Mann was asked to comment, and in extemporaneous remarks said that he could support the resolution: the schools could indeed ameliorate the ills of society, and those who worked for the common schools were "devoted to the most sacred of causes." This conviction of the ultimate importance of the common school never left him; in his ninth report his enthusiasm led him to say that "This institution is the greatest discovery ever made by man; we repeat it, *The Common School is the greatest discovery ever made by man.*" In another context he stated that the establishment of free schools was the boldest innovation ever promulgated since the commencement of the Christian era.[34] Throughout his twelve years as secretary his overriding concerns were the improvement, expansion, and support of the common schools.

His was by no means a one-man crusade, although during some of the controversies which embroiled him Mann felt like a lonely martyr. But the cause was worth the sacrifice, as he wrote to Henry Barnard, his friend and colleague in Connecticut: "when I look afar into the future and see the beautiful and glorious development it shall have in other hands, I find not satisfaction in my toils, merely, but I feel a pride in being stationed at this most honorable post of labour. Let us go on and buffet the waves of opposition with a stout arm and a confiding heart."[35] Mann had, however, little justification for self-pity. In fact there was widespread support, particularly in Massachusetts, for the common schools. The time was ripe for Mann and his fellow reformers.

In the second quarter of the nineteenth century Massachusetts began to feel the effects of industrialism and its twin concomitants, immigration and urbanization. Substantial industrial growth began around 1830 and during the next three decades the economy of the state was transformed. Between 1845 and 1855, for example, the volume of cotton cloth manufactured almost doubled, while the value of agricultural produce fell to below 20 per cent of the total value of manufactured goods.[36] New machines in the increasingly larger cotton mills and shoe factories made openings for the unskilled labor of immigrants, most of whom came from Ireland.

From 1830 to 1850 the population of Massachusetts increased by nearly 60 per cent,[37] and in one year alone, 1847, 37,000 immigrants arrived in Boston.[38] The combination of industrialism and immigration created a town proletariat. Lowell, for example, which did not exist in 1820, had a population estimated at 15,000 in 1833, more than one-third of which was employed in the cotton mills.[39]

Changes such as these destroyed the ethnic homogeneity of the state and contributed to the rise of a large working class, a small but powerful group of owner capitalists, and a movement of social and educational reformers. All these groups provided the impetus and arguments for educational change. In 1830 workingmen in Boston formed a political organization, Working Men, Mechanics, and Others Friendly to their Interests, which resolved "That the establishment of a liberal system of education, attainable by all, should be among the first efforts of every law-giver who desires the continuance of our national independence."[40] Leaders of this emerging labor movement argued that a system of free and universal education could be employed to destroy class distinctions and guarantee social and economic equality. This deep faith in the power of education was revealed by Seth Luther, a leading figure in the New England labor movement. His 1832 "Address to the Working Men" depicts the working class as ruined by the want of education and as a result "rendered miserable in the extreme, and incapable of self-government; and this by the grinding of the rich on the faces of the poor, through the operations of cotton and other machinery."[41]

This picture of degradation and inhumanity in the New England mills did not, however, lead Luther to advocate revolution or even to propose radical social legislation. His major reproach to the "aristocracy" was their neglect of public education, and his suggestion for redeeming the republic from the twin curses of poverty and corrupting riches was a system of common schools. This widespread demand among working men for public schools was based on one fundamental proposition: universal and effective education depends on legislation. For some years the belief persisted that once common schools were permanently established other forms of legislation would not be necessary.

This belief that a system of universal education would modify the evils of industrial capitalism was shared by humanitarian reformers. Robert Rantoul, for example, was a lawyer, a member of the state Board of Education, and a friend of labor. In an address to a group of workingmen he urged that with the improvement and extension of free schools "we need have no fear of the aristocratical tendencies of accumulated masses of capital." Horace Mann was also conscious that Massachusetts was exposed to the "fatal extremes" of great wealth and desperate poverty. Its population, in the 1840s, was more dense and its supply of capital greater than that of any other state in the Union. The danger, Mann thought, was that all capital would be thrown into the hands of one class, and all labor into another. The only effective instrument to counteract this threat was universal education. If education were equally available it would attract wealth, and a populace whose intelligence had been cultivated by education would not remain permanently poor.

> Education, then, beyond all other devices of human origin, is the great equalizer of the conditions of men—the balance-wheel of the social machinery . . . it gives each man the independence and the means by which he can resist the selfishness of other men. It does better than to disarm the poor of their hostility towards the rich; it prevents being poor.[42]

In addition to the arguments that universal education would prevent class differentiation and reduce if not eliminate poverty, there were other considerations advanced. Education would yield pecuniary benefits by increasing productivity, and public schools could be powerful agents in the reduction of crime and the preservation of civic order. By no means all industrialists favored tax-supported public schools, but a significant number regarded them as vital to the country's prosperity. One of these, Abbott Lawrence, a prominent manufacturer and politician, warned his colleagues in Massachusetts that no effort should be spared to increase the general level of intelligence through education. Both popular education and special technical schools were needed to raise the levels of skill, initiative, and productivity which, in turn, would make the cotton mills and shoe factories more remunerative. "Let the common school system," he wrote to a friend, "go hand in hand with the employment of your people; you may be quite certain that the adoption of these systems at once will aid each other."[43] Educational leaders such as Alonzo Potter and George B. Emerson argued that a laborer whose mind has been disciplined by education would be more careful of property, work more steadily and cheerfully and therefore more productively than one who, as a child, was left in ignorance and idleness.[44]

Mann devoted a substantial part of his fifth report to the pecuniary benefits of education. Through a lengthy letter and follow-up interviews he questioned a number of Massachusetts businessmen regarding the economic effects of common schooling. He asked them to examine their books over a number of years to judge the quality and quantity of work performed by their employees and included several of their replies in his report. One came from an owner of mills and factories employing some 3,000 workers who was unequivocal in his belief that the best cotton mill in New England would never yield a profit if manned by illiterate operatives. Mann's report was widely circulated throughout New England, the New York legislature alone ordering

18,000 copies, including a German translation for the German-speaking population of the state. Some twenty years later John Philbrick, superintendent of schools in Boston and a national figure in education, observed that Mann's fifth report had "probably done more than all other publications written within the past twenty-five years to convince capitalists of the value of elementary instruction as a means of increasing the value of labor."

Education reformers buttressed their argument for prosperity by adding another based on security. The secretary of the Board of Education of the State of Maine put the question quite bluntly in his 1847 report: "What surer guaranty can the capitalist find for the security of his investments, than is to be found in the sense of a community morally and intellectually enlightened?" Mann published a condensed version of this report in the *Common School Journal.*[45] Conservatives, too, saw education as a means of preventing social upheaval. Daniel Webster supported public schools in Massachusetts on the grounds that they would maintain the social and political status quo against "the slow but sure undermining of licentiousness," and "open violence and overthrow." Governor Edward Everett welcomed the education of mechanics since "an intelligent class can scarcely be, as a class, vicious."[46]

Mann did not have to be reminded of the dangers of mob violence; he had had first-hand experience near his own door. Three weeks before he became secretary he made this entry in his journal: "A riot of almost unheard-of atrocity has raged for several hours this afternoon between the Irish population of Broad Street and its vicinity, on one side, and the engine-men and those who rallied to their assistance, on the other."[47] Later the same year, as he prepared to move out of his office to new living quarters, he recorded that the building had been set on fire twice by incendiaries. In 1834 a mob had gathered outside the Ursuline convent in Charlestown, across the river from Boston, and its leaders ordered the sisters to leave the building. The rioters then stormed the convent, desecrated its chapel, and set fire to the entire structure. The next day the mayor of Boston appointed a committee of citizens to investigate the event, its first task being to appoint an attorney to organize and conduct the investigation. The committee selected Mann, who worked on the investigation for ten days "almost without intermission" but then fell ill and was unable to continue.

The threats to the existing order and the dangers to property rights through mob violence became part of the arsenal of arguments used by education reformers. Mann, in his eleventh report, was convinced that "the great body of vices and crimes which now sadden and torment the community, may be dislodged and driven out from amongst us, by such improvements in our present common School system, as we are abundantly able immediately to make."[48] This emphasis on security also included the protection of the republic and its cherished form of government. That popular education could preserve these was not a new idea. It had been stated by Jefferson ("If a nation expects to be ignorant and free, in a state of civilization, it expects what never was and never will be."), and by James Madison ("A popular Government, without popular information, or the means of acquiring it, is but a Prologue to a Farce or a Tragedy; or, perhaps both. Knowledge will forever govern ignorance: And a people who mean to be their own Governors, must arm themselves with the power which knowledge gives."). Mann recognized that the necessity of general intelligence under a republican form of government had become, as with all great truths, rather shopworn. But education for life in a republic must consist not only of intellectual components; it must also be concerned with moral elevation and the development of values. "Never will wisdom preside in the halls of legislation," he said, "and its profound utterances be recorded on the pages of the statute book, until Common Schools . . . shall create a more far-seeing intelligence and a purer morality than has ever existed among communities of men."[49]

In his stress on moral education Mann was well within the Massachusetts tradition. The constitution of the Commonwealth required the state to "countenance and inculcate the principles of humanity and general benevolence, public and private charity, industry and frugality, honesty and punctuality . . . sincerity, good humor, all social affections and generous sentiments among the people." The School Law of 1826 expressly charged all instructors of youth to impress these many virtues upon the minds of their pupils. But now a dilemma developed. Many of these virtues were normally regarded as religious principles, but the same law specifically provided that no books should be used in the public schools that were "calculated to favor any particular religious sect or tenet." By the late 1830s sectarian instruction had largely disappeared from Massachusetts schools,[50] but the dilemma persisted: how could schools separate teaching morality from instruction in religion when it was generally believed that moral principles were derived from a religious source? More precisely, the question was whether or not morality depended on a particular kind of religion.

Mann's answer to non-sectarianism was, paradoxically, Protestant Christianity. His views on moral and religious education are set forth in his twelfth report. In one passage he observes: "In this age of the world, it seems to me that no student of history, or observer of mankind, can be hostile to the precepts and doctrines of the Christian religion. . . . or opposed to Bible instruction for the young."[51] What he had in mind was a non-denominational but nevertheless Protestant Christianity and the King James version of the Bible. He was convinced that there was a common core of Christian ethical concepts, and that this "non-sectarian" consensus could be used to teach morality in the common schools. The other means of providing a moral foundation lay in the use of the Bible, without comment, in religious exercises. For Mann, the Bible should be allowed "to speak for itself."

Because Massachusetts was still predominantly Protestant in the mid-nineteenth century (in 1858 there were over 1,500 Protestant and sixty-four Roman Catholic churches in the state) it was generally believed that a teacher with the New Testament in his hand need not be a sectarian teacher. Mann reported in 1848 that in his twelve years as secretary he had never heard an objection made to the use of the Bible in the schools. It appears that the Protestant sects had declared a truce and accepted Mann's compromise of "common denominator" Christianity.

The Roman Catholic hierarchy could not, however, accept Mann's compromise. Eight years earlier when compulsory Bible-reading in the public schools was a major Catholic grievance in the school controversy in New York, a spokesman for Archbishop John Hughes said:

> The Holy Scriptures are read every day, with the restriction that no specific tenets are to be inculcated. Here we find the great demarcation principle between the Catholic Church and the Sects introduced silently. The Catholic Church tells her children they must be taught by *authority.* The Sects say, read the Bible, judge for yourselves. The Protestant principle is therefore acted upon, slyly inculcated, and the schools are Sectarian.[52]

After heated controversy and a bitter struggle to obtain the church hierarchy and Catholic parents realized that parochial schools could a child secure an education in Catholic doctrine. By the end of the first decade of the t tury over a million children were enrolled in parochial sc public schools the Protestant consensus, for which Mann ful advocate, held until well into the twentieth century

On the whole, Mann's vision of the common school his deeply grounded belief in "the *absolute right* of every that comes into the world to an education."[54] Such would, at a minimum, enable each individual to perform social, civil, and moral duties required of a citizen of a this it followed that [the United States needed a new kind would enrol the whole child population, a common scho that it was open to the children of all the people, not in t ing a school for the common people. If such schools we able they would have to be free, otherwise large segmen lation would be excluded, and they would have to be o not inferior "pauper schools" but equivalent to then- vate schools.] Bishop George Doane of New Jersey so the reformers' views and repudiated the idea of the pau Mann reprinted extracts from his address to the state le *Common School Journal.* "The Common School," decla *common,* not as inferior, not as the school for poor men as the light and the air are common. It ought to be the cause it is the first school. . . . "[55]

Now if every child has the God-given right to free sc quality, and if the state is dependent on the common sc tinued existence and well-being, it is the state's duty necessary public funds. Mann's justification for taxatio mon schools, a contentious issue in his day, is a dis unique, advocacy for the support of public education. port he discusses the morality of property and answers men of Massachusetts who were reluctant to pay taxes cation. Such a stance, declared Mann, was nothing less tion from duty" because it stemmed from their false right to hold property. The ownership of property, in hi an absolute right but rather a transitory possession created not for any one man or even one generation, bu collectively, to be possessed and enjoyed in succession." Subject to reasonable man-made regulations, nature ordains a perpetual transfer of property from one generation to another. In short, wealthy men may not argue that taxation for public schooling is confiscation. Mann summarizes his ideas on the stewardship or trusteeship of wealth and the related implications for the common school system of Massachusetts by offering three propositions:

> The successive generations of men, taken collectively, constitute one great Commonwealth.
>
> The property of this Commonwealth is pledged for the education of its youth, up to such a point as will save them from poverty and vice, and prepare them for the adequate performance of their social and civic duties.
>
> The successive holders of this property are trustees, bound to the faithful execution of their trust, by the most sacred obligations; because embezzlement and pillage from children and descendants are as criminal as the same offences when perpetrated against contemporaries.[56]

A New Pedagogy

In 1837, while Mann was preparing for the role of secretary, he read George Combe's *The Constitution of Man.* Combe was a Scottish barrister turned philosopher, and a lecturer and writer who interpreted the new science of phrenology in the United States. The phrenological theory of brain structure originated in Austria with Franz Joseph Gall and Johann Spurzheim at the end of the eighteenth century. It is remembered today as a mid-nineteenth-century cult whose practioners read character from the contours of the skull, but in origin it was an experimental science based on the theory that anatomical and physiological characteristics have a direct influence on mental behavior. In fact, it was a primitive form of behavioristic psychology that held that the mind is composed of some thirty-seven independent faculties, aptitudes, or propensities which could be catalogued, such as combativeness, acquisitiveness, cautiousness, and benevolence. These were localized in different "organs" or regions of the brain. In later and popular interpretations of phrenology it was held that development of these organs affected the size and contour of the cranium so that a practitioner could make a moderately accurate character analysis by studying the shape of a subject's head.[57]

When Gall and Spurzheim published their theories, a long and savage review appeared in the *Edinburgh Review*. Spurzheim hurried to Edinburgh and arranged a public demonstration during which he dissected a brain and at the same time carried on a running conversation in which he answered his critic. His audience included the medical and literary intelligentsia of the city, among whom was George Combe. Together with his brother and other enthusiasts, Combe formed a phrenological society in Edinburgh and decided to abandon the law and make a career in lecturing and writing about phrenology. By the 1830s it had become a movement with a dozen societies, its own journal, and a substantial literature, including *The Constitution of Man*. First published in 1828, this book was translated into French, German, Spanish, Swedish, and Italian. In the United States it went through twenty editions in seven years.[58] Spurzheim visited the U.S. in 1832 and was enthusiastically welcomed by the faculties of Harvard and Yale and the Boston Medical Society. He lectured to large audiences at the Boston Athenaeum and elsewhere. It is highly probable that this heavy schedule of lectures and conferences contributed to his death in Boston later in the year. Three thousand Bostonians attended his funeral.

American interest in phrenology mounted again when George Combe made a lecture tour of the major cities of the eastern states in 1838–40. Over an eighteen-month period he gave two-hour lectures to audiences of three to five hundred. He was cordially received by the intellectual and social elite of Boston and became an intimate friend of William Ellery Channing and Horace Mann. In the spring of 1840 Mann and the Combes toured the West together (as far west as Ohio and Kentucky, that is, but nevertheless completing a journey of nearly 3,000 miles) and they continued to correspond for the rest of their lives. Combe wrote of Mann: "He is a delightful companion and friend," and Mann was no less enthusiastic about Combe: "There is no man of whom I think so often; there is no man of whom I write so often; there is no man who has done so much good as you have." In Combe's phrenology Mann found a convincing rationale for his belief in education. If the faculties of the mind could be developed through appropriate exercise, and if this growth of mind and character was in man's own hands, the goals of improving man and society were not beyond possibility. Mann could thus write to Combe: "We see that there will be a new earth, at least, if not a new heaven, when your philosophical and moral doctrines prevail . . . they are doctrines which cause a man's soul to expand beyond the circle of his visiting-cards; that recognize the race as beings capable of pleasure and pain, of elevation or debasement."[59] In Combe's optimism Mann found a welcome antidote to the Calvinistic doctrines of original sin that had blighted his childhood.

Before phrenology fell into the hands of charlatans and became an amusing and harmless quackery it was a guide in determining the goals, curricula, and teaching methods of the common schools. In fact, Mann regarded Combe's *Constitution* as the finest of pedagogical textbooks and in a letter to his sister, Lydia, said: "Its philosophy is the only practical basis for education."[60] With their "evidence" that a scoundrel was one whose mental organs had not properly developed, and that a vice was a product of an under- or overdeveloped faculty, phrenologists believed that these conditions could be corrected, or as one speaker observed, "Your *organism* and *not your fate*, is at fault."[61]

Education reformers combined phrenology with the theories of the European educators, Heinrich Pestalozzi and Friedrich Froebel, and produced a pedagogy that foreshadows the progressive education movement of later years. Children should learn by doing rather than by hearing; a teacher should try to understand each pupil and encourage by praise rather than punishment; children should be responsible for their own behavior; schoolwork should be practical and concrete; and because the mind and body are intimately connected a child should be taught the laws of health and given ample time for play and exercise.

Whether Horace Mann's concern for the teaching of physiology and what he called the laws of health and life stemmed from phrenology, or from his own chronic ill health caused by a boyhood of grinding toil and later grief and exhaustion, it is impossible to say. We do know, however, that when he wrote his sixth report, well over half of which was given over to the science of health, he almost ruined his own health from overwork. The returns from school committees showed that in 1842 only some 400 children in the public schools of Massachusetts were studying physiology. Mann was upset by this information and for sixty pages argued that instead of ranking eighth among the subjects taught in the higher elementary grades physiology should rank first.

In stressing the importance of studying the working of the body, together with the need for well-ventilated classrooms, frequent exercise in the open air, and loose rather than constrictive clothing, Mann was clearly a pioneer. He specifically recommended that children of seven or eight should have fifteen minutes of outdoor recess for every fifty minutes spent in the classroom and he buttressed his case for health education by including letters he had solicited from eminent physicians. These men corroborated Mann's opinion that a large proportion, probably one-half, of sickness and physical debility could be attributed to ignorance of physiological principles already discovered, as distinct from causes that were not known. It pained Mann to report that thousands of young people were studying algebra and geometry, rhetoric and declamation, and Latin and Greek while the science of health and life was neglected. He was also distressed to find that other practical subjects were given short shrift, that nearly twice as many pupils were studying algebra as bookkeeping, that geometry took precedence over surveying, and that rhetoric had twice as many followers as logic.

In the spring of 1843 Mann secured permission from his board to visit Europe. His intent was to become acquainted with the system of public instruction in those countries "which had long enjoyed the reputation of standing at the head of the cause." The trip was also a honeymoon. Years earlier Mann had met the Peabody sisters, Elizabeth and Mary, in Mrs. Clarke's boarding house in Boston. He was attracted to both these young women, then in their late twenties, Elizabeth for her enthusiasm and brilliant conversation, Mary for her beauty and quiet grace. They were overwhelmed by his table conversation, as Mary wrote to her sister Sophia: "And then Mr. Mann is so intolerably witty, and has a fine anecdote, a story or a saying for every emergency and tells them with such full effect that he well nigh destroys me." Both Elizabeth and Mary with well-bred delicacy and restraint told Mann, largely through correspondence, of their respect and affection. But his grief for the memory of Charlotte swept over him at intervals, and often quite unexpectedly, for the next several years. And he was in no position to marry while under the burden of debt he had inherited from his brother. Thus Elizabeth and Mary waited and suffered for ten years. Suddenly, however, Mann's indecision snapped and in March 1843, only six weeks before his departure for Europe, he proposed to Mary. As one of Mann's biographers has commented, she must have been the most surprised and relieved woman in Boston.[62] They were married on 1 May and on the same day sailed from Boston bound for Liverpool on the Cunard steamship *Britannia*.

Within thirteen days of leaving Boston the Manns were visiting schools in England. From there they travelled to Ireland and Scotland, thence to several German states, and finally to The Netherlands, Belgium, and France on a six-month trip which Mann later emphasized was undertaken at his own expense. His observations and reflections on this journey are incorporated in his seventh report. Mann was critical of education in England. Among the European nations conspicuous for civilization and resources, England alone had no national system of education. It was here, too, that the greatest contrasts existed between the intelligence and wealth of the upper classes and the ignorance, poverty, and crime of the lower orders. Private schools, Mann found, not only reflected the structure of English society but also deepened class divisions. By contrast, Mann was tremendously impressed by Prussia's system of public schools even though, as he was well aware, it was sustained by arbitrary power.

Mann's chief object was to examine the modes of teaching used in European schools. His observations tell us as much about him as the schools he described. In Scotland, for example, he was delighted with the thoroughness of the method used in teaching reading, a subject on which he had written at length. He was also impressed with the level of mental activity in Scottish classrooms. The most lively and active schools he had ever seen in the United States must, he commented wryly, be regarded as dormitories when compared with the fervid life of schools in Scotland. He was told by a government inspector that the first test of a teacher's qualification was his power to excite and sustain the attention of his class:

> I have seen a school kept for two hours in succession, in this state of intense mental activity, with nothing more than an alternation of subjects during the time, or perhaps the relaxation of singing. At the end of the recitation, both teacher and pupils would glow with heat, and be covered with perspiration.[63]

On the continent the Manns spent almost two months visiting the schools in Prussia, Saxony, and half a dozen other German states. In most instances Mann was not escorted and teachers did not know in advance that he was coming. He carried letters of introduction but produced them only as he was about to leave. The Prussian teachers appear to have impressed him most. He was heartened to find that they had made the important discovery that children have five senses, together with various muscles and mental faculties, all of which must be kept in a state of activity. The Prussian teachers had found profitable and enjoyable employment for these powers and thus did not need to use the rod either to stimulate or to stifle their operation. Committed as he was to Combe's phrenology, Mann found what he wanted in the Prussian classroom, where children's "perceptive powers," "reflecting faculties," and "moral sentiments" were exercised and developed.

In Prussia, as in Scotland, teachers were vigorously animated and their "rhetorical vehemence" created interest and response in their pupils, even during lessons in handwriting or phonics. Mann learned that vivacity, wit, anecdote, and the power to arouse and retain the attention of his pupils were all requirements for a Prussian teacher. This lively style of teaching led Mann to notice that teachers never heard a recitation while sitting down and never taught with a book in their hands. But he was also struck with what he did not see: "I never saw a blow struck, I never heard a sharp rebuke given, I never saw a child in tears. . . . I heard no child ridiculed, sneered at, or scolded for making a mistake."[64] Mann learned that while corporal punishment was permitted in German schools it was rarely used, which led him to observe somewhat sadly that it would be unlikely for a visitor to spend six weeks in the schools of Massachusetts without seeing a child in tears. But then, he went on to say what he had said before: teachers were only as good as public opinion demanded.

There was no doubt in Mann's mind that "the beautiful relation of harmony and affection" that existed between teachers and pupils and the high quality of instruction in Prussian schools were related to the seminaries for teachers and the rigorous qualifications public school teachers were obliged to meet. In some parts of Prussia students attended a preliminary institution for six months, during which time it was discovered whether or not they qualified for entry to a seminary. The three-year seminary instruction offered both academic and pedagogical courses. Mann was also impressed with the qualifications of

Scottish teachers, most of whom were graduates of or had attended university before becoming teachers. He admired their enormous energy but condemned their heavy use of corporal punishment. If that evil could be eradicated the Scottish teacher would be a model for the world.[65]

There was, however, much about Europe that Mann criticized. Its class distinctions, extremes of wealth and poverty, and the denial of political and religious liberty brought forth all of Mann's republican instincts and patriotic fervor. In mid-nineteenth-century Europe he found a society in which, by his own estimate, less than half the adult population could read or write in any intelligible manner, fewer than one-third were comfortably housed or fed or clothed, and not one in 500 had a voice in the choice of rulers. He then goes on to say: "It was from a condition of society like this . . . that our ancestors fled . . . the colonization of New England was like a new creation of the race. . . . This transference of the fortunes of our race from the Old to the New World was a gain to humanity of at least a thousand years."[66]

Mann's seventh report was well received, at least in establishment circles. Mann's friends and colleagues in Massachusetts praised it warmly, government bodies in England and Prussia reprinted it, and in London the *Athenaeum* gave it a favorable review. But a group of thirty-one Boston schoolmasters who felt they had been slandered by it prepared a 144-page pamphlet in which they countered practically all Mann's observations and recommendations related to classroom teaching, teacher training, and the use of corporal punishment. This publication, entitled *Remarks on the Seventh Annual Report of the Hon. Horace Mann,* sparked a classic controversy that reverberated throughout Massachusetts and beyond. "We object," the masters stated, " . . . to the idea that the relation of a pupil to his teacher is one of affection first, and then duty. We would rather reverse the terms. . . . " Duty implied instilling respect for authority through fear and wise punishment. Fear of physical pain, they believed, would have its place so long as "men and children continue to be human; that is, so long as schools and schoolmasters and government and laws are needed." A wholesome application of the rod in youth, they said, may save their pupils from "the dungeon and the halter in maturer life," and they recalled the firmness and stern virtue of the Puritan founders of free schools.

The controversy continued for the better part of a year with Mann issuing a *Reply,* the schoolmasters a *Rejoinder,* and Mann returning with an *Answer,* all of which were lengthy and acrimonious rebuttals. The conflict ended, however, not in polemical but political action. A group of Mann's supporters gained a strong footing in the Boston School Committee and seized control of the annual common schools examinations. In place of the traditional oral questioning, this group of reformers imposed a written test. The results were disastrous and a report written by Samual Gridley Howe, one of Mann's close friends, was sufficiently influential to persuade the school committee to dismiss or transfer a good number of the thirty-one masters, to reduce the use of corporal punishment, and to adopt written tests as standard procedure. For the moment, at least, Mann and his reformer friends had won the battle for a more humane pedagogy based on a benign view of the nature of man. In an age of progress the Calvinist theory of childhood was outmoded.

Congressman and College President

When John Quincy Adams, former president and later congressman for Massachusetts, died in February 1848, Mann's friends urged him to become a candidate for the vacancy. He did not take long to make up his mind. After nearly a dozen years as secretary he was weary of controversy and ready for new challenges. Besides, he thought the crusade for the common school cause had been won in Massachusetts and was, as he wrote to a friend, "so consolidated . . . that nothing could overturn it. It was only annoyances and obstructions that we had to look after. . . . "[67] There were, too, other factors. In Washington he could carry his crusade for education to the national level, particularly if an Office of Education were established and he were appointed its secretary. For a far more down-to-earth reason he accepted the nomination: he badly needed a congressman's salary. He had recently opened two new state normal schools and from his own pocket had covered the deficits incurred on each site. When wealthy industrialists failed to respond to his appeals he wrote, "I live by tapping my own veins and sucking my own blood."

As a member of the House of Representatives from 1848 to 1852, Mann made five major speeches, all about slavery. On at least two occasions before going to Washington Mann had made clear his position on segregation. When he learned that the New Bedford Lyceum refused to accept blacks as members, he cancelled his agreement to deliver a lecture; and when a black student, newly enrolled in the West Newton Normal School, could find no family willing to offer her board and room, Mann and his wife, who had recently settled in the village, gave her their spare room. In his formal letter of reply to members of the Whig Convention who had offered him the nomination Mann pledged that his voice and vote would on all occasions "be exercised in extending and securing liberty to the human race."

Mann arrived in Washington one day in April when the peach trees were in bloom. As he walked about the city, a tall figure in a well-tailored frock coat, he saw both the magnificence of the Capitol and the squalor of slavery. But in spite of entreaties from his supporters in Boston he made no speeches in the House. In May and again in June his friend, Charles Sumner, pleaded with him to take a stand: "A speech from you on the slavery question and the morality of politics would have an important influence on public sentiment. . . . Yours is a voice of power. What you say must produce an echo."[68] Finally, on the last day of June, Mann made his maiden speech to a packed chamber on the issue of "Slavery in the Territories." He argued, from legal precedents, that Congress did indeed have a clear right to legislate on the matter of slavery in the new territories, and then went on to examine the economic and moral aspects of slavery. He ended with this peroration:

> Sir, on the continent of Europe, and in the Tower of London, I have seen the axes, the chains, and other horrid implements of death, by which the great defenders of freedom for the soul were brought to their final doom,—by which political and religious liberty was cloven down; but fairer and lovelier to the view were axe and chain, and all the ghastly implements of death ever invented by religious bigotry or civil despotism to wring and torture freedom out of the soul of man;—fairer and lovelier were they all than the parchment roll of this House on which shall be inscribed a law for profaning one additional foot of American soil with the curse of slavery.[69]

In 1850 Mann failed to secure the Whig party's nomination and instead fought his second election as a Free Soil candidate. The Free Soil party opposed the extension of slavery into new territories acquired from Mexico. Mann won his way back to Congress by a margin of only forty-one votes, and in the next session spoke out passionately against the Fugitive Slave Law. In 1852 he was nominated as the Free Soil candidate for governor of Massachusetts and although he campaigned strenuously he lost the election. His political career was over and he could now return to his first love, education.

Several months earlier Mann had made an extended lecture tour through New York state, giving addresses on education or temperance or a new topic, "A Few Thoughts on the Powers and Duties of Women." Mann felt obliged to make these tours as a means of reducing his debts, but his health suffered as a result; on one tour he travelled 1,000 miles in a week, lecturing four times and sleeping in a railway coach for three successive nights.[70] In Lima, New York, he met the Reverend Eli Fay, a representative of the Christian Connexion, a religious group which intended to found a college. When Mann learned that the college would be non-sectarian and co-educational he was responsive and his interest grew as the Reverend Fay added that his committee was looking for a man of national stature to become its president at a salary of $3,000 a year. Mann blew hot and cold over the prospect of presiding over a college, yet to be built in Yellow Springs, Ohio; and Mary was concerned that fever and ague would attack the family, which now included three boys. However, Fay and Mann continued to correspond and on 15 September 1852, Fay's committee appointed Mann the first president of Antioch College.

A year later 3,000 people came by train or coach, horseback, or farm wagon to see the governor of Ohio and other dignitaries and to hear Horace Mann, educator and statesman from the East, give his inauguration address. He did not disappoint them; indeed, he held their attention for two hours, during which he confidently predicted that nineteenth-century men and women could so harness the forces of nature and accelerate the rate of progress that human perfectibility could be achieved in a world free of war, poverty, and disease. Modern man could achieve this millennium through educational institutions of high quality, and it was his pledge to shape Antioch accordingly. Mary Mann was on the platform and wrote afterward, "I shall not soon forget the sea of eager upturned faces which met my view from the platform. . . . They have a way here of groaning out 'Amen' . . . when they like anything."

But the enthusiasm of opening day evaporated when the faculty marked the admissions examination given to some 200 applicants. Only six men and two women were adequately qualified to enter the freshman class; the others entered a preparatory department which, fortunately, was part of Mann's plan. But greater disappointments, in fact crises, awaited him. Almost from the day it opened Antioch was bankrupt, and the only reason that it could continue to operate was the chaotic state of its bookkeeping. Mann discovered this state of affairs during his first year as president and for the next five years the college lurched from crisis to crisis as Mann worked desperately to raise the needed funds. He and his faculty accepted reduced salaries or, in some years, none at all; professors who were also ministers returned to the pulpit during vacations and Mann made repeated lecture tours through the Midwest. He was in as much demand as ever and could command $50 for each engagement. By the spring of 1859, however, Antioch finally declared bankruptcy and all its assets were sold to a group of Mann's friends for $40,000. A new board of trustees then secured unencumbered title to the property.

Despite his financial burdens Mann had accomplished much at Antioch. He established a basic curriculum of Latin, Greek, English, mathematics, history, and the natural sciences and required all students to take physiology and hygiene. Through his own classes he introduced new methods of teaching. Instead of the traditional memorize-and-recite pattern, students were encouraged to engage in individual study projects and report their results to the class. The glen adjacent to the campus became an outdoor laboratory. Under Mann, Antioch was one of the first American colleges to incorporate study of the theory and practice of teaching into the undergraduate curriculum. Months before he accepted the presidency Mann wrote to Fay that one attraction of the plan for a new college was "that of redressing the long-inflicted wrongs of woman by giving her equal advantages of education—I do not say in all respects on identical education, but equal advantages of education—with men."[71] Mann also assured Fay that, if appointed, he would appoint women to the faculty. This was not a new revelation. For years he had urged the appointment of women teachers in the common schools of Massachusetts and two of the first three state normal schools were co-educational at their founding.

But the struggle to keep Antioch, and his own family, solvent had taken its toll. As he attended to all the details of the 1859 commencement and drafted his own baccalaureate address he realized that he probably would never deliver another. That may be why he spoke so directly to his audience: "I yearn for another warfare in behalf of right, in hostility to wrong, where, without furlough, and without going into winter quarters, I would enlist for another fifty-years campaign and fight it out for the glory of God and the welfare of men . . .. But alas! That cannot be; for while the Phoenix spirit burns within, the body becomes ashes."[72] He ended his last address with the humanitarian vision that had pervaded his life:

> So, in the infinitely nobler battle in which you are engaged against error and wrong, if ever repulsed or stricken down, may you always be solaced and cheered by the exulting cry of triumph over some abuse in church or state, some vice or folly in society, some false opinion or cruelty or guilt which you have overcome! And I beseech you to treasure up in your hearts these my parting words: *Be ashamed to die until you have won some victory for humanity.*[73]

Within a few days Mann's body was wracked by a fever that recurred throughout the summer. On 2 August 1859, he died. He was sixty-three.

The Measure of Mann

Horace Mann had his blemishes. In controversies he was unnecessarily harsh and vindictive, using, as his friend Theodore Parker said, a forty-eight pound cannon to kill a mosquito. Mann recognized this quality of melodramatic intensity as a family trait and mentioned it to his sister, Lydia: "we are all inclined to make too serious matters of small ones; and when matters are really serious, they absorb us, and irritate us, to a degree which our physical organization is not fitted to bear. We all have a tendency to extremes." Try as he might to slough off his early Calvinism, he never lost the urge to moralize, a tendency that drove him to ask Richard Henry Dana to revise *Two Years before the Mast* because "a narrative, a description, had no value except as it conveyed some moral lesson or some useful fact."[74] Such revisions would make the book suitable for Mann's school library series. In his crusade he seemed, at times, to welcome martyrdom and eagerly to accept suffering, but it is difficult to know whether he martyred himself for the cause or for his own glory. Perhaps Emerson saw more clearly: "Take egotism out, and you would castrate the benefactors, Luther, Mirabeau, Napoleon, John Adams, Andrew Jackson," to which group Emerson added, "and our newer servants—Greeley, Theodore Parker, Ward Beecher, Horace Mann, Garrison—would lose their vigor."

Whether the victory was to be for humanity or for self, Mann and his fellow reformers could point to an impressive list of results. During Mann's period of office, Massachusetts increased its appropriations for public schools by over 60 per cent and spent $2 million improving its schoolhouses. Teachers' salaries increased by more than 50 per cent and there was a marked increase (nearly 40 per cent) in the number of women teachers. Taxes for the support of schools were raised and small district schools were consolidated into larger units. One month was added to the average length of the school year, and three normal schools had begun to raise the qualifications for teachers.[75] Although there was a noticeable increase in total school enrolment to keep pace with a growing population, there was no increase in the proportion of children who attended public schools. That proportion remained at about 62 per cent.

Mann reveals these figures in his tenth report and his disappointment is clearly evident. In the years following his term as secretary, however, there were significant developments. Massachusetts established compulsory education in 1852, and by 1860 a majority of states had established systems of public education in which at least half the nation's children were enrolled.[76] When Mann resigned, the Board of Education had already asserted the educational role of the state. In subsequent years, although power was delegated to towns and districts, the ultimate mandate of the state to supervise the efficiency and quality of its schools was established. Larger cities—such as New York, Boston, and Chicago—developed school systems of their own. Boston, for example, changed from having what was, in effect, a miscellaneous collection of village schools supervised casually by primary school trustees to a more coherent system whose first superintendent claimed that "in organizing a system of popular education, the same practical judgment is to be exercised in making special adaptations of means to ends, as in any manufacturing enterprise." Large city school systems in fact created a hierarchy, similar to that in industry, in which responsibility was delegated and employees' performance monitored. In schools that became crowded as urban population grew and became more ethnically diverse, heavy emphasis was placed on order and discipline. And, ironically, a movement that had envisaged enlightened teachers giving children individual care through benign pedagogy became, by the end of the century, a bureaucratic system in which public apathy, political interference, incompetent teaching, and rote learning were all too common.

This unlovely picture of the public school system in the urban United States forces us back to the tangled roots of the common school revival in the middle third of the century. Were Mann and the humanitarian reformers largely responsible for institutionalizing the system of common schools, a movement that began in the East and spread to every state? Or did economic and social forces stemming from immigration, industrialization, and urbanization provide the primary dynamics? The reform movement was itself a product of a society that was increasingly more urban and industrialized. Leaders of the humanitarian movement attempted to convince both capitalist and working man that common schools would mitigate the evils that accompanied industrial capitalism: pauperism, crime, intemperance, and unemployment. Conversely, a system of universal education would produce more literate and intelligent workers who would in turn stimulate the economy, improve production, and increase profits. Thus, reformers could secure support by arguing that expansion of schooling would aid the growth of an urban and industrial society and at the same time cure the malaise created. New England could have it both ways.

Through his intellectual stature, bull-dog integrity, and the extent and quality of his addresses and writings, Mann did more to publicize the cause of education than any man of his generation in the United States. That was because he was so integrally a part of his generation. His beliefs—in progress, the perfectibility of man, and the reform of society—were part of the fabric of the mid-nineteenth-century United States, and Mann as both mirror and burning glass reflected and documented, accentuated and exaggerated, these convictions. That the new republic had a special mission in the world was an idea he accepted and then shaped into a crusade for a unique system of common schools. His proposal for a non-sectarian liberal Christianity as the basis for moral instruction was, in his day, as acceptable compromise and in proposing it Mann thundered his conviction that teaching morality was one of a school's prime functions. He also recognized the decline of Calvinism and believed that a more liberal and humane pedagogy eventually would be widely accepted. In a period of great optimism about the future of the Republic tinged with unease over the social and economic ferment, Mann stilled doubts and fed the confidence of his countrymen when he spoke with such vigor and certainty of education as a panacea for all ills. He was, indeed, in time with the national music of the United States.

Even his oratory, with its flights of rhetoric, striking images, and powerful peroration, was the style of the times. Here is the closing paragraph of his twelfth report, his farewell as secretary of the Board of Education.

> The Massachusetts system of Common Schools . . . is a *Free* school system. It knows no distinction of rich and poor, of bond and free, or between those who, in the imperfect light of this world, are seeking through different avenues, to reach the gate of heaven. Without money and without price, it throws open its doors, and spreads the table of its bounty, for all the children of the State. Like the sun, it shines, not only upon the good, but upon the evil, that they may become good; and like the rain, its blessings descend, not only upon the just, but upon the unjust, that their injustice may depart from them and be known no more.

In the sense that the term is used in this book Horace Mann was not an innovator. The *idea* of the common school, the normal school, or a new pedagogy did not originate with him. He helped to rescue and breathe new life into common schools, to transplant the normal school from Europe, and persuasively wrote and spoke on matters ranging from the practicalities of schoolhouse design to the stewardship of property. He supported all manner of innovative ideas and practices—grading of pupils, compulsory attendance, school libraries, teachers' institutes, longer school terms, more women teachers—but a substantial number of other school reformers were advocating the same ideas.

Mann's uniqueness was different. Not since Jefferson had there been a public figure of superior mind who gave deep thought to public instruction. Mann was clearly the first illustrious American to devote fifteen hours a day (by his own testimony) for twelve years to the cause of the common schools. The position of secretary gave him no stated responsibility other than the collection and spreading of information. Yet with this modest mandate Mann became one of the most influential leaders of his time. Through his annual reports, addresses and lectures, annual conventions and public controversies he was one of the best known and most visible public figures of his day. He filled halls on his lecture circuits, and his reports were read widely at home and abroad. Education leaders in virtually every state wrote to him for advice on appointments or matters of policy and he was in heavy demand as a conference or convention speaker. Through editorship of the *Common School Journal* he revealed his skill as a publicist in the common school cause and through his former colleagues in the Massachusetts General Court he saw his ideas become legislation. At the age of forty-five he was awarded Boston's highest honor—the invitation to deliver the 4th of July oration. Thus as a prophet at home and abroad, and a deeply dedicated humanitarian reformer, Mann made the secretaryship into a position of influence and respect. In so doing he became an educational statesman. This was the measure of his creativity and innovative capacity.

THREE

Mary Lyon
1797–1849

Mary Lyon: The Liberal Arts College for Women

Mary Lyon, reprinted with permission from Mount Holyoke College Library/Archives.

Frugality, Piety, and Knowledge by Handfuls

When the eighty young women began arriving by stage coach and carriage at the new five-storey building of the Mount Holyoke Female Seminary in South Hadley, Massachusetts, on 8 November 1837, they found no front steps, sparse covering on the floors, and little furniture. One trustee, Daniel Safford, a well-to-do Bostonian, was on his knees tacking down straw matting, and his wife, "a royal woman with a lovely face," as one student described her, was washing crockery in the kitchen. Presiding over this bustle and confusion was Mary Lyon, "her face all aglow under the traditional turban," managing to oversee household details yet greeting each student as she arrived as a mother would welcome her daughters. By four o'clock the matting was down and two local clergymen, also patrons of the new seminary, appeared for opening exercises—a prayer and a short address. Supper was late that night, and Miss Lyon then directed those girls for whom no residence beds were yet available to village homes. At four the next morning she was supervising preparations for breakfast. The girls seemed to have caught the spirit of their principal as they made the best of inconvenience, carried wood and water from the basement to their rooms, and accepted the scheme of "domestic labor" under which students did all their own cooking and cleaning. As one student recalled, there was a further reason for accepting hardship in that first year: "We were so glad to have a place in the seminary, for we knew that more than twice our number had been refused for want of room."

Mary Lyon was born in 1797 on a small rockbound farm in the hill country of Massachusetts, where her parents practised necessary frugality and active piety. Her father died when Mary was five and when her mother married again and moved with her two youngest daughters to a nearby village Mary stayed on the family farm and at thirteen became her brother's housekeeper. Her schooling was intermittent and in some years possible only when she found a village family who gave her bed and board in return for help in the house. At the age of twenty-two she returned to the district school of her home village of Buckland, first as a pupil but soon as an assistant teacher. In the early 1820s she was alternating as a student and teacher in several Massachusetts academies and seminaries.

One of her most influential teachers was the Reverend Joseph Emerson, principal of the seminary he had opened in 1818 at Byfield, north of Boston. At the age of twenty-four Mary Lyon enrolled at Byfield for the six-month term. A graduate with distinction of Harvard and a Congregational minister, Emerson was experienced as a teacher, lecturer, and preacher. Mary was at once impressed: "He renders every recitation attractive. Never have I attended one, from which I might not gain valuable information, either scientific, moral or religious. . . . You ask if I am contented, and if I am satisfied with my school. I am perfectly so. I can complain of nothing but myself."[1] Emerson had wide-ranging intellectual interests and could communicate his excitement for books and ideas to his young students. But at the centre of all his instruction were his religious convictions, and to him the Bible was "the book of books, for schools, academies, colleges —the book of books, not only to direct the conduct, convert the soul, and save the world; but to discipline the faculties." An evangelical, fundamentalist, nineteenth-century Puritan, he believed implicitly in the millennium and an intellectually stimulating life in heaven.

The other side of Emerson was his love of language, literature, and philosophy. "It is thinking," he said, "close thinking that makes the scholar," and his teaching was less traditional recitation than Socratic dialogue. His concern for a more enlightened pedagogy and particularly his emphasis on a knowledge of English were to influence Mary Lyon's later work. It was at Byfield that she read the poetry of Milton, Pope, Gray, and Cowper for the first time. Emerson's enthusiasm was contagious and his estimate of the intellectual powers of women was, for schoolmasters of his time, unusually high. In a tribute to Emerson after his death, Mary Lyon explained that

> he treated ladies and gentlemen essentially in the same manner. . . . If a lady advanced an opinion, to which he could not assent, he did not hesitate to object because it was the opinion of a *lady;* for he appeared to believe that she had a mind capable of weighing an argument. . . . The tendency of the course he pursued was to inspire ladies with a modest confidence, not only in their own individual powers, but also in the native abilities of their sex. . . . [2]

To Mary Lyon this kind of teacher was a revelation, and her friend, Amanda White, also a student at Byfield, wrote home to say that Mary was gaining knowledge by "handfuls." Emerson recognized the quality of her mind and spirit and confided to his assistant that better disciplined minds had come to his seminary but none had equalled Mary Lyon's in power. This may have been Emerson's greatest gift: he revealed Mary to herself.

Byfield Seminary and its principal left other influences on Mary Lyon. Early in the term Emerson asked his students to decide which of them were true Christians and which were unbelievers. Mary was much agitated in making this decision and only after hesitation joined those who "hoped they had been renewed by divine grace." She began to attend weekly prayer meetings on Saturday evenings and in a letter to her mother spoke of an increasing concern for a revival in the seminary. The conflict between her intellectual ardor and her commitment to Christianity surfaced for the first time at Byfield and troubled her for years afterward. She did, however, make a public profession of faith when she joined the Congregational Church in Buckland in March 1822. And when she founded her own seminary, revivals and conversions were an integral part of its life. It was also at Byfield that she learned about the beginnings of American foreign missions. Emerson's sister-in-law was one of the first women missionaries and the Byfield students heard many details of her heroic life in Burma. Throughout the next three decades Mary Lyon gave foreign missions her enthusiastic support and encouraged both her staff and alumnae to serve the missionary cause abroad.

That golden summer of 1821 had one further benefit: the beginning of a friendship with Emerson's assistant teacher, Polly Zilpah Grant, then twenty-seven and from contemporary accounts a young woman of quick intelligence, commanding presence, and elegant appearance. Like Mary, she had grown up on a New England farm, had learned frugality and piety from her mother, and during adolescence had suffered the doubts and torments of a Calvinist training. In contrast to Mary, who at twenty-four was a sturdy, well-built countrywoman, unsophisticated in manner and unconcerned about her appearance, Zilpah was tall and dignified but had little of Mary's physical energy and health. Their common search for peace through religious commitment and a passion to teach drew them together, and within three years of meeting at Byfield they opened their own seminary.

THE FEMALE SEMINARY

Emma Willard

The forerunner of the female seminary was the private day or boarding school exported to the colonies from England. A typical advertisement for such a school appeared in the *New York Gazetteer* of 7 April 1774: "J. and M. Tanner inform the public that they intend moving to another residence where they will set up a boarding school for young ladies." They proposed to teach reading, writing, and arithmetic as well as needlework, music, dancing, drawing, French, embroidery, and "every polite accomplishment." The method of teaching would be "similar to that of the most approved English Boarding Schools." One voice urging the new republic to break away from English models was that of Benjamin Rush, a leading citizen and physician in Philadelphia who had signed the Declaration of Independence and had become an influential voice in the early United States. Speaking at the commencement exercises of the Female Academy of Philadelphia in July 1787, he urged adoption of a set of principles for the education of young ladies that would be "accommodated to the state of [American] Society, manners and government." American women should be capable of assisting as "stewards and guardians of their husbands' property," and adequately prepared to instruct their children in the principles of liberty and a republican form of government. In particular, "it is incumbent upon us to make ornamental accomplishments yield to principles and knowledge, in the education of our women."[3]

In the first quarter of the nineteenth century, both girls and boys attended common schools, though little more than this elementary education was considered necessary for girls. Only a few cities maintained high schools for girls and the one established in Boston in 1826 closed after two years, the victim of its own success. The city fathers could see no point in spending eleven dollars a year to educate a large enrolment of girls who would either soon marry or find jobs in the new factories. And Boston matrons feared that the source of housemaids would dry up if daughters of the Irish immigrants began to attend high school. There were, of course, no colleges for women and no prospect of women finding their way into the men's colleges: the American college was designed primarily as a preparation for the professions and these were not open to women. Thus, generally speaking, education beyond the common school was available to girls only in private institutions.

The governor of New York, De Witt Clinton, was distressed that his state allocated no funds for the education of girls beyond the common schools and in 1819 recommended to the legislature that it consider legislation for improving women's education. Behind his appeal lay a document, *A Plan for Improving Female Education,* sent to him by Emma Willard, then principal of a female academy in Middlebury, Vermont. At Middlebury she and her husband formed polite relationships with the president and faculty of Middlebury College (then a college for men), who accepted her invitations to attend the final examinations and closing exercises of her academy. Not once, however, was she or her staff invited to the commencement exercises of the college. This experience made Willard bitter about the disparity in educational facilities between the two sexes and fired her ambition to create a school for girls with higher standards than those of existing seminaries and academies.

In 1818, when her *Plan* was in its final revision, she turned to the governor and legislators of New York State. Five of her pupils had come from Waterford, New York, and through them she made connections which encouraged her to write directly to Governor Clinton, enclosing the *Plan.* Nearly a year later she received his reply. He had read it with "equal pleasure and instruction," and he encouraged her to have it printed. It was read widely both in the United States and Europe, but a recommendation to grant $5,000 to a projected academy in Waterford was defeated by the New York legislature. In spite of this reversal the Willards did not give up; they moved from Middlebury to Waterford, where Emma Willard took charge of a new seminary for which the legislature had at least granted a charter. A year later Governor Clinton again appealed to the legislature to grant public funds to the academy and pointed out that the new school represented "the only attempt ever made in this country to promote the education of the female sex by the patronage of government." But this appeal also failed.

Willard's *Plan* was not original but it marshalled familiar nineteenth-century arguments. Women of dubious competence had opened female seminaries for private profit; young women attending these temporary institutions were poorly housed and badly taught, in some instances by instructors who taught as many as ten different "branches" or subjects. These frequently included showy and ornamental accomplishments. By comparison, colleges for young men, chartered by public authority, were endowed with funds and, with a board of trustees, were permanent institutions. Thus, they could determine the qualifications for entrance, designate the number of years of required study, and provide superior instruction and equipment. But Emma Willard made it clear that while she was recommending that female seminaries should possess the respectability, permanence, and uniformity of operation enjoyed by the men's colleges, she emphatically was not proposing the same mode of education for men and women. Indeed, twice in her *Plan* she insisted that her proposed seminaries would be as different from the men's colleges as the female character and duties were from those of the male.

Her central arguments were based on two themes: that the stability of the republic depended on the character of its citizens, and that the formation of character cannot be left to poorly educated mothers. It is within the power of women to give society its tone with respect to manners and morals. Another benefit would accrue from the education of women: female seminaries would improve the common schools by supplying them with teachers. Here Willard reveals that while she passionately believed women needed to be better educated she was not essentially concerned about equality. Young women would go out from the seminaries and probably would make better teachers than men, but they could afford to accept lower salaries. Men thus released from teaching would be at liberty to add to the wealth of the nation by entering occupations from which women were, as she said, necessarily debarred.

In 1821 Willard responded to an offer from Troy, New York, whose citizens agreed to provide both a building and continuing support if she would move her school there. Troy became one of the leading female seminaries in the country, with a high reputation for the quality of its teaching and its pioneering efforts in teaching science. Its graduates were in demand as teachers across the country, as were the textbooks that Emma Willard wrote in geography and history. For nearly twenty years she continued as principal but it was not until 1837, a year before she stepped down and turned her school over to Sarah Lucretia Willard, her daughter-in-law, that the seminary was incorporated and granted money from the literary fund of the state legislature. The academic standards she set at Troy, the lectures she gave to teachers and superintendents, the network she created of Troy alumnae, and her own regal bearing all made Emma Willard into a public figure, not then a customary role for a woman. She was, however, unable to realize her main goals—a minimum age of sixteen, a three-year course for all students, full residential accommodation, a faculty made up of specialists, and permanent legislative support.

Catharine Beecher

Another national figure in the growing discussion of women's education was Catharine Beecher, who was born in 1800, the oldest child in a family of thirteen and the favorite daughter of her father, Lyman, the nationally known revivalist and preacher. At sixteen her mother died and several years later her fiancé, an instructor of mathematics at Yale, was drowned in a shipwreck. To cope with grief and loneliness she turned to good works and benevolence and in 1823 opened a female seminary in Hartford. Within three years enrolment had grown from fifteen to eighty and the school had moved from quarters above a harness shop to the basement of a church. All instruction was conducted in one room, and the staff of three taught up to twelve subjects a day with practically no equipment. After three years of suffering this "round of haste, imperfection, irregularity and the mere mechanical commitment of words to memory," Catharine Beecher presented a plan to the leading citizens of Hartford for a new school with an assembly and study hall ample enough to hold 150 pupils, and ten other rooms for instruction.

Most of the city fathers ridiculed her proposal, but with the aid of a group of influential women a stock company was formed to which some $5,000 was subscribed. Her appeal for a permanent endowment of $20,000 was, however, not successful. In the new building each of the eight teachers had her own classroom and was expected to teach only one or two subjects. Pupils were divided according to ability and previous preparation into small classes ranging in size from six to twenty. A governess reigned over the study hall to see that perfect quiet was preserved. This highly structured scheme of organization was Beecher's reaction to the earlier years of chaos and a reflection of her belief that if teachers were responsible for fewer subjects and accepted responsibility for making policy, a seminary could become more like a college.

Throughout her long life Catharine Beecher believed that the Creator had assigned to men and women widely different spheres of responsibility. She accepted the traditional view that a woman's role was that of wife, mother, and housekeeper, to which she added teacher. All were demanding responsibilities that required training and Beecher's major contribution to the debate on women's education was her insistence that a woman needed to be trained for her profession. Toward the end of her life when the land grant colleges were beginning to offer systematic instruction in agriculture she commented somewhat bitterly:

> The care of a house, the conduct of a home, the management of children, the instruction and government of servants, are as deserving of scientific treatment and scientific professors and lectureships as are the care of farms, the management of manure and crops, and the raising and care of stock.[4]

In one of her early books, *Suggestions Respecting Improvements in Education,* which she read to her trustees in Hartford in 1829, she laments that teaching had not been made an honorable profession but instead was looked upon as "the resource of poverty or as a drudgery suited only to inferior minds." But now that common schools were opening across the land more teachers were needed, women particularly, and "we see a *profession,* offering influence, respectability and independence, thrown open to women." The need, in fact, was great. By the mid-1830s Beecher estimated that well over a million children were without schools, 30,000 teachers were needed at once, and an additional 4,000 were needed every year to cope with the increase in population. A young nation that believed itself an experiment was calling for help and instead of "the fainting, weeping, vapid, pretty play-thing, once the model of female loveliness,"[5] what the United States needed were young women who realized "the obligations imposed by Heaven to live and do good." For Catharine Beecher every young woman at the close of her school education should be qualified to serve as a teacher; the education necessary to fit her for that role would also prepare her for domesticity.

Catharine Beecher's vigor and dedication were not, however, instrumental in founding a permanent institution for the higher education of American women. Her influence was felt more through the strength of her personality and the extent of her writing. In all she wrote thirty-three books, and between 1841 and 1856 her *Treatise on Domestic Economy* was published in three editions and reprinted fifteen times. As a member of the upper middle class she was opposed to women entering the world of business and industry. She also opposed the suffrage movement, in part at least because it would give the vote to "that vast mass of ignorant women whose consciences and votes would be controlled by a foreign and domestic priesthood."[6] On the other hand, with considerable political astuteness, she used a national stage to persuade women that they had a distinctive and honorable, if limited, role to play in both home and classroom, and that it was their right and duty to agitate for training appropriate to their calling.

Derry and Ipswich

The same year that Catharine Beecher opened her seminary in Hartford, a well-to-do bachelor, Jacob Adams of Derry, New Hampshire, left the first bequest ever made in the United States exclusively for the education of girls. The endowment was used to found Adams Female Academy in Derry and with some trepidation a committee of its trustees consulted Joseph Emerson on the choice of principal. Would his assistant, Zilpah Grant, be suitable? And could he release her? Sorry as he would be to lose Miss Grant he recommended her, and when her appointment was confirmed he bade her Godspeed saying, "If you can put into operation on right principles a permanent seminary for young ladies, you may well afford to lay down your life when you have done it." Within weeks Zilpah wrote to Mary Lyon inviting her to join her staff. It was the beginning of a partnership that continued for ten years and had lasting consequences for the education of women.

It was not only the prospect of working with her friend that attracted Mary Lyon to Adams Academy. Soon after her appointment as principal, Zilpah Grant had drawn up a prospectus for the new academy that held a strong attraction for Mary. The school would be divided into junior, middle, and senior classes with entrance requirements for each. Below these would be a preparatory division. Subjects would be taught in sequence and graded in difficulty from year to year. In the senior year, for example, the curriculum would include natural philosophy, chemistry, and astronomy. The scriptures would hold a central position and, as a condition of her appointment, Zilpah Grant insisted that one-seventh of study time would centre on the Bible. Furthermore, there would be special instruction for those planning to become teachers. The prospectus closed with this entreaty: "It is earnestly requested that all who attend will enter at the commencement and continue during the term." This prospectus was an expression of the goal that Willard, Beecher, Grant, and Lyon were prepared to battle for: the raising of the standards of education for young women. In place of the seminaries that allowed girls to skip from school to school spending only a year, often less, at each, these women favored a three-year course of graded studies and systematic methods of instruction. In 1824 the new school opened with an enrolment of sixty for a summer term of thirty weeks.

For the next ten years Mary Lyon served her apprenticeship as a teacher and assistant principal. Adams Academy under Zilpah Grant lasted for only four years. The trustees became increasingly dissatisfied with the emphasis on religious instruction and Grant's efforts through revival meetings to secure the salvation of her pupils' souls. When Board members finally took action they adopted an ingenious solution. Instead of condemning the religious activity they voted to add music and dancing to the curriculum, and at the same time reappointed Grant as principal and doubled her salary. As expected, Grant resolutely refused to sanction dancing and the trustees declared all teaching positions open and advertised for another principal. Within a month Zilpah had found a new school at Ipswich with a commodious rent-free building and a contract that gave her complete autonomy. She persuaded Mary to stay with her and, in effect, they moved their school to Ipswich, taking a substantial number of pupils with them. Both at Derry and Ipswich the school year initially consisted of a summer session only and for six years Mary organized her own winter schools (November to April) in the hill towns of Buckland and Ashfield.

She became a highly effective teacher in these years and realized that she could administer her own school. The winter schools initially gave elementary instruction to girls who would become teachers in the common schools, but gradually "higher branches" were added and as enrolment increased to 100 pupils Mary added assistants to her staff. Her reputation spread throughout western Massachusetts and it was not unusual for visitors to appear on more than half the days of the school term, winter weather notwithstanding. These schools gave her great satisfaction and toward the end of her second winter she wrote to her friend Amanda White: "I enjoy [school] so much that I sometimes almost fear lest I may have all my good things in this life."[7] But these were also years of anxiety and depression. In a letter to Zilpah she says, "I have a pleasant school, but one thing is wanting, and when I think of this, my heart is sad. Amidst all my blessings, I feel that the frown of God rests upon me. Pray for me and for my dear pupils."[8] She suffered from deep doubts about the quality of her attachment to her Savior and about her capacity to lead her students to salvation.

So strong was Mary Lyon's attachment to Zilpah Grant that she left her winter schools in 1830 to become Grant's full-time assistant principal in Ipswich. Before making this decision Mary had refused an offer from Catharine Beecher ("Will you please write me immediately if there is *any* prospect that I could induce you to join the *faculty* of H.F. Seminary.") and had resisted the entreaties of a county ministerial association in western Massachusetts to continue her work there on a year-round basis. For the next four years Zilpah and Mary instituted both a summer and a winter term, raised admission requirements, set the minimum age for entry at fourteen, and deliberately refused to teach the "ornamental branches" or drawing room accomplishments. Mary taught arithmetic, chemistry, and history and for a year and a half served as acting principal while Zilpah was recovering her health. By 1834 Ipswich with an enrolment of 200 and a teacher/student ratio of 1:15 had become one of the leading seminaries, comparable to those presided over by Emma Willard and Catharine Beecher. There was a strong emphasis on thoroughness and accuracy, and throughout the school year students studied no more than two or three subjects in cycles of several weeks. Questions could be raised and an atmosphere of free discussion prevailed in such courses as mental philosophy, but the climate of the school was Calvinistic, as Mary Lyon's first biographer makes clear:

> The government of the school was a kind of theocracy, the teachers standing between the pupils and God, to assist them in learning his will. . . . The regulations were referred to the immutable standard of right and wrong. Is it right? Is it in accordance with the law of love? were questions constantly pressed home, with the hope of leading the scholar habitually to ask them for herself. Conscience was brought to bear on courtesy, neatness, dress, and everything which affects personal character and usefulness.[9]

At Ipswich, Mary Lyon gained experience she would later find useful. As acting principal she had a brief apprenticeship in the craft of school administration; in placing her students as teachers she became known to principals in New England, the South, and the Mississippi Valley; and in conducting the school's religious exercises she learned the art of giving short sermons on a scriptural text. Successful as Ipswich undoubtedly was, it had no permanent endowment nor did it own adequate residence accommodation for its students. And its fees were sufficiently high to limit admission to girls from upper-middle income families. The appeal for funds that Zilpah and Mary launched in February 1831 began with a letter to the trustees in which they revealed two requisites for establishing a female seminary: a building containing classrooms, laboratory, library, reading room, and assembly hall; and a contiguous residence for 150 boarders, "pleasant and airy, so finished and furnished as to give ladies as favourable a situation . . . as is afforded to young men in our colleges." Meetings followed, prospective donors were identified, and Zilpah received pledges for nearly half the estimated needs, but that was the winter her health failed and she left both the school and the campaign in Mary's care.

For the better part of the next two years Mary Lyon learned the uncertainties and realities of fund-raising from an unobtrusive position in the background. In fact, the Ipswich Seminary campaign was a trial run for one of the main events of her life. She learned, for example, that she and Zilpah must not appear too aggressive and that plans for the seminary "should not seem to originate with *us,* but with benevolent *gentlemen.* If the object should excite attention, there is danger that many good men will fear the effect on society of so much female influence, and what they will call *female* greatness."[10] On the other hand, when asked by the trustees, she drew up a succinct prospectus entitled *New England Female Seminary for Teachers.* The main object of the proposed institution (it was never made clear whether the location would be at Ipswich or elsewhere) would be to prepare women of mature minds for active usefulness, especially to become teachers; its religious character would be strictly evangelical. The prospectus ends with the unabashed observation that no similar institutions were then in existence and that the one proposed would "lead the way toward the establishment of permanent female seminaries in our land."[11] For a variety of reasons the appeal failed: most of the seven trustees appointed to lead the campaign showed little enthusiasm and failed dismally to secure contributions from wealthy benefactors, and there was disagreement over the location of a new seminary. By April 1833, the board of trustees for the prospective seminary had been dissolved and Mary was writing to Zilpah that there were more than nine chances out of ten that "the door of Providence will be closed against all future operations towards founding a permanent institution."[12]

Her depression was, however, temporary and it lifted during a three-month journey to New York and Philadelphia and through Ohio, Michigan, and Illinois in the summer of 1833, the only occasion during her life that she spent any extended period away from New England. When she returned to Ipswich she had recovered her enthusiasm and wrote: "During the past year, my heart has so yearned over the adult female youth, in the common walks of life, that it has sometimes seemed as though a fire were shut up in my bones. I should esteem it a greater privilege to labor in this field than in any other on which I have ever fastened my attention."[13] She had also become convinced that the campaign for the new seminary then taking shape in her mind should not use the Ipswich appeal as a model. The precedent that appealed to her more was Amherst College, funds for which had been collected not from the rich but from "liberal Christians in common life." A year earlier she had confided her sense of the future to Zilpah Grant:

> If I should separate from you, I have no definite plan. But my thoughts, feelings, and judgment are turned toward the middle classes of society. For this class I want to labor, and for this class I consider myself rather peculiarly fitted to labor. To this class in society would I devote, directly, all the remainder of my strength (God

> permitting)—not to the higher classes, not to the poorer classes. This middle class contains the main springs, and main wheels, which are to move the world.[14]

Mary and Zilpah agreed through correspondence that 1834 would be the final year of their partnership, and with Zilpah's full approval Mary launched from Ipswich the first stage of the campaign for Mount Holyoke.

I AM ABOUT TO EMBARK IN A FRAIL BOAT . . .

Mary Lyon's next three years were filled with the triumphs and disappointments of campaigning: soliciting funds throughout the state, working with a committee of benevolent gentlemen and quietly persuading them to accept her judgment, drafting and redrafting, usually through several versions, her detailed plans for a new seminary, and answering the criticism and opposition her proposals aroused. The very fact that in the 1830s a woman had the audacity to launch such a campaign was in itself cause for criticism, and although she was known in the towns of western Massachusetts, Lyon was breaking all conventions when, as a single woman, she crisscrossed the state by stage coach and arranged meetings to further the cause of advanced education for women. Little wonder then that in the summer of 1834 she wrote to her youngest sister, "I am about to embark in a frail boat on a boisterous sea. I know not whither I shall be driven, nor how I shall be tossed, nor to what port I shall aim."

She began her campaign with a two-page brochure first printed in February 1834 and entitled *To the Friends and Patrons of the Ipswich Female Seminary,* the first of seven publications in which she appealed for funds and interpreted her plans. The essence of her appeal in this first publication was the need to found a new seminary, similar in academic quality to Ipswich, for those numerous and promising young women who, "for want of pecuniary means," were denied its privileges. If a building and residence could be provided by voluntary contributions, if the teachers appointed were possessed of a missionary spirit and were willing to labor cheerfully for a modest salary, domestic work were performed by members of the school, and a style of living were adopted that was "*neat,* but very plain and simple," it should be possible to reduce the cost of board and tuition from one-third to one-half the figure then current at Ipswich and other reputable seminaries. The brochure was reprinted in September 1834 and carried the names of seven members of an ad hoc committee who would serve until appointment of a permanent board of trustees. Four of the seven were clergymen. Also listed were ten prominent men, including Lyman Beecher and Herman Humphrey, president of Amherst College, who endorsed the proposal. There was no indication that Mary Lyon had written the appeal and of course no mention of the fact that the committee had held its first meeting in her Ipswich parlor.

At this meeting the committee resolved that $1,000 was needed at once to cover the expenses of mounting the later campaign and thereby assure donors that no portion of their gifts would be diverted to agents or advertising. Lyon undertook to secure this sum exclusively from women and in her last two months at Ipswich raised nearly the full amount. An appeal to the students and teachers at the seminary accounted for a quarter of the total figure, and a house-to-house canvass persuaded the wives (and their husbands) of Ipswich and vicinity to give $475; the remainder came from former students who responded to Lyon's scores of urgent letters. All this she accomplished while she was in complete charge of the seminary and Zilpah was on a five-month trip to the West. In late October 1834 Mary finally left Zilpah and went to spend the winter with Professor Hitchcock and family in Amherst. As she had written to her mother five months earlier, "I very much want six months or a year to read, write, plan, and do a thousand other things. I do not expect to be idle."[15]

In December she was back in Ipswich making herself available for consultation at a meeting of her ad hoc committee. In January she was in Worcester, where the committee settled the question of location for the new seminary. Also at this meeting were representatives of three Connecticut River valley towns which were bidding for the proposed seminary. The committee decided on South Hadley, on condition that the contribution pledged be changed from $5,000 to $8,000 and that it be raised in fifteen days. Lyon did not actually attend either meeting but she was in an adjoining room ready to be summoned if needed. There is no evidence that she objected to this treatment. She realized that if her project were to succeed it needed the leadership of men and she would have to create and maintain a delicate balance between their leadership and her own. Furthermore, she was not a militant feminist and was prepared to accept the conventions of her time. "It is the mark of a weak mind," she once told her students, "to be continually comparing the sexes and disputing and making out the female sex as something great and superior." She did not, however, give her committee free rein and through individual and small group consultation prior to committee meetings she usually was persuasive.

One example of her influence over the committee came late in 1835 when the campaign was not going well. In a mood of desperation several committee members proposed that Zilpah Grant be asked to join Mary as co-head of the proposed seminary. Grant's reputation and personal charm would, they felt, give added prestige to the project. Initially, Mary agreed to this proposal but then changed her mind. The secretary of the committee met her after the October meeting at which this matter was discussed and asked for her views. He later recorded her response: "She opened not her mouth. Her whole appearance indicated a disinclination for such a connection." And he confided to his diary, "It is very evident that Miss L. does not wish for Miss G. to be associated with her."[16] There is no record of further discussion of the matter within the committee. At the time it was an issue of some importance; although the two women were close friends, remained so, and had worked closely and well together for several years, Zilpah did not share several of Mary's ideas for the new seminary. Indeed, with Zilpah as co-head a very different institution would have emerged.

Raising money among the women of Ipswich convinced Mary Lyon that this direct, personal appeal for small donations must be continued. A full-time agent, the Reverend Roswell Hawks, was employed and Mary frequently accompanied him or went alone to schools, churches, or farm homes. With her green velvet money-bag she became a familiar figure on the main stage coach routes of southern New England and was usually recognized by fellow travellers. In the summer of 1835 she wrote to her mother of her nomadic life. It was clear that it took all her faith to sustain her: "I wander about without a home, scarcely knowing one week where I shall be the next. In this way, I expect to live, *at least* until one year from next spring, the earliest possible time that our new institution can open. . . . But I have no doubt that I am following the leadings of Providence."[17] And when her friends remonstrated with her over the impropriety of these wanderings she protested vigorously.

> What do I do that is wrong? . . . I visit a family where I have been previously invited, and the minister's wife, or some leading woman, calls the ladies together to see me, and I lay our object before them. Is that wrong? I go with Mr. Hawks, and call on a gentleman of known liberality at his own house, and converse with him about our enterprise. What harm is there in that? . . . My heart is sick, my soul is pained with this empty gentility, this genteel nothingness. I am doing a great work. I cannot come down.[18]

A visit to the small hill town of Heath brought in $1,200, and a meeting of distinguished ministers and laymen in Boston resulted in pledges of over $4,000. Contributions ranged from six cents to $1,000 and one list gives the names of more than 1,800 subscribers who contributed or promised a total of $27,000. Sufficient funds were in hand to allow construction to begin in 1836, but by the end of the year when Mary knew more funds were needed, she wrote 100 letters urging women in the towns and villages of New England to organize a drive to collect fifty or sixty dollars to buy furniture and bedding for dormitory rooms. Meanwhile, the state legislature had issued an act of incorporation which established a board of trustees and in October 1836, the cornerstone was laid. In a letter to Zilpah, in which there is no sign of strain in their relationship, Mary speaks of this ceremony: "The stone and brick and mortar speak a language, which vibrates through my very soul. . . . This will be an era in female education. The work will not stop with this institution. . . . It is a concession on the part of gentlemen in our behalf which can be used again and again."[19]

Those who supported Mount Holyoke Female Seminary were not left in doubt as to the plans and ideas of its founder. Between 1835 and the opening two years later Mary Lyon found the time and energy to write a detailed prospectus, a circular to accompany her letters appealing for funds for furniture, and a *General View of the Principles and Design* of the seminary. There is, of course, a good deal of repetition in these documents, and, in keeping with the style of public statements of the period, a wealth of florid language. But among the bursts of rhetoric the essential features of the new institution can be found. Admission was to be limited to adult young women, with enrolment eventually growing to 200; every student was to live in residence; "an elevated standard of science, literature and refinement" was to be offered at a moderate standard of expense; and it was to be assumed that a large proportion of graduates would become benevolent, self-denying teachers or enter "other spheres of usefulness." A self-perpetuating board of trustees composed of responsible men would assure the institution's permanence. An unusual feature of the seminary would be the plan of domestic work in which all students would participate gratuitously, and finally, the new institution would contribute in however modest a way to the salvation of the world.

> [The present generation] looks abroad on a world lying in wickedness. It beholds with painful interest the slow progress of these United States in carrying the blessings of salvation to the two hundred millions, who are the estimated proportion of the inhabitants of this benighted world to be converted to God through our instrumentality. And as it attempts in vain to calculate the time, when the work shall be accomplished, it would fain increase its progress a hundred fold, by training up the children in the way they should go.[20]

The three months before opening day were filled with excitement and anxiety for Mary Lyon. From some 200 applications she had to choose the most eligible eighty, but the shortage of furniture for student rooms was still desperate. There was no certainty as to when the building could be occupied, yet a date for the opening had to be agreed on well in advance; her head was "full of closets, shelves, cupboards, doors, sinks, tables, etc.," and it is not surprising that she had "more sick days with headache the last few weeks than usual." Yet, characteristically, she assured Zilpah Grant that "on the whole I am very much sustained by a kind Providence." Behind these more immediate concerns was the economic crisis of 1837, which made it impossible for many pledges to be honored. Nevertheless, the date for opening in November was decided and advertisements were placed in Boston, New York, and local papers as early as mid-August. And on 8 November Mary Lyon welcomed her students to the first school or seminary to be established in the United States by an appeal to public philanthropy.

A Peculiar Institution

When the Reverend Dr. E. N. Kirk, president of the board of trustees, gave the commemorative address to more than

600 of Holyoke's daughters at the twenty-fifth anniversary celebrations in July 1862, he spoke of the seminary as "a peculiar institution." By that he meant unique or special. Neither Great Britain nor other European nations had developed a system of thorough intellectual training combined with religious cultivation for its young women. The United States had, however, "more distinctly perceived than any other people, that the best condition of human society will never be attained until the women of the great middle class of the nation become thoroughly educated, intellectually and spiritually."[21] At the time of the founding of Mount Holyoke there were in the United States some 120 colleges for young men and it was Mary Lyon's determination to found a seminary that would give young women an education of equal quality. Her aim was not to achieve equal rights for members of her sex or to thrust women out of their so-called appointed sphere, but rather to cultivate women's intellect so that as wives, mothers, teachers, and missionaries they could better serve the Christian cause. The evangelical Christian atmosphere of Mount Holyoke under Mary Lyon can scarcely be overemphasized. For roughly 100 years New England passed through several periods of religious fervor, starting with the first "Great Awakening," from 1720 through the 1740s, a second beginning at the turn of the century, and a final burst of zeal in the revival period of the 1840s. The "Great Boston Revival" of 1842 was reported to be "one of the most remarkable spiritual quickenings in all the annals of American revivals,"[22] and leaders of this movement, particularly Lyman Beecher and Edward Norris Kirk, were well known to Mary Lyon. It is not surprising then that revivals were held at Mount Holyoke in eleven of the twelve years she served as principal. As one teacher recorded, the year 1843 was "one rich in blessing." A careful division of responsibility was made among the teachers and of the thirty-six students who entered the school that year "without hope," only six remained destitute of it.

The religious emphasis that permeated the seminary was expressed in a number of ways. Mary Lyon normally gave a short sermon each day during morning prayers, small groups gathered for prayer meetings on Sunday, teachers conducted Bible classes, and at least once a month students met to hear about foreign missions, frequently from missionaries home on furlough. The seminary was, however, nondenominational and churches had given relatively little to Lyon's appeal for funds. During the 1840s the number of missionaries bound for foreign lands under the auspices of the American Board of Commissioners for Foreign Missions increased noticeably. Mary Lyon was a strong supporter of the A.B.C.F.M. and enthusiastically encouraged both her teachers and students to enlist for service abroad. Thus began the long tradition of Holyoke alumnae becoming part of the missionary enterprise; at the seventy-fifth anniversary celebration the 250 and more graduates and non-graduates who had gone out to nineteen countries were appropriately honored.

Several features of the "Domestic Plan" at Mount Holyoke were unique. Originally devised not as an essential feature of the seminary but as a "mere appendage" to reduce expenses, Mary Lyon later defended the scheme of creating a family atmosphere for her students. By taking responsibility for washing, ironing, sweeping, baking, washing dishes, and every other domestic task (there were no servants) her girls enjoyed the benefits of an hour of exercise every day, the sociability that came from working in small groups, and the "union of interests" that helped create a sense of community. But these were advantages only when the plan was operating smoothly. In the opening weeks the superintendent of the domestic department "broke down" and had to leave; Lyon comforted her, gave her a parting gift, and took over her responsibilities. This meant scheduling and supervising the work crews and it was only after three or four months during which she did not leave the seminary for even half a day that she considered her family to be organized.

A well-run and orderly school was high on her list of priorities. In 1842 she reported: "We have had a very prosperous year in worldly things. Everything is systematized and Miss Moore and Miss Whitman urge forward the wheels so beautifully that all seems more than ever like clockwork."[23] And a few months later: "Our young ladies are very youthful, more and more so, every year; but there is so much docility, such a sweet atmosphere all around, that I feel, from day to day, that our home is a sweet home."[24] Yet, characteristically, she was resolutely pessimistic about the spiritual tone of her school: "Alas! one thing is lacking—the direct and powerful influence of the Holy Spirit."[25]

Academic standards were higher than in the great majority of the female seminaries and admission requirements were demanding. Emily Dickinson, whose home was at Amherst, attended Holyoke for one year (1847–48) at the age of seventeen. Of her entrance tests she wrote: "I cannot be too thankful that I got through them as soon as I did, and I am sure that I never would endure the suspense which I endured during those three days again for all the treasures in the world."[26] Textbooks were chosen and courses of study designed as nearly parallel to those of Amherst College as possible: the Amherst and Mount Holyoke catalogues for 1841 to 1849 list twelve texts used in common.[27] Mary Lyon repeated the experiments in chemistry she had observed in the classes of Professors Eaton and Hitchcock. Latin was added to the list of optional subjects in 1839–40, and examinations at the end of the year were open to the public. On one occasion Edward Hitchcock overheard the conversation of two college presidents who were on the platform after students in one of Lyon's classes had been examined in Butler's *Analogy of Religion,* which in the men's colleges was usually taught to senior students by the president. "How is it that these young ladies recite on Butler so much better than our senior classes?" "I do not know," replied the other, "unless it be that they have a better teacher."[28]

In 1846 the *Springfield Republican* reported on the commencement exercises and commented on this "highly useful institution" which was educating so many young women "in the most thorough manner" at very low cost.[29] Throughout her twelve years as principal Mary Lyon kept the cost of tuition, room, and board at sixty dollars per year. This modest fee, approximately a third of the charges made by other seminaries of comparable standing, could be continued because of the Domestic Plan, the self-denial of teachers and their principal, the increasing enrolment, which allowed for economies of scale, the growing endowment, and Lyon's sagacity in managing accounts. She set the example in self-denial by refusing to accept a salary of more than $200 per year plus board and heat, and although her trustees urged her to take more, she always refused. Teachers' salaries in the first decade ranged from $125 to $200, a scale Catharine Beecher sharply criticized and invited Mary to discuss with her. (In the delicate state of her health Beecher imperiously asked Mary to come to her home but not to talk "in a very animated way" and to come prepared to be "calm as a clock" and "not too interesting.")

By the end of the third year (1839–40) enrolment was 119, the school was financially sound, and both the number of applicants and academic standards were rising. Mark Hopkins, president of Williams College, had given the commencement address, and trustees were discussing the addition of a new wing to the original building. But during the nine-week vacation word arrived at South Hadley of the illness and death of seminary students from typhoid fever. Some forty students had contracted the disease and nine had died. This was a shattering blow to Mary Lyon and, as she wrote to Zilpah Grant, "None but my heavenly Father knows how great a trial this was to my heart."[30] When the seminary reopened in September only eighty students appeared, but the waiting list was sufficiently large to bring enrolment back to normal. By 1844, with the addition of the south wing, it was over 200, and by 1848, it reached 235.[31] By 1851 the total value of gifts for land, buildings, and furniture had reached $68,500, the seminary was out of debt, and the trustees had a surplus of $1,800, which in the years ahead would grow into a substantial endowment.[32]

In the fall of 1846 Lyon was ill for three months with a severe cold which affected her lungs. There is evidence that several years earlier she had contracted tuberculosis.[33] Early in 1849 while suffering from influenza she caught erysipelas from one of her students. She died on 5 March and was buried in the seminary grounds. In May that year a shaft of Italian marble was placed over her grave carrying the inscription, "There is nothing in the universe that I fear but that I shall not know all my duty, or shall fail to do it." If Holyoke was a "peculiar institution," one of its unique characteristics was the quality of its founder and first principal.

Her rigid Calvinism, passionate devotion to duty, and inexhaustible energy made Mary Lyon a formidable woman. Yet she had another side. Her personal warmth and wit, deep affection for her students and staff, and capacity to cope with difficulties, together with her piety, made her an example of womanhood that New England parents were only too glad to accept as an influence on their daughters. In her evangelical religion and acceptance of the traditional role of women she was a woman of her time, but in her belief that the intellectual ability of women was equal to that of men and her confidence that young women could survive the rigors of a seminary that was as demanding as many of the men's colleges she was well ahead of her contemporaries. In creating a seminary of high academic quality for mature young women of moderate means, stressing the necessity of permanence, insisting on residential accommodation, selective admission, and a well-ordered course of study she created the model for the liberal arts college for women. And although her seminary did not officially become a college until 1888, when other women's colleges had been established for years, Mount Holyoke to this day proclaims in its literature that it is "the oldest continuing institution of higher education for women in the United States." No Holyoke alumna leaves her alma mater without immersion in the legend of Mary Lyon.

From Seminary to College

In 1887 when Mount Holyoke celebrated its fiftieth anniversary the atmosphere of the seminary was still deeply religious: revivals and conversions were conducted quietly, evangelists such as D. L. Moody had recently visited the campus, and meetings of the Women's Christian Temperance Union were enthusiastic and well attended. In the early eighties the principal, Julia Ward, had said, "I would a thousand times rather see it [the seminary] blotted from the face of the earth than to see it secularized. It is my deep conviction that the highest intellectual and religious culture must here exist together."[34] The course of study had been extended to four years; Latin was required; Greek, French, and German courses were available; and faculty from over a score of men's colleges regularly lectured in the sciences. Instruction during the first half century was marked by vigorous discipline and thorough mastery of the subjects being studied.

What they learned Holyoke alumnae wanted others to know. Not only did they become teachers and missionaries but they founded seminaries and colleges on the Holyoke model in the United States and abroad. By 1887 there were Holyoke daughter schools on a Cherokee Reserve, in Ohio (Western Seminary in Oxford and Lake Erie Seminary in Painesville), Michigan Seminary at Kalamazoo, and Mills College in California. Fidelia Fiske, one of Mary Lyon's teachers, founded a school in Oroomiah in what was then Persia, and other transplants had been established in Turkey, South Africa, Spain, and Japan.[35] For its first forty years (1837–77) Holyoke kept in touch with some 2,300 students. Of that number, 73 per cent became teachers for varying periods of time, and nearly 9 per cent entered the service of foreign missionary boards.[36]

The original building had additional wings used for residences, library, and gymnasium, and a new building for science and art opened in 1876. In traditional Holyoke fashion some 500 people had contributed either money or scientific specimens to the building and its collections. In its wisdom the board of trustees, after several years of agitation by alumnae groups, had appointed three women to its membership, the principal ex officio, and two others. There were, however, dark periods in the years after Mary Lyon's death, when the principal's authority declined and the board of trustees exercised greater control. In the 1860s the seminary had a debt over $25,000. The most effective way of liquidating it appeared to be a legislative grant. However, only on a third attempt and with legal advice did board and faculty members convince committees of the legislature that Holyoke Seminary merited state aid no less than such colleges as Tufts, Amherst, and Williams. The request for $40,000 was approved by the legislature. When this news reached Holyoke the campus was illuminated and the girls gathered under the principal's window to sing, "Praise God, from whom all blessings flow." Not only was the debt discharged but a system of steam heating replaced the original coal stoves.

In 1881 the principal submitted to the trustees a request that the seminary be converted into a college. The request was referred to a committee, debated for a year, and then tabled. It was not a new issue. Seventeen years before when a request had been made for a state grant a legislative committee accepted the fact that Mount Holyoke Seminary "in propriety and strength of claim falls not below those institutions of learning which have been the recipients of material assistance from the state"[37]—that is, the men's colleges. This statement was recalled at the fiftieth anniversary celebrations as the alumnae addressed themselves to the college question. A resolution was adopted which stated: "The time has fully come when this seminary should itself take the name Mt. Holyoke College, and also establish a curriculum befitting the name."

Again the trustees appointed a committee and meetings of alumnae groups submitted appeals for action. Conservative voices on the board forced a compromise solution: to retain the seminary course but in addition to establish two collegiate courses leading to bachelor degrees, and to change the name to Mount Holyoke Seminary and College. In spite of public controversy created by Boston newspapers, the proposed bill passed the Massachusetts House of Representatives and Senate without a dissenting vote and in March 1888 the seminary and college was authorized to grant both diplomas and degrees. So heavy were the March snows that year that it was not until nine days later that these glad tidings reached South Hadley. Again the campus was illuminated, the girls sang the doxology, and the principal at supper read

Deuteronomy 28:1–14. Afterward, as one student reported, "We were all out of doors as much as we wished for an hour, and had a merry time."

Then began the task of developing the curriculum for classical and scientific courses, raising entrance requirements, and upgrading faculty qualifications. Since Mary Lyon's time Holyoke teachers had been chosen from among Holyoke graduates and in 1887 only three members of staff had been educated in other institutions. Within a year of the new charter the non-Holyoke group had increased to eight and there was "a veritable scramble by members of the teaching staff to extend their training by postgraduate study"[38] through leaves of absence and attendance at summer schools. With a better qualified staff the new principal, Elizabeth Storrs Mead (herself not a Holyoke graduate), introduced a new course of study leading to the degree of Bachelor of Literature. This literary course soon absorbed most of the students enrolled in the seminary curriculum and by 1892–93 only eight seminary students remained. By contrast, enrolment in the college course had risen to over 300.

The transition from seminary to college was possible largely because Mary Lyon had founded a strong seminary. Nevertheless, there was a sense of uneasiness, as the *Seminary and College Journal* of 28 March 1889, reveals. After giving the alumnae full details of recent developments, the editor concludes: "You can easily see that in connection with the new position of the school and the changes contemplated, there are many perplexities and temptations, and some real trials, which call for abundant grace and wisdom. How shall we blend the spirit of Mary Lyon and the spirit of the times?"

Women's Colleges

Women's colleges had appeared before the Civil War in the United States but they were few in number. Probably the first was the Georgia Female College, which opened in Macon in 1839. Chartered as a college and authorized to grant degrees, its founders intended it to be equal to existing colleges for men. Its first president, George F. Pierce, was nothing if not enthusiastic: "The prospect is novel; it stands out on the map of world history alone—isolated—a magnificent example of public spirit and Catholic feeling—of devotion to literature, and of zeal for Female Education."[39] Unhappily, how ever, President Pierce soon had to face a difficult choice: he could maintain collegiate standards and lose his students, or he could compromise and enrol sufficient students to pay his bills. He chose the latter option, admitted girls at the age of twelve, and adjusted the course of study accordingly.

The earliest co-educational college to grant degrees to women was Oberlin, which opened in 1833 and admitted young women to its college course in 1837. All students worked for four hours a day, the men on the 500-acre farm or in the workshops, the women carrying out domestic chores. This pattern of paid manual work was common in the evangelical schools of the period and allowed farmers' sons to work their way through theological training. The first women's college in the East to establish requirements comparable with the men's colleges was Elmira Female College, chartered in 1855, and recognized as a college by the Board of Regents of the state of New York. One condition the Regents laid down was periodic visitation by them. It was also during the 1850s that Matthew Vassar, a wealthy Poughkeepsie brewer and a bachelor with no direct heirs, began to consider how he might dispose of his considerable fortune. His original intention had been to build a hospital but his advisers, who were not disinterested—one became the first president—persuaded him to found a women's college. Once convinced, Vassar became interested in both the cause and the curriculum of women's education and in his first address to trustees of Vassar College said: "It occurred to me that woman, having received from her Creator the same intellectual constitution as man, has the same right as man to intellectual culture and development."

Vassar opened in 1865 in Poughkeepsie, New York, with some 350 students and a faculty of thirty, twenty-two women and eight men. In the first year not one student could meet the full requirements for entry to the freshman class and thus all had to be assigned to the preparatory course. Only gradually did the four-year classical and scientific courses develop. By the time of his death in 1868 Matthew Vassar had bequeathed close to $800,000 and in the quality of its faculty, the number of courses available, its accommodation and equipment, his college was far enough ahead of the seminaries to be seen as a new kind of institution.

By giving women the opportunity to prove their capacity for work outside their traditional sphere, the Civil War was a powerful factor in preparing the way for women's colleges. In hospitals, on farms, in offices and industry, and more than ever in schools, they gave their services, which in themselves made an effective case for equal rights, particularly the right to the same kind of education that men received. The war gave women confidence that their minds were not inferior and, slowly but inevitably, they became interested in a wider variety of careers. In 1870 93 per cent of all women workers were in seven occupations: domestic service, and as agricultural laborers, seamstresses, milliners, teachers, textile mill workers, and laundresses.[40] Nevertheless, there were modest signs of change. The 1870 census of occupations listed at least one woman in each of the 338 occupations in its classification, and nearly two million women were in paid occupations. Precedents were being established: there were 525 women physicians, sixty-seven among the clergy, and five women lawyers.[41]

The final quarter of the nineteenth century was a period of great economic vitality in the United States, when huge personal fortunes were made and private philanthropy created a tradition of generous endowment for higher education. Smith and Wellesley both opened in 1875 with large benefactions. Henry Fowler Durant, a wealthy Boston lawyer, founded Wellesley, first as a female seminary on the model of Holyoke, of which he was a trustee and about which he is reported to have said, "There can't be too many Mount Holyokes." By the time it opened in 1875 in Wellesley, Massachusetts, the state legislature had changed its name to Wellesley College. Smith College was founded when Sophia Smith, perplexed by the burden of disposing of two fortunes, her own and that of her brother, took her pastor's advice and provided in her will for a college "with the design to furnish my sex means and facilities for education equal to those which are afforded in our Colleges for young men." When it opened, Smith College in Northampton, Massachusetts, was uncompromisingly "equal" in setting admission requirements that were substantially the same as those at Harvard, Yale, and Amherst. Its freshmen were examined in Greek, Latin, algebra, geometry, geography, English, and history. The unhappy result was an entering class of twelve the first year and sixteen the second. Smith refused to create a preparatory department but compromised by admitting "special students," a polite term for girls who could not meet the admission standards in mathematics and classics, and enrolment soon grew to the point that a quota had to be placed on the number of special students. Bryn Mawr, which opened in 1885 through the generosity of a Quaker physician and businessman,

Joseph Taylor, also intended to give women "all the advantages of a college education which are so freely offered to young men." It too had no preparatory department but did introduce one unique feature, a graduate school to train teachers, particularly college teachers.

By 1888 when Holyoke was granted its college charter the report of the Commissioner of Education of the United States listed eight women's colleges in Division A, those which were "organized and conducted in strict accordance with the plan of the arts college," and 190 in Division B, the majority of which were seminaries, collegiate institutes, and women's colleges with lower standards.[42] Both lists were incomplete and by 1890 the commissioner had added Elmira and Barnard to Division A. The seven colleges—Barnard, Bryn Mawr, Holyoke, Radcliffe, Smith, Vassar, and Wellesley, later known as the Seven Sisters—formed the vanguard of the women's college movement at the turn of the century. Holyoke had survived a disastrous fire which destroyed Mary Lyon's original building in 1896, its enrolment almost doubled during the nineties, and its teaching staff was increased to maintain a faculty to student ratio of 1:11. Its reputation was no doubt enhanced when President and Mrs. McKinley arrived in June 1899 for their niece's graduation.

The majority of women students enrolled in higher education at the turn of the century were not, of course, attending women's colleges. Over two-thirds were in co-educational colleges, or state and private universities, most of which had been founded since the Civil War. Under the Morrill Act of 1862, state legislatures could use the proceeds of federal land grants to endow colleges of the agricultural and mechanical arts which later became state universities. The stimulus of a rapidly expanding population and a buoyant economy created new careers in industry, agriculture, and the professions for those with the advantages of university training. Thus state universities grew in number and prestige in the late nineteenth century. At their founding, or soon thereafter, most were co-educational. Early in the twentieth century all state universities admitted women with the exception of three in the South—Virginia, Georgia, and Louisiana.[43] Similarly, several universities founded in the same period by private philanthropy—Boston, Cornell, and Stanford, for example—were co-educational, as were many small colleges that evolved from seminaries or academies. This expansion of higher education was made possible in good part by the remarkable growth of the public high schools. In the three decades following 1870 the number of public high schools increased sixfold, and it was their students who entered the state universities.

In the eastern states, particularly in New England, the success of the women's colleges was achieved in the face of doubt and scepticism about the value of higher education for women. Would college study destroy a woman's femininity, or affect her chances of finding a husband? There was a lingering doubt about whether or not women's minds were of equal quality to men's, and a basic prejudice toward the educated woman. The most vigorous debate, however, centred on health. In 1873 Dr. Edward Clarke, a prominent Boston physician and a professor at the Harvard Medical School, wrote *Sex in Education*, an allegedly scientific treatise on the physiological effects on young women subjected to the rigors of college study. For its time the book was a best-seller and it was widely discussed in the seventies and eighties. Clarke attempted to show that the critical stage in a woman's physiological development coincided with the years of a college education and he argued that "The same system never does two things well at the same time. The muscles and brain cannot *functionate* in the best way at the same moment." He warned mothers and daughters that too much study could have dire effects, and that if higher education for women continued it required "no great prophet to tell that the wives who are to be mothers in our republic must be drawn from transatlantic homes."[44]

The women's colleges rallied to defend themselves. The resident physician of Vassar challenged Clarke's "facts" about a fourteen-year-old Vassar student, and other testimony emphasized that Clarke had made his case on too little evidence, essentially only six case studies. The Association of Collegiate Alumnae, later known as the American Association of University Women, surveyed 705 women graduates from twelve colleges and universities and found that "the seeking of a college education on the part of women does not in itself necessarily entail a loss of health or serious impairment of the vital forces." President Seelye of Smith spoke of his first graduating class: "The health of the students had not been impaired. All of them were as well and most of them stronger than when they entered college." Clarke's *Sex in Education* thus did little to diminish women's enrolment in higher education, yet it was an important book for the widespread debate it created. As a result of that debate both co-educational and women's colleges increasingly concentrated their attention on their students' health through sound nutrition, courses in physiology and hygiene, and programs of physical education. These were not new developments for Holyoke students; Mary Lyon had included calisthenics in her 1835 prospectus and later stressed that one virtue of the Domestic Plan was the exercise it offered. Her students were also required to walk a mile a day.

When Charles William Eliot was inaugurated as president of Harvard in October 1869, he warned that "the world knows next to nothing about the mental capacities of the female sex. Only after generations of civil freedom and social equality will it be possible to obtain the data necessary for an adequate discussion of woman's natural tendencies, tastes and capabilities." He did not believe it was Harvard's responsibility to gather such data because he was unalterably opposed to co-education: "the difficulties involved in a common residence of hundreds of young men and women of immature character and marriageable age are very grave. The necessary police regulations are exceedingly burdensome." Other eastern colleges, including Yale, Amherst, and Dartmouth, were opposed to co-education, and Cornell, whose founder's intention was to establish "an institution where any person can find instruction in any study," agonized for two years before admitting women students. This opposition to co-education by the eastern men's colleges gave strong encouragement to the founding not only of women's colleges but also of "annexes," later to become co-ordinate colleges, such as Radcliffe (Harvard), Barnard (Columbia), and Pembroke (Brown). The idea of an annex for women students came from England. Girton and Newnham colleges were established in Cambridge and Somerville and St. Hilda's at Oxford in the late nineteenth century. All were separate, and not equal.

Presidents of the men's colleges breathed more easily after Vassar, Wellesley, Smith, Mount Holyoke, and Bryn Mawr were chartered and the faculty of men's colleges were delighted to accept part-time appointments at the new colleges. In fact, less than a year after his inauguration President Eliot was congratulating Vassar graduates at the 1870 commencement: Latin, German, and French which he had heard in classes was superior to that of Harvard seniors. Amherst professors who taught at Smith reported that the average scholarship of Smith students was higher in the same studies than in their Amherst classes, and it was well known within the academic community that the women's colleges in the northeast insisted on high standards for admission and required students to undertake a program of study quite as rigorous as that of the leading men's colleges. Thus by the turn of the century women had proved that they were men's intellectual equals. Those who worried about the intellectualization of women could take comfort in the remark of Alice Freeman, president of Wellesley: "It is not possible to annihilate the womanliness of our American girls by anything that you can do to them in education."

Three Presidents

The question was no longer, "Should women pursue a higher education?" but rather, "Of what kind?" and "To what purpose?" Such questions had been raised earlier. When Alice Freeman became president of Wellesley in 1881 she at once articulated her ideal of the educated woman and shaped Wellesley accordingly. Her aim was to create a delicate balance between womanliness and intellect so that women could use their intellectual training in pursuing their roles as wives, mothers, teachers and, as they were later to be called, social workers. "Learning alone is not enough for women," she said, and her ideal woman would be a sensitive, high-minded, generous, and courageous person who would excel in "characteristic employments of housekeeping, teaching and ministering to the afflicted."[45] Freeman's formulation of the ideal life for women did not conform to the realities of her own life, although she tried to reconcile the conflict by thinking of herself at Wellesley as head of a large family and attempting to create a homelike atmosphere for students, whom she referred to as "my girls." This reconciliation between her considerable administrative ability and her views on the role of women was shattered when in 1884 she met George Herbert Palmer, professor of moral philosophy at Harvard. Two years later they were in regular correspondence and in a barrage of letters he used her own pronouncements to persuade her to resign from Wellesley and become his wife. She surrendered and in a published poem wrote:

> Great love has triumphed. At a crisis hour
> Of strength and struggle on the heights of life
> He came, and bidding me abandon power
> Called me to take the quiet name of wife.

A later Wellesley president, Caroline Hazzard, echoed Palmer's sentiments. "The maternal power of love and sacrifice is our greatest glory," she said in an address given in 1904. At Smith's quarter century anniversary in 1900 an early graduate in her address on the theme of home and family said, "the bearing and rearing of children is the capstone of a liberal education." Other women's colleges also supported the domestic role of women, and while they offered a higher standard of academic training than the seminaries and academies, they did not represent a radical departure from the womanly ideal of dedication to home and family.

There was, however, at least one college president who showed little enthusiasm for this acceptance of women's traditional role. Martha Carey Thomas, president of Bryn Mawr from 1894 to 1922, did not denigrate gentle breeding, high standards of behavior, and "the usages of culture," but her ideal, particularly in her early years as president, was the scholar, indeed the celibate scholar. After graduation from Cornell she had enrolled for graduate work at Johns Hopkins. She was permitted to attend lectures by sitting behind a curtain but was excluded from seminars. Like many other American students in the late nineteenth century she travelled to Germany and was welcomed to the classrooms of Leipzig but not permitted to take its doctorate. She then transferred to the University of Zurich, where she completed her degree and soon after wrote to her family, "I should love to have the presidency of Bryn Mawr. I believe I could make it the best woman's college there is . . . and I do not believe any other person . . . would have the interests of other women so at heart. . . . "[46] She joined the faculty of Bryn Mawr in 1883 as a professor of English but within a year, by a majority of one, the trustees elected her president.

In striving to make Bryn Mawr the best women's college in the United States, Thomas imposed high entrance requirements, introduced a graduate department, and gave her faculty, most of whom were men because she could not find enough highly qualified women, every incentive to engage in original research. Students were not expected to be responsible for the care of their rooms or do domestic labor; practically all their time was to be used for academic purposes and they would live a life of "intellectual renunciation." The curriculum allowed few electives and such subjects as Greek, mathematics, and philosophy were emphasized, as they could best train the mental faculties. Thomas regarded the college years as the most formative period of a woman's life: "A woman's college is a place where we take those wonderful, tender and innocent freshmen with their inherited prejudices and ancestral emotions and mould them by four years of strenuous intellectual discipline into glorious thinking, reasoning women fit to govern themselves and others."[47]

In her addresses to students Thomas spoke with evangelical fervor of the "college woman" and more particularly, the "Bryn Mawr woman." In welcoming students at the opening of the 1899–1900 academic year she referred to the "type of Bryn Mawr women which will, we hope, become as well known and universally admired as the Oxford and Cambridge man or as the graduate of the great English public schools." To create such a type a college must be a residential, self-contained, and isolated community where the outside world did not intrude and the life of the mind could be cultivated without distraction. Women would win liberation through higher education. It was during the years 1884 to 1910 that Carey Thomas reserved her highest praise at college commencements for young women who entered graduate schools, joined college faculties, and sacrificed their lives to advancing "the bounds of human knowledge." She believed that commitment to such a career was incompatible with marriage:

> Women scholars have another and still more cruel handicap. They have spent half a lifetime fitting themselves for their chosen work and then may be asked to choose between it and marriage. No one can estimate the number of women who remain unmarried in revolt before such a horrible alternative.[48]

The influence of Carey Thomas and the Bryn Mawr environment was impressive. Of all Bryn Mawr graduates in the classes of 1889–1908, 61 per cent went on to some form of advanced study, and 10 per cent began a career in college teaching.

After some twenty-five years President Thomas mellowed somewhat and in her address as a guest at the seventy-fifty anniversary of Mount Holyoke in 1912 she said: "The next advance in women's education is then to throw open to the competition of women scholars the rewards and prizes of a scholar's life and to allow women professors like men professors to marry, or not, as they see fit." She also had become much less emphatic about academic isolation and intellectual renunciation. There were careers for women aimed at "social reconstruction and human betterment'' and she increasingly gave her own time and support to the suffrage, prohibition, and international peace movements. Under pressure from both faculty and students she accepted changes in both Bryn Mawr's curriculum and entrance requirements. Electives were added and Greek was no longer required; courses in social work and pedagogy were introduced, but Thomas refused to accept music and home economics. In 1921 she established a summer school for working women, an indication that Bryn Mawr had moved out of its isolation and single-minded emphasis on scholarship toward involvement with the social concerns of the time. But Thomas never lost her passion for the cause of women. At Bryn Mawr's fiftieth anniversary celebration in 1935 she quoted the alumna letter she treasured most: ''I have forgotten everything I learned at Bryn Mawr but I still see you standing in chapel and telling us to believe in women.''

Mary Emma Woolley, who became president of Mount Holyoke in 1901, stands somewhere between Alice Freeman Palmer and Carey Thomas in her convictions of what a college for women should strive to be. Woolley was one of the first two women to receive a bachelor's degree from Brown University and prior to her appointment at Holyoke had been professor of biblical literature and history at Wellesley. In her inaugural address she emphasized that the purpose of a college education is preparation for life, ''which is only another way of saying, preparation for service in its broadest sense. . . . '' Avenues of service include not only the home and school, particularly the elementary school, where the college graduate has ''a chance to impress character in its most formative period,'' but also social work.

> The outlook for the college woman in social work has no horizon, no boundary line. In the complex civilization of our times, with its economic unrest, its social inequalities, its broad gulf between the enormously wealthy and the bitterly poor, the evils of intemperance and crime of various sorts, let no man or woman complain that there is not a place for labor.[49]

The problems of the city require both sympathy and research, ''a sympathy held in leash by the discipline of a trained mind.'' Other careers are open too: inventors and designers in industry, research in scientific and historical projects, and, of course, participation in foreign mission fields. But in their enthusiasm to equal or excel men's colleges, colleges for women must cultivate characteristics "which belong more distinctly in the feminine realm": the value of intuition, the insight into human nature, and "the ability to 'feel' what one cannot explain by logical processes." Toward the end of her address Woolley included a paragraph that delighted the assembled Holyoke alumnae:

> I have a fancy for the old word "gentlewoman." It carries with it a suggestion of the courtliness which springs from a royal heart, of courtesy which is based on unselfishness and consideration of others. A synonym for "college woman" should be "gentlewoman"; the sacrifice of gracious womanhood is too high a price to pay for knowledge, a price which is not asked. Rather, education should bring out the best in speech and in manners as well as in thought.[50]

Women Graduates and Their Careers

In her stress on opportunities for women in social work Mary Woolley reflected a trend that accelerated late in the nineteenth century and continued well into the twentieth. In the women's colleges the ideal of usefulness was well grounded, but an increasing awareness of social problems led to new avenues of usefulness. Industrialization, urbanization, and immigration were changing the face of the United States, and for college-trained American women the city became a new frontier where not only secretarial and clerical positions were available but where opportunities existed to help the less fortunate and promote social reform. In the 1890s the Association of Collegiate Alumnae recognized the need for a professional corps of social workers and through its conferences and publications concentrated on the theme that here was a career that called forth the feminine qualities of sympathy and compassion but also required the interests, knowledge, and intelligence of the college graduate, in short, a union of womanliness and intellectuality. "Thus the social service occupations might satisfy the college woman who was torn between domesticity and a desire to make use of her special preparation."[51] Women's colleges responded by introducing appropriate courses as electives at the undergraduate level. In 1888 Bryn Mawr offered a course in "Charities and Corrections" which was adopted by Vassar in

1894. And before relinquishing the presidency of Bryn Mawr, Carey Thomas founded a School for Social Work, thus giving the new profession additional status.

Most college women who engaged in social service were part-time volunteers, not full-time career women. Of 5,065 Holyoke graduates, for example, who responded to an alumnae questionnaire in 1936 only 144 or 2.7 per cent were professional social workers compared with 2,462 or 46.8 per cent who were involved in volunteer social and civic organizations.[52] Early in the century, women's colleges had recognized the importance of the volunteer movement as a part-time career for their graduates. In 1915 Dean Virginia Gildersleeve of Barnard organized a Volunteer Service Department whose purpose was to match volunteers with assignments in New York City. Holyoke students in 1912 could prepare for volunteer work of several kinds. They could join the campus branch of the YWCA, which four-fifths of the students did, or become involved in social work in the depressed districts of the town of Holyoke. In 1929 Wellesley offered a course in group leadership which was admittedly avocational and designed "to help women to use leisure fruitfully" and to become sensitive to contemporary social problems. The aspirations and expectancies of the women's college graduates continued well into the twentieth century to be the "nurturing professions" of motherhood and homemaking, teaching and social work, to which was added the community-minded volunteer.

There were, of course, varied reasons for the widespread acceptance of volunteer work. It gave the college woman the opportunity to expand her "natural functions" outside the home on a part-time basis at times that did not seriously interfere with her responsibility as wife, mother, and homemaker. Furthermore, during the better part of the first century of higher education for women in the United States most professions were closed to them. In 1908 the president of Barnard urged members of the Association of Collegiate Alumnae to take up careers in social service because the number of women in law, medicine, and theology was not increasing markedly.[53] At the seventy-fifth anniversary of Mount Holyoke the Alumnae Association president reported on the careers Holyoke's 4,000 living graduates had entered, but she could discover only "about thirty" who had made their way into medicine and only "a few" who were lawyers.[54] Twenty-five years later the numbers for the same professions were thirty-one and seven.[55] In her address at the Holyoke centenary celebrations, Frances Perkins, Franklin Roosevelt's secretary of labor and the first woman cabinet minister, pointedly referred to the handful of college women who held senior appointments in the state and federal governments. Similarly, when Bryn Mawr in 1970 made a comprehensive survey of the living alumnae of its undergraduate college who had held full-time jobs, the proportion who became engineers, architects, or lawyers was less than 1 per cent and only 3.2 per cent became physicians.

There is little evidence that the women's colleges fought vigorously to open the doors of the professions or the higher reaches of government, industry, or commerce to their graduates:

> It was almost as if there existed a kind of unspoken and perhaps even subconscious non-aggression pact: the women's colleges would provide educated wives but not professional competition for the men of Amherst, Yale, Harvard, Dartmouth, Princeton and the rest; in return the men's institutions assumed a distant but real paternal interest in the Sisters, serving as sources for administrators, trustees, faculty, and, not least, financial support as alumnae husbands. The inevitable uncertainties of the women's college graduates, heightened and sharpened by a superior education that ultimately proved irrelevant to the larger society, were assuaged by the promise of leadership in good works for social causes, offering the women self-validation and society a free ride.[56]

Women's Colleges and the Women's Movement

The official beginning of the women's rights movement in the United States is usually dated from the Seneca Falls convention of 1848. A group of five women, including Elizabeth Cady Stanton and Lucretia Mott, organized this meeting to discuss "the social, civil and religious rights of woman" and presented a Declaration of Sentiments which was a paraphrase of the Declaration of Independence.

> We hold these truths to be self-evident: that all men and women are created equal, that they are endowed by their Creator with certain inalienable rights: that among these are life, liberty and the pursuit of happiness. . . .

> The history of mankind is a history of repeated injuries and usurpations on the part of man toward woman, having in direct object the establishment of an absolute tyranny over her. To prove this, let facts be submitted to a candid world.

The facts were listed as a series of eighteen grievances among which were these:

> He has monopolized nearly all the profitable employments, and from those she is permitted to follow, she receives but a scanty remuneration. . . . He has denied her the facilities for obtaining a thorough education, all colleges being closed against her.[57]

For two days the conference discussed and adopted twelve resolutions, all but one of which were unanimously endorsed. This one was the ninth, which advocated women's suffrage, and its failure to secure unanimous approval reflected the fear of some women that a demand for the vote might jeopardize progress in other directions.

Early advocates of higher education for women did not want to jeopardize their cause by supporting women's suffrage. Like Mary Lyon, they did not want to risk antagonizing those benevolent men who were needed to support their movement. Furthermore, their faith led them to believe that once education had become universal other problems would soon be settled. Carey Thomas and Mary Woolley, however, did support the suffrage movement and publicly endorsed the organization of the Equal Suffrage League in American colleges. Prior to the First World War the League had nearly 200 members at Holyoke and was sending representatives to march in suffrage parades in Boston and Hartford. Sixty years later, however, a survey of Mount Holyoke alumnae found that only 3.3 per cent who returned the questionnaire had participated in a women's liberation group.[58] It would appear that when the women's colleges had achieved their single-minded goal—a standard of higher education for young women equal to that provided for young men—the colleges abandoned other goals in much the same way that American women abandoned feminism for nearly forty years once they had won the right to vote.

Paradoxically, a significant number of women's movement leaders attended the seminaries and women's colleges. Lucy Stone, who became one of the foremost orators of her day in speaking for both the rights of women and the abolition of slavery, briefly attended Mount Holyoke Seminary in its early years. She later recalled that Mary Lyon rebuked her for placing copies of William Lloyd Garrison's anti-slavery magazine, *Liberator,* in the seminary reading room. Stone graduated from Oberlin in 1847 but refused to write a commencement address because she would not be permitted to read it herself. She was, however, charitable toward Oberlin, as were other early women's rights leaders, and she referred to its opening as "the gray dawn of our morning." Harriot Stanton Blatch, an 1878 Vassar graduate, organized the Equality League of Self-Supporting Women, later known as the Women's Political Union. This body initiated the parades which became both an alarming and successful form of suffrage agitation. And Inez Mulholland, Vassar 1909, organized her suffragette supporters in a graveyard when the president of Vassar forbade meetings of such groups on campus. Among the luminaries of the more recent women's movement are Gloria Steinem and Betty Friedan (Smith), Sheila Tobias (Wellesley), Caroline Bird (Vassar), and Catharine Stimpson (Bryn Mawr).

These and other leaders have deplored the modest involvement of the eastern women's colleges in the feminist movement. Catharine Stimpson on a return to Bryn Mawr in 1974 sensed that many students were finding the new feminism "preachy, unfair to motherhood, or excessively frank about sexuality."[59] Liva Baker has documented that up to 1975 women's colleges were singularly inactive in sending representatives to congressional hearings on such issues as the Equal Rights Amendment, wage and employment discrimination, and the improvement of vocational and physical education for women.[60] Caroline Bird, after a detailed study of the participation of the women's colleges in events related to the women's movement between 1961 and 1971, has concluded that "At Vassar, as well as at her sister colleges, there has long been a kind of intellectual disdain for the whole subject of the special qualities and duties of women."[61]

There has been, historically, a disinclination in women's colleges to invite women as Commencement speakers. Smith waited forty-four years before inviting a woman to speak at its commencement, and Lucy Stone asked publicly in 1891, fifty-four years after Holyoke was founded, why only men were invited to speak on Founder's Day. Women have fared better as presidents: Wellesley has always had women presidents, as has Barnard, except for three brief interim or acting appointments. Smith, however, waited a century before appointing its first woman president. Holyoke, by contrast, went for a full century with women as principals of the seminary and presidents of the college. When this tradition was broken on Mary Woolley's retirement in 1937 she was so incensed that she never again set foot on the campus.

A somewhat different interpretation of the function of the relationship between a women's college and the women's movement was given in 1974 by David Truman, then president of Mount Holyoke.

> Let me emphasize that it is not my intent that the women's college should be a base or bastion for women's liberation or any other social movement. Our concern is not with movements but with the development of individuals of talent, individuals who in the present and prospective circumstances of the society are most likely to find their talents wasted, their potential unfulfilled unless their college years assist them in reassessing and revaluing themselves and their opportunities. That, as I see it, is the mission of the women's college. . . . [62]

As might be expected, the proportion of women on the faculty of women's colleges has been high, particularly in the early years of this century (see Table 3). The founder of Wellesley stipulated that there be an all-woman faculty, and when advanced degrees were not a condition of employment the women's colleges preferred a predominantly female faculty. As the pressure mounted for a stronger sprinkling of faculty doctorates, and as women's college enrolments grew faster than the output of women Ph.D.'s (as late as the 1960s only 11.6 per cent of doctorates in the United States were awarded to women)[63] the proportion of male faculty members increased. Nevertheless, women's colleges have maintained a higher proportion of women on their faculties than either the men's colleges or the co-educational colleges and universities.

Men continue to dominate the co-educational institutions. In 1981 over 75 per cent of all faculty and 90 per cent of full professors were male. In the women's colleges 55 per cent of all faculty and 43 per cent of full professors were female.[64] In neither type of institution are women winning the battle for equality; in the co-educational institutions the number of women faculty is increasing very slowly and in women's colleges the proportion of women is dropping, in some instances as a matter of policy. Holyoke, for example, believes that young women should be taught by both men and women and through a deliberate effort to increase the number of men on its faculty achieved a 50:50 ratio in 1972. This policy does not endear their alma mater to feminist alumnae, one of whom has asked: "Founded by women, supported by women, for the higher education of women, why are we now hiring any men if women, as well qualified, are having difficulty getting jobs?"

Table 3
Women Faculty Members in Thirteen Colleges (%)[65]

	1919 %	1974–75 %	1980–81 %
Amherst	0	7	20
Barnard	100	59	58
Bryn Mawr	55	40	40
Dartmouth	0	13	20
Haverford	0	12	16
Mount Holyoke	90	46	51
Oberlin	29	17	18
Radcliffe	0	—	—
Smith	68	40	39
Swarthmore	30	21	22
Vassar	80	39	40
Wellesley	82	55	54
Williams	0	16	16

STATUS OF COLLEGES
Amherst: co-educational since 1975
Barnard: college for women affiliated with Columbia University
Bryn Mawr: college for women with co-operative arrangement with Haverford
Dartmouth: co-educational since 1972
Haverford: co-educational since 1980
Holyoke: college for women
Oberlin: co-educational; first degrees awarded to women 1841
Radcliffe: Harvard faculty has been responsible for Radcliffe instruction since 1943
Smith: college for women
Swarthmore: co-educational since its founding in 1864
Vassar: co-educational since 1970
Wellesley: college for women
Williams: co-educational since 1970

THE BEST OF BOTH WORLDS

In the early 1980s only some 135 of the more than 3,000 colleges and universities in the United States were designated as "women's colleges" or "primarily women's colleges."[66] Two decades earlier the number was 300. Why the decline? Because of high costs and falling enrolments some colleges have declared themselves bankrupt. (Institutional euthanasia is sometimes difficult. When the trustees of a women's college in Pennsylvania decided it was time to close with dignity, the alumnae sued and the court ruled that the college could not close.) Others were absorbed into or united with larger institutions, and most became co-educational. Among the Seven Sisters Vassar is co-educational, Radcliffe is fully integrated with Harvard, and Barnard remains a college for women with a special relationship to co-educational Columbia. The others agonized about co-education before deciding against it. Holyoke, for example, polled its alumnae, faculty, and students, and held interminable discussions for two years before the chairman of the board of trustees made this announcement on 6 November 1971:

> The Board of Trustees of Mount Holyoke College voted today to reaffirm its commitment to the principle of women's education and remain a college devoted to the liberal arts. While maintaining its historic tradition, the College will nevertheless continue to welcome qualified men as exchange students or visitors in residence, and will continue to explore possibilities for further Five College cooperation with Amherst, Hampshire and Smith Colleges and the University of Massachusetts. This can give us the best of both worlds: an institution where the education of women can continue to be our major commitment, yet one in which we can explore numerous options and opportunities for exchange and cooperation.[67]

It was, both for Holyoke and the other colleges that had maintained their historic tradition, a difficult decision. The report of the Holyoke Fact-Finding Committee on Coeducation had revealed a dramatic decrease in the number of applications to women's colleges and since all the selective men's colleges in the East except Amherst had become co-educational the total pool of highly qualified women applicants might well decline further. When the decision was made there was no hard evidence that women's colleges that had become co-educational would attract large numbers of candidates of either sex. In addition to strictly practical considerations there were arguments for co-education at the level of principle that had to be answered—an educational institution that segregates by sex is indulging in a form of discrimination; only in an environment that includes the opposite sex can women prepare themselves for "real" life after graduation; the presence of men in the classroom adds to the variety of intellectual and cultural viewpoints; and the historical reason for the founding of colleges for women, equality of opportunity at a time when only men entered higher education, no longer obtains.

The case for the women's college reverses these arguments and adds several more: segregation does not discriminate against women: it is on the contrary a form of freedom. Discrimination is far more serious at the co-educational institutions where men normally dominate both the classroom and the extracurricular program. Only at a women's college do women become first-class citizens, independent of stereotypes and traditional expectations and free to choose from a wide variety of majors. One result, as the Holyoke literature points out, is that students in women's colleges are twice as likely to major in sciences and mathematics as women at co-educational institutions.[68] There is also "the opportunity to develop their leadership potential in every aspect of campus life in an environment free of prejudice and role restrictions often encountered in society at large."[69] This experience as a first-class citizen prepares a young woman to go into the post-graduation world with the confidence to demand to be treated in the manner to which she has become accustomed.

These arguments have been buttressed by recent research. A 1976 study[70] on the undergraduate origins of American scientists and scholars found that for the period 1920–73 more women from Mount Holyoke earned Ph.D.'s in the physical sciences than from any other college or university in the country. As an early teacher of chemistry this evidence would have warmed the heart of Mary Lyon, as would another study that showed a strong positive correlation between the ratio of women faculty to women students and the proportion of women students later cited for their career achievement in *Who's Who of American Women.*[71] That is to say, in colleges where there are many adult women on the faculty—in administration, and chairing important committees, women who are married and unmarried, with and without children—woman students have a wealth of role models through whom they gain support and confidence. That a high proportion of American women may need to develop confidence in themselves has been demonstrated by the research of Matina Horner, who became president of Radcliffe in 1972. In her explorations of the differences between the two sexes in motivation toward achievement she found among women what has been termed "the motive to avoid success." Early in life American society tells its women that "it really isn't ladylike to be too intellectual," and women students affected by the cult of femininity tend to doubt their abilities and be reluctant to use them.

Horner commented in 1969:

> She [the American woman] is warned that men will treat her with distrustful tolerance at best, and outright prejudice at worst, if she pursues a career. She learns the truth of Samuel Johnson's comment, "A man is in general better pleased when he has a good dinner upon his table than when his wife talks Greek." So she doesn't learn Greek, and the motive to avoid success is born.[72]

In both their arguments for maintaining their present status and in their recruiting literature the women's colleges emphasize that the fear of success is not fostered on their campuses. Indeed, quite the opposite is the case, as a Mount Holyoke Faculty Committee declared:

> [Here] the woman student has an unequalled chance to discover and develop her qualities of leadership as well as academic capacities, her confidence in these capacities and a respect for those of other women, a sense of herself as a full individual, an awareness of her range of roles and choices, and to do so unrestricted by the various social, psychological and cultural pressures exerted in fully coeducational institutions.[73]

Such a statement clearly implies that the cult of femininity is fostered on the co-educational campus. This view has been restated by an associate professor of English at Mount Holyoke—"I think women in a learning situation can do best if free of the need to be seductive and silent and timid in order to attract men"[74]—and by David Truman, president of Mount Holyoke when the decision was made to continue as a college for women, who in one speech created the image of "a woman on a coeducational campus . . . who feels she must both compete *with* men and *for* men" and who may thus find it "much easier . . . to become a pom-pom girl."[75]

Holyoke does not regret its decision. Applications for admission did not decline and by 1980 the freshman class of 505 was selected from 2,300 applicants. A drive for funds which began in 1972 raised $37 million in less than a decade and in 1981 the president announced a new campaign to raise $13 million in two years. Co-education is no longer debated on campus and neither faculty nor students are inclined to reopen the issue. But Holyoke is not simply a liberal arts college for women. It is a very special place with an able faculty, a generous faculty/student ratio, a splendid library, forty well-equipped buildings, and nineteen residence halls each with its own dining room. It has long since lost its isolation and its image of a nunnery, which was an indictment made by one of Mary Lyon's students. A shuttle bus takes students to the other members of the Five College Plan (Amherst, Hampshire, Smith, and the University of Massachusetts) and each year some 500 Holyoke women register for courses on these other campuses, none of which is more than ten miles away.

Curriculum options at Holyoke include internships in Washington, in business and industry, or abroad. All students are required to enrol in a non-Western course devoted primarily to study of some aspect of Asia, Africa, Latin America, the Middle East, or the non-white peoples of North America. Students may spend a year of study abroad or at a college in the Twelve-College Exchange Program. A vigorous recruiting campaign has attracted a modest number of black students and generous financial aid consisting of grants, loans, and work on campus has made it possible to continue the Mary Lyon tradition of enrolling daughters of middle and low income families. Few colleges can boast a campus of 800 acres of rolling lawns, wooded hills, and two lakes.

But perhaps the major strength and chief attraction of Holyoke and its sisters is their selectivity. It is part of American folklore that several dozen colleges and universities are difficult to enter and hence attractive to bright students. Recent studies by Alexander Astin and Lewis Solomon have confirmed that employers and graduate schools tend to give preference to the graduates of these select institutions.[76] Thus Holyoke and its sisters have advantages in recruiting students, employing faculty, raising funds, and placing their graduates that most other other women's colleges do not enjoy. In this sense they are elitist and their excellence (a favorite word in the recruiting literature) will continue through the loyalty and support of their alumnae. In recent years Holyoke graduates have contributed more than $3 million annually, and a network of alumnae is active in searching for bright candidates. To her that hath shall be given—

In October 1978 Elizabeth Topham Kennan was inaugurated as president of Mount Holyoke, the first woman to be appointed since Mary Woolley retired in 1937 and the first alumna of the college to serve as president in this century. A medieval scholar and historian with graduate degrees from Oxford and the University of Washington in Seattle, she provides a sharp contrast to the gentlewomanliness of Mary Woolley and the religious passion of Mary Lyon. As a wife and mother she knows the dilemmas and conflicts of the professional woman and when she accepted the presidency and her husband resigned his position and joined her in moving from Washington, D.C., to South Hadley her students took note. She regards herself as a feminist in that she is committed "to seeing that society provides women with opportunities for equal employment, pay and advancement."[77] Presidents may serve as models for their students but they also reflect student values and expectations. In 1979 and 1980 every Holyoke graduate appears to have secured a job or entered graduate school. As the director of Career Services reported, "They are entering virtually every profession, working for every kind of employer, and being admitted to an array of graduate programs." In 1979 and 1980 over 30 per cent of the graduating classes were admitted to graduate programs and professional schools, the majority in law and medicine. In comparison with earlier years, teaching and social work were not popular choices and no one had decided to become a missionary.

Because of her students' expectations that their education in a selective women's college will prepare them to join the ranks of the new professionals, President Kennan can speak with some confidence of women and power:

> I suspect that the true radical potential of feminism lies in the individual women who are willing to make the sacrifice of self that is entailed in exercising authority. For these women there may be occasional loneliness as decision makers must always, in the final analysis, be lonely. But they retain the responsibility to strengthen, to listen, to understand, to provide for this generation and the next.

> Women in power have enormous potential: we have only to seize it.[78]

In the call for a sacrifice of self there are echoes of Mary Lyon, and the challenge to exercise authority to make the world more hospitable for future generations recalls Mary Woolley. But Elizabeth Kennan's confidence that women are inevitably moving into positions of power and that power can be exercised within a moral framework for human betterment is a phase of the feminist movement that the women's colleges have not hitherto embraced.

Through curricular changes and innovations, exchange and internship options, and commitment to the training of morally responsible leadership, Mount Holyoke under Elizabeth Kennan appears to be shedding some of its conservatism without losing touch with its traditions. Its official pronouncements and the public statements of its president reflect both the confidence and sense of authority which now permeate women's colleges in the United States.

FOUR

James Tompkins
1870–1953

Moses Coady
1882–1959

James Tompkins and Moses Coady: The Antigonish Movement in Nova Scotia

James Tompkins, reprinted with permission from St. Francis Xavier University; Moses Coady, reprinted from *Coady Remembered* by Malcolm MacLellan with permission of St. Francis Xavier University.

Flaming Prophet

On a bitterly cold day in December 1922, Father J. J. Tompkins arrived in Canso, a poverty-stricken fishing village on the northeast tip of the Nova Scotia mainland. He was fifty-two and this was his first parish. For fifteen years he had been vice-president of St. Francis Xavier College, but his enthusiasm for a proposal to merge the colleges of the three Maritime Provinces into a federated university in Halifax was not shared by the Bishop of Antigonish or the St. Francis Xavier Board of Governors. Tompkins and other clerics who had supported the merger were transferred to rural parishes. For Tompkins, Canso was, initially at least, a lonely exile. His parishioners were poor and a high proportion were illiterate; schools were poorly equipped and badly taught; his church was deep in debt yet needed further repairs; his house, he reported, was so draughty that a man "might be blown off his feet in a corridor," and during a serious illness in the spring of 1923 he told a visitor why he had changed his bedroom: "Foghorn's driving me mad. It's worse in the other rooms. But it's colder over here."

This short and wiry priest with white hair and a high-pitched voice came from an Irish family which had settled in the Margaree Valley of Cape Breton Island in the early nineteenth century. With minimal qualifications (sporadic schooling and a year of tutoring by an uncle) he began teaching at seventeen in the French-speaking Acadian community of Cheticamp, and for the next several years alternately taught and studied at St. Francis Xavier. Eventually Tompkins passed the examinations in the twenty-one subjects required for an A teaching licence (equivalent to a headmaster's certificate) in Nova Scotia and in 1895 was graduated from St. Francis Xavier. This kind of persistence persuaded the college to offer him a position as a teacher of Greek and mathematics. On the recommendation of his bishop, John Cameron, Tompkins was awarded a scholarship at the Urban College of the Propaganda in Rome and after four years of study among students from various parts of the world he returned to Nova Scotia, celebrated his first mass in South-West Margaree, and was instructed by his bishop to return to St. Francis Xavier.

The college had then been in operation for nearly half a century. Founded first at Arichat on Cape Breton and intended to supply priests and teachers for parishes in the diocese, it moved to Antigonish in 1855 and became the College of St. Francis Xavier. The provincial legislature conferred full university powers in 1866.

Its graduates would form a large proportion of the Roman Catholic clergy of eastern Nova Scotia and both these clerics and members of the college faculty would become directly involved in the everyday affairs of the fishermen, farmers, and industrial workers of the diocese. But the college has never been "parochial." Its founder, Bishop Colin MacKinnon, had studied theology in Rome. Bishop John Cameron, who did much to strengthen the college in the late nineteenth century, was a legendary figure who became comfortable in seven languages during his eleven years at the Urban College. When he returned with doctorates in philosophy and divinity he came to be referred to as "the learned Cameron" by the Roman Catholic hierarchy in Canada. Both the bishops of Antigonish and rectors of the college identified promising young men and encouraged them to enrol for graduate work in Rome, or in European and American universities. This tradition of study abroad gave the faculty a breadth of view and a liberal spirit which was unusual in a small denominational college.

One example was "Little Doc Hugh," Monsignor (and Dr.) Hugh MacPherson, who joined the faculty in 1900 after study at Lille. As head of the new Engineering Department, his formal teaching was in science and engineering subjects, but he also taught piano, violin, German, French, Latin, and Gaelic. He became the first official Representative of the Nova Scotia Department of Agriculture and worked closely with farmers in advancing the application of science in agriculture. In 1914 he helped them to form the first producer co-operative. Both the diocese and the college had unique features, as Daniel MacInnes has written:

> The Diocese of Antigonish was extended over the entire region of Eastern Nova Scotia through its parish structure; it was centralized in its administration and higher education; it was comprehensive in social services through the media of parish priests, schools and hospitals; it was generally well integrated with respect to priest-people relations since they shared ethnicity and similar social backgrounds; and finally, it contained a clerical resource of talent that may best be described as a locally-born but foreign-bred intelligentsia.[1]

On his return from Rome to the St. Francis Xavier faculty, Tompkins soon revealed his restless mind and enormous energy. Not content simply to teach Greek and algebra, he became college librarian, then a fund-raiser and, within five years, vice-president. He persuaded Dr. J. E. Somers of Cambridge, Massachusetts, and Neil MacNeil, a Boston contractor, both wealthy native Nova Scotians, to contribute handsomely to a building program that allowed the college to expand both its program and enrolment. He began an association that would continue throughout his life with the Carnegie Corporation of New York, which was permitted by its charter to make grants for education in the British Dominions.

In the summer of 1912 Tompkins crossed the Atlantic in a cattle boat to make sure that St. Francis Xavier was represented at a conference of the universities of the Empire. This appears to have been the occasion that ignited his interest in adult education and on this and later visits he learned of the Workers' Educational Association in England, attempts by the Catholic bishops of Ireland to create a university that would address itself to poverty, and the pioneering work of the University of Wisconsin extension department.

Tompkins also began to contribute articles to an eastern Nova Scotia weekly newspaper, *The Casket,* and in 1918 when the paper was for sale he persuaded the majority shareholder to sell his shares to Bishop James Morrison. Thus *The Casket* became a diocesan paper and a column "For the People," inspired by Tompkins, became a regular feature. In the issue of 15 August 1918, Tompkins wrote on what had now, for him, become an insistent theme—the widening role of colleges and universities:

> The time has come when our colleges should not only be homes of learning, but leaders of thought adapting themselves to modern problems and modern requirements, racy of the soil, the light and power stations in their respective constituencies. What they can do for the people is only limited by the ability and enlightened public spirit of those who are guiding their destinies.

Before going on sabbatical leave in 1920 Tompkins was involved in many activities. For example, he negotiated a grant of $50,000 from the Carnegie Corporation to endow a professorship of French, a decision that delighted the leaders of the Acadian community, who had appealed to St. Francis Xavier for help in keeping their language and culture alive. His ideas for adult education were taking shape as he worked with a committee of priests and laymen to create a People's School that would bring adults to the university for a residential course. He discussed such a school in Ottawa with W. L. Mackenzie King, soon to become prime minister of Canada, and took away with him a letter of introduction to the secretary of the Rockefeller General Education Board. King explained that Father Tompkins was "seeking to develop People's Schools similar to the Agricultural High Schools of Denmark" and that the board could place their entire confidence in him. In the same year Dalhousie University of Halifax conferred on Tompkins the honorary degree of Doctor of Laws.

During his leave Tompkins wrote the thirty-one page pamphlet *Knowledge for the People,* a seminal statement in the literature of adult education in Canada. Following the First World War, Tompkins sensed that a new spirit was abroad and that nowhere was that spirit more in evidence than in education. "Men and women everywhere are clamoring for the equal opportunity that education and intellectual training give." There was a way to satisfy this demand:

> With this movement for universal education, transcending all existing schools and all ordinary avenues of training, has come inevitably a change in the theory and practice of our colleges and universities and the development of what is known as *University Extension.* University Extension implies an organized effort to give to the

> people not in college some of the advantages enjoyed by the one-half of one per cent who are able to attend college. It reaches out to the farmer, the workman and the average citizen and says to each: "If you cannot go to your college, your college will come to you." Agricultural Extension makes better farmers, and general Extension makes more effective and successful men and better citizens.[2]

Tompkins then reveals his grasp of adult education programs in Great Britain and Ireland, the United States and Canada. In England the W.E.A. had organized two tutorial classes in 1907 under the auspices of Oxford; ten years later there were over 2,100 branches scattered across England and Wales. Irish manual workers were attending classes at University College, Cork, under the sponsorship of the Gaelic League. As early as 1891, twenty-eight American states had begun university extension in some form. For Tompkins the University of Wisconsin was "the great pioneer and classic example of a people's university." In his view the province in Canada that had done more for "the real betterment and happiness of the rural classes" was Quebec, and the heroes were the rural clergy, particularly the agricultural missionaries who were introducing methods of scientific farming. In Saskatchewan 1,000 students were enrolled in extension courses, double the number of intramural students. This demand for extension classes was, in the words of the president, "one of the most hopeful and far-reaching movements of recent years." In Nova Scotia the educational climate was more bleak. The formal school system was scarcely responding to the clamor for equal opportunity, at least not in 1919, when the report of the superintendent of education revealed that fewer than 10 per cent of elementary school leavers entered high school.

But the university must not wait for the provincial government and local authorities to develop a comprehensive elementary and secondary school system. In the final section of his pamphlet Tompkins issues "The Call to St. Francis Xavier's," a plea for "an independent beginning immediately, on however modest a scale." With these modest beginnings the university must proceed with great caution in deciding what to teach:

> In this matter we must take and follow the opinion of the people themselves. For us, what the people most need to learn must be

> what they most want to learn. Let there be the least trace of superiority or propagandism in our attitude, let the people once think of us as academic persons come to force our preconceptions upon them, and the undertaking is dead.[3]

The teachers, lecturers, and workers in this new endeavor should come from the clergy. A cadre of priest-teachers should be recruited, although such efforts might meet with the objection that "lecturing and class-holding are not a priest's business. If I am to be a priest let me do a priest's true work." To which Tompkins's reply was that the proposed kind of education was "the most effective shape in which the spirit of charity can express itself in these times."

In *Knowledge for the People* are the seeds of the Antingonish Movement. It reveals Tompkins's deep faith in the power of education to become an instrument for social and economic change. "How," he asks, "if not through education, are the people to be raised to better and happier living?" When he asks, "How are they to improve their lot if we do not show them how they may?", he gave his college a new sense of mission in the seven counties that make up the diocese of Antigonish.

The first project was the People's School, which opened at the college in 1921 with an enrolment of fifty-one, all of whom were men ranging in age from seventeen to fifty-seven. The main subjects were English, economics, public speaking, mathematics, and agriculture. The course lasted two months, teachers donated their services, no entrance examination was required, and no fee was charged. A similar school was held the following year with sixty enrolled, and there were later two further sessions in Glace Bay, in the industrial area of Cape Breton. At a conference Tompkins organized for diocesan clergy in 1921 the agenda revealed an increasing interest in industrial problems: collective bargaining, remedies for unemployment, labor legislation, and social insurance. During the summer that year he again attended the Congress of the Universities of the Empire at Oxford and gave a paper on adult education. En route to England he visited New York to see William Learned, assistant to the president of the Carnegie Corporation and by now a close friend.

Such were Vice-President Tompkins's many interests, but by the end of 1921 the issue of the federation of the colleges of eastern Canada was his overriding concern. At the request of the colleges and the government of Nova Scotia, the Carnegie Corporation agreed to undertake a survey of higher education in the Maritime Provinces. William Learned and Kenneth Sills, president of Bowdoin College in Maine, conducted the study and in their report[4] recommended a federated system with a "central institution" in Halifax to which the other colleges would be affiliated. Controversy soon became intense. Tompkins strongly supported federation on the grounds that existing colleges would retain their autonomy and denominational identity; with generous aid from Carnegie the central university could become a first-rate institution comparable to McGill or the University of Toronto. Furthermore, Tompkins argued, "the small college is going to have great difficulty in financing itself." His opponents were outraged at the thought of the denominational colleges becoming local institutes (the term used in the report) or junior colleges that would serve as feeders of the university in Halifax, where students would complete the last two years of the arts course. James Morrison, Bishop of Antigonish, appointed a committee to study the plan and advise him and the board of governors of St. Francis Xavier. In October the committee submitted its report[5] with the recommendation, based on both pedagogical and religious grounds, that the college should "decline with thanks the invitation to get gobbled up."[6]

> After our students have had a course in a thoroughly Catholic college they will be better prepared to meet the dangers of secular teaching. . . . We believe that the greatest contribution Catholics can make to the economic prosperity of our country is to stand four-square against the secularization of education and to develop our Catholic college as much as possible. . . . Our Catholic young men are entitled to the best. And the best is an independent St. F.X.[7]

Fortified with this report, Bishop Morrison, himself strongly opposed to federation, met with the board of governors, and the proposed federation plan went down in defeat. It was quietly buried by a decree from Rome in 1923.

The merger issue is important not only because its resolution meant the continuation of St. Francis Xavier as an independent Roman Catholic college but also because it was a temporary victory for the conservative wing of the Church. Tompkins and his colleagues' stress on scientific agriculture, People's Schools, and educational conferences, and their enthusiasm for the federation plan were seen to be moving too quickly into situations over which the Church would have little control. Add to these such movements as the formation of a Farmer's party and the rise of labor militancy and the Church might well have to give way to secular agencies in coping with social and economic problems. Thus four liberal clerics of the St. Francis Xavier faculty—James Boyle, John R. MacDonald, Michael Gillis, and James Tompkins—were sent to rural parishes.

EASTERN NOVA SCOTIA: SETTLEMENT AND DECLINE

Some parishes in the Antigonish diocese had been settled a century earlier by Scots Catholics who were victims of the Clearances, a tragic period in Scotland's history when lairds and landlords cleared the Highland crofts to make way for sheep and drove men, women, and children from their homes. The immigration to eastern Nova Scotia was largely unassisted. The landlord's concern was to get rid of his tenants, the agent collected his fee of 12 shillings per head, and the ship's captain wanted to unload his cargo at the nearest harbor. New arrivals usually found no one to assist them on landing and thus had to fend for themselves. They had come from a treeless land and now had to cope with a forest wilderness; they had no experience in clearing land and little knowledge of tillage. They came and remained as community groups from the Highlands and the Islands (208 sailed from Rhum alone in 1828), and they drew strength as well from their faith. Above all, for the first time in their lives they were free of landlords and could own land.

Kinship and clan affiliations were kept alive in the new settlements and family farms developed a subsistence economy that lasted late into the nineteenth century. Scots Presbyterians from the Highlands and French-speaking Acadians settled in separate communities. On the other hand, Loyalists (American colonists who remained loyal to Britain during the American Revolution) and the Irish who left their homeland during the years of strife and famine tended not to develop separate or distinct settlements. Through this immigration the population of Cape Breton increased sixfold during the twenty-year period 1815–38, that is from an estimated 6,000 to over 35,000.[8] In the area that later became the diocese of Antigonish, three counties on the mainland and four on Cape Breton, Scots Catholics formed by far the majority. But whatever may have been their origin or their religion, practically all immigrants to eastern Nova Scotia in the late eighteenth and the first half of the nineteenth century were refugees and displaced persons who felt themselves to be enforced migrants.

For a brief period of about thirty years in the mid-nineteenth century the coastal communities of Nova Scotia enjoyed prosperity because of water, wind, and wood (fish, sail, and shipbuilding). But as early as 1839 the age of sail was threatened when Samuel Cunard, a native Nova Scotian, signed a contract with the Imperial government to establish regular communication by steam between the British Isles and North America. The next year the first Cunarder arrived in Halifax twelve days out from Liverpool. There were confident predictions that Halifax would become "the centre of steam navigation for the whole American continent."[9] There was as well an air of confidence in the 1852 report of the lieutenant governor to the colonial secretary:

> All the great interests of the province exhibit revived activity. Its staples . . . command high prices. The population are fully employed, and the Revenue collected under a tariff steadily increases yielding . . . a large surplus for the protection of the fisheries, the encouragement of agriculture, the maintenance of schools, and for internal improvements of various kinds.[10]

Coal mining was becoming a major industry in the Sydney-Glace Bay area and by the 1860s over 3,000 men and boys were employed. The mines were not only providing jobs and contributing to the urbanization of northern Cape Breton, but were also assisting the lumbering, shipbuilding, and shipping industries by providing a major cargo.

This short-lived "golden age" benefited seaport towns and had relatively little effect on the Scots communities of eastern Nova Scotia, where subsistence farming continued. By the final quarter of the century these communities had, however, run out of land and there was a labor surplus. At the same time the province's economy, particularly the commercial economy of the coastal towns, was in decline. The option was, of course, emigration. By the 1880s, the agricultural Scots with their small plots, limited production, and increased population were in a predicament similar to the one their forbears faced before leaving Scotland. They could move to the industrial towns of Sydney and Glace Bay or board the recently completed railroad for central

Canada or New England. In the decade 1891–1901 the population around Sydney increased more than threefold.[11] Emigration was by no means confined to eastern Nova Scotia, however, nor was it brief: between 1881 and 1931 the Maritime Provinces lost 100,000 persons each decade.[12] Most were the young and able from rural areas. They left behind on the farms and in the fishing villages a legacy of apathy and despair which Father Tompkins, the new parish priest of Canso, soon discovered.

When he arrived in Canso the First World War depression had deepened eastern Nova Scotia's despair. Cod was selling at 1½¢ a pound, lobster from 3 to 9¢ a pound, and on average a fisherman's income was less than $400 a year. It did not take Tompkins long to realize that here was a testing ground indeed for his theories of adult education. In one of his first sermons he spoke of theft in the community and asked his parishioners why they took a fish net, a pair of boots, or a piece of pork from one another. Was it because they did not have enough money and food to keep body and soul together, and if that were the case would it not be better to find ways of working together? He would throw in his lot with theirs and would keep on asking questions. Throughout his parish he warmed to his task and with breezy informality talked to fishermen wherever he met them asking about the price of fish or the cost of equipment and then invariably handing out clippings, leaflets, and pamphlets. Frequently these dealt with co-operatives and credit unions. Within a year of his arrival Tompkins was in correspondence with government officials, the local member of parliament, and the president of Dalhousie, exploring the possibility of setting up a research centre at Canso to study fishery problems. He maintained a lively correspondence with the president of the Carnegie Corporation, even sending him literature on co-operatives. With one adult education leader in the United States he shared his thoughts:

> Culture, art, literature, etc. offer little consolation to degrading poverty and to an empty belly—and there are more of the latter than there ought to be, at least in Canada. Men have been happy, and even inspired, in a garret, but today we need an economic basis for culture, art, religion, etc. . . .
>
> I notice in Canso for instance—an important fishing centre—that the people are poorer and more dependent today than they were twenty years ago. They damn the place, their employment and their

> employers. They do not know what the matter is, and they are too poor and ignorant to find out for themselves. The reason back of it all is that they are being exploited by fish firms owned by men in Montreal and anywhere else but Canso. . . . And so we become a branch people, and a few places hundred or thousands of miles away skim off the cream, which goes into the pockets of a very few —not the best place to keep cream, but you will forgive the figure.[13]

Also in 1924, through the urging of two of the exiled priests, Michael Gillis and John R. MacDonald, the annual conferences for the diocesan clergy were revived at St. Francis Xavier. Their topic was the decline of rural communities. At that conference a resolution was adopted requesting the college authorities "to form a department of extension work which will organize People's Schools in the central points of the diocese, and direct study clubs in all sections. . . . "[14] For the next four years these meetings, first known as Agricultural and later as Agricultural and Industrial Conferences, discussed and debated rural and urban issues and invariably urged the university to establish an extension program. Pressure was also applied from other sources, one of which was the Scottish Catholic Society. Founded in 1919 and dedicated to the preservation of Gaelic culture, the Society encouraged greater use of Gaelic and the revival of traditional music. But the continuation, indeed the survival, of Scottish and Catholic traditions was also related to improving the standards of living in rural areas. Both the Scottish Catholic Society and the St. Francis Xavier Alumni Association joined the campaign for an extension department and by 1928 took direct action. Alumni representatives met with the board of governors to demand action, and the Scottish Catholic Society threatened to raise $100,000 to develop its own extension program. This may well have been a bluff; if so, it worked. "The heather was on fire" and in November the board of governors ceased to procrastinate and voted to establish an extension service.

Meanwhile, Tompkins had not been idle in Canso. The sixtieth anniversary of Canadian Confederation was on 1 July 1927, but the men and women of Canso had little heart for celebration. Instead, Tompkins proposed a meeting in the parish hall. One by one the men spoke of their plight and on the suggestion of the chairman, John Chafe, Tompkins's closest friend in the village, decided to send a petition to Ottawa demanding that government representatives come to Canso and see at first hand the conditions of the fishing industry. Thirty-nine men signed the petition. For weeks there was no response. Tired of waiting, Tompkins telephoned the editor of the *Halifax Chronicle,* who himself came to Canso and in a series of seven articles told the story of the condition of fishermen and their families, thus precipitating a second meeting at which the local member of parliament and an official of the federal Department of Fisheries felt obliged to be present. Tompkins then took his case to the diocesan priests' annual retreat and secured forty signatures on a resolution calling for the appointment of a royal commission to investigate the fisheries of the Maritime Provinces and the Magdalen Islands.

In October the MacLean Commission (its chairman was A. K. MacLean, president of the Exchequer Court of Canada) was appointed and began its work immediately. It held hearings throughout the Maritime Provinces and called for evidence from the fishermen themselves. At its hearing in Halifax, Moses Coady, a member of the St. Francis Xavier faculty, asked to testify. The essence of his brief was a threefold program: the organization of shore fishermen and their involvement in making policy for the industry; the use of science and technology in the fisheries; and promotion among the fishermen of produce and consumer co-operatives. When the Commission issued its report in May 1928, one recommendation was worded as follows:

> We recommend . . . that the establishment of co-operative organizations of fishermen be assisted by the Department as soon as possible, and that an organizer, experienced in co-operative methods, be appointed and paid by the Federal Government for the required period to initiate and complete this work.[15]

A Giant of a Man

The obvious choice for this appointment was Moses Coady, then forty-six, a giant of a man whose face and body looked like rough-hewn granite. He had an intense vitality and the urgency of a man in a hurry. He too was born in the Margaree Valley and did not leave it until he was twenty-three. Late in life he said that if he had any creative imagination and "a soul that tends to poetry and idealism" he owed it to the natural beauty of the Margaree.[16] He helped his parents clear the forest and build a home: "We were carpenters, coopers, woodsmen, fishermen, farmers all in one. I was doing a man's work when I was ten."[17] He did not go to school regularly until he was fifteen, but tutoring at home prepared him for high school, where he found the most influential teacher of his life, Chris Tompkins, brother of James.

Throughout his youth and early manhood Coady was, in fact, a protegé of the Tompkins brothers. During his high school years James, then in Rome, showered him with books and pamphlets and corresponded regularly. After a year in the Provincial Normal School, Coady became both teacher and principal in the rural school he had attended. He studied Latin through correspondence with Tompkins. Two years were enough to allow him to graduate from St. F.X.; then he was off to Rome for five years in theology and philosophy at the Urban College and back to St. F.X. to teach at the campus high school. Off again three years later to study education at the Catholic University in Washington, he returned to succeed Tompkins as principal of the high school.

During the twenties, as a member of the St. Francis Xavier faculty, Coady had taken part in the People's School and Rural Conferences and was familiar with co-operative movements in various parts of the world. When asked in the fall of 1929 by the federal Department of Fisheries to undertake the organization of fishermen he accepted the appointment and immediately began a ten-month journey to the fishing villages along the 8,000 miles of coastline in eastern Canada. Appropriately enough, his first meeting was in Canso, where 600 fishermen and their wives were waiting for him in the Ideal Theatre. He covered most of Cape Breton before winter set in. In January he started up the coast of New Brunswick by horse and sleigh, attempting to cover thirty-five miles and hold four meetings a day. In some villages Coady is alleged to have introduced himself by saying, "I'm a 20th Century John the Baptist; I've come to organize you."[18] By mid-year his mission was completed and in June he brought together in Halifax 208 delegates from the fishing villages. The outcome of this meeting was the formation of the United Maritime Fishermen, a body that over the years has become a marketing agency through which local co-operatives can sell their products on world markets.

Coady could now return to St. Francis Xavier and the main line of his career. Two years before when the board of governors had created the Extension Department he had been appointed its first director and given six months' leave to study adult education in Canada and the United States. In a letter written from New York, Coady sketched in what he called the high spots of the extension program he had in mind. The primary need was for educational programs that would result in economic ventures. "The Maritimes need economic restoration before anything else." Some form of residential labor college on British lines was needed to train leaders in educating adults. "We have no such thing in Canada and St. F.X. could well afford to lead in this matter." The Extension Department should draw, like the University of Wisconsin, on various faculties for its workers, and one or two good men should give their whole time to research in "the economic and scientific fields." This letter was addressed to A. B. MacDonald, who in 1930 was appointed Associate Director of the department.

MacDonald, when an undergraduate at St. Francis Xavier, had been selected for further training and with a little persuasion from Tompkins decided to enrol at the Ontario Agricultural College. He worked for eight years among farmers in Ontario and was a school inspector in Nova Scotia at the time of his decision to join Coady. In the words of an enthusiastic contemporary, "What a team they were! Dr. Coady, learned, dynamic, impressive, yet humble, zealous and kind; A.B., charming, jovial and good natured, but at the same time ambitious, practical, and with a rare genius for organization. It will probably be a long time before such a combination will be seen in action again."[19] The team went into action almost ten years after Father Tompkins had published *Knowledge for the People.* During those ten years the campaign to create the Extension Department was largely led by the exiled priests who, from their parishes, used the columns of *The Casket* and reorganized the rural Conferences at which resolutions advocating an Extension Department were adopted annually. Possibly the most tireless and persistent figure behind the founding of the Extension Department was Michael Gillis, who after his "transfer" from St. Francis Xavier served for twenty-five years in rural parishes. Through the Rural and Industrial Conferences, the Alumni Association, and the Scottish Catholic Society, he worked so effectively that Coady later paid him this tribute: "The person most responsible for the creation of the St. Francis Xavier Extension is, of course, Father Michael Gillis, former parish priest of Boisdale. . . . "[20]

The Antigonish Movement: Strategy and Techniques, 1930–51

The early annual reports of the Extension Department show that St. Francis Xavier had carried on a form of extension for years and that the conferences, people's schools, and consultation with farmers of the kind initiated by Hugh MacPherson would continue. The new emphasis, however, would be on adult education in small groups for those unable to come to the university. In the first year of operation the department, that is Coady and MacDonald, organized 175 study clubs in rural areas, most of which decided to study the business side of farming, particularly marketing. Box libraries of twenty-five books were placed at centrally located points for study clubs to use. Fishermen also formed study clubs and within two years both fishermen and farmers had organized produce and consumer co-operatives. Study clubs had appeared in the coal-mining towns of Cape Breton which would, the department felt confident, serve as "a great antidote to the extreme radicalism that threatens the people of this area."[21]

A field office had opened and a young miner named A. S. MacIntyre, who had renounced his membership in the Communist party, was placed in charge. Two additions were made to the Extension staff—James Boyle and Michael Gillis—who would share their parochial duties with young assistants and thus have more time to work with fishermen and farmers. The Departments of Agriculture and Fisheries had been asked to supply expertise to the Cranberry Growers and Lobster Canning Co-operatives, and the provincial legislature passed a bill to enable the people of Nova Scotia to organize credit unions. This considerable activity prompted the Carnegie Corporation to grant $35,000 to the department and encouraged Coady and MacDonald to give an optimistic and confident annual report for 1932: "It may be said in a general way that this eastern country is throbbing with new life."

Gradually, an organizational strategy and a set of techniques were adopted. The first stage in the approach to a new community was the mass meeting, which a member of the Extension Staff with the support of parish priests carefully arranged and publicized. Coady would then arrive in the school house or parish hall for what he called an "alarm clock meeting" at which he would wake from their lethargy and apathy all those who came to listen. Once he had his audience's attention he would "lay on the rawhide lash," often by homely anecdotes: "I meet a farmer who complains that there is no market for his products. If the city of Montreal were suddenly dumped in his pasture what good would that market be to him? What does he have to sell? Three sheep, two scrawny cows and a pig and a half." After laying on the lash he would "pour oil on the wounds" by telling his listeners of ways they could take toward a better life, and in graphic detail he would recount the experience of ordinary men and women who had organized study clubs and then co-operatives in Nova Scotia villages; or he might refer to the success of co-operatives in Sweden and Denmark. But always his purpose was twofold: to shatter the people's complacent acceptance of their economic lot, and to rouse them to want to do something about it.

Coady was often at the height of his power and influence at these meetings. He would thunder against the "vested interests" and condemn the extremes of capitalism as immoral and unchristian. "You have to put the screws on the capitalist system . . . set up institutions to force capitalism to change its ways . . . we must reject the old idea of capitalism as a total economic system." There were ways that this could be done in the villages of Nova Scotia if people would come together and use the instruments of group action and economic co-operation. This, he said, "is the form of business that has legitimacy over all others . . . people doing things for themselves." For Coady the best economic system for Canada, as he stated repeatedly, was a sensible and balanced mixture of co-operatives, public ownership, and what he called old-fashioned private enterprise. To challenge the existing order by teaching doctrine like this from dozens of public platforms was, for that time, an act of daring for both Coady and his university.

Before the mass meeting closed, local leaders, usually the parish priests, made arrangements for the formation of study clubs. These neighborhood groups, seldom with more than twelve members, were usually composed of both men and women who met once a week in homes, hence the term "kitchen meetings," or in a vacant store, school, or barber shop. They had a clearly defined goal: for a year, more or less, they would study the formation of a credit union, a co-operative store, or a marketing co-operative, that is, they would have a project that would result in economic action. The Extension Department would send them books, pamphlets, and leaflets on the topic being studied, and once a year their volunteer leader would be invited to take a short course at the university. Coady wrote a pamphlet, *Would You Be a Leader?*, in which with a light touch and many examples he described a good study club leader. Some characteristics were dignity, a proper reserve, and the capacity to be silent at the right moment. His example was Von Moltke, the German general in the 1870 war with France who was said to have been silent in seven languages.

Once a month all the study clubs in a local community would meet to compare progress. The basic assumption underlying the network of study clubs was that adults do not need didactic teaching. Through selective reading followed by discussion the members of the group could identify their problems and plan how to solve them. Their motivation was high because they were discussing problems vital to their livelihood. As with all adult education movements there was a good deal of attrition; not every study club member stayed the course and only a minority of clubs formed co-operatives. But the results were encouraging, as Table 4 reveals.

Table 4
Activities in Nova Scotia Related to the Extension Department, 1932–39[22]

	1932	1933	1934	1935	1936	1937	1938	1939
Study clubs	179	350	650	940	860	1,013	1,100	1,300
membership	1,500	5,250	6,000	10,650	8,000	10,000	10,000	11,000
Credit unions	8	19	27	45	65	90	142	170
membership							22,000	30,000
Co-op stores	2	4	6	8	18	25	39	43
Co-op buying clubs			3	10	5	3	4	4
Co-op fish plants		3	5	5	10	11	11	11
Co-op lobster factories		8	12	14	17	17	17	17
Other co-ops			2	2	2	7	7	10
Leadership course attendance		86	44	30	63	78	132	130
Staff: full-time	3	4	5	5	5	7	11	11
part-time	2	2	2	3	4	9	4	7

Other encouragement came from Rome. In a letter dated 8 March 1938, Cardinal Pacelli, Secretary of State for Pope Pius XI, wrote to the Bishop of Antigonish:

> The world today which is hostile beyond measure to right living, brings many causes of grief to the Holy Father. Of late, however, something that is taking place in your country has come to his knowledge which has brought him great joy and which is an earnest of better things for the time to come.
>
> I speak of your effort in the social sphere, which, far and wide, is known by common designation as the Antigonish Movement. And since this redounds to the great glory of yourself and the teachers of St. Francis Xavier University, the Holy Father gladly adds, to the general expression of admiration and congratulation, his own tribute of praise.

Fundamentally, the Antigonish Movement's social and economic aims were to be achieved through adult education. Movement leaders were critical of the existing school system. Years earlier in *Knowledge for the People,* Tompkins had been sharply critical of rural schools: "The rural schools do not respond even remotely to the needs and demands of the time. In fact they are a menace to the future well-being of the province." Thirty-five years later, Malcom MacLellan, a member of the St. Francis Xavier faculty and a leader of the Antigonish Movement, was no less critical:

> The truth is, unfortunately, that Education, kidnapped by the forces of reaction, functions mainly for the perpetuation and protection of the economic and social system of individualistic capitalism. Instead of being in the vanguard of social and spiritual progress, the school and its official leaders are but marionettes on the mimic stage of finance capitalism, manipulated by the unseen strings of economic despotism. Education has become a glorified wooden head reechoing the voices of financial ventriloquists who monopolize our wealth and determine our destiny.[23]

Coady regarded formal schooling as the trap door that enabled the bright and vigorous few to escape into the professions. In his view, education had created classes in a supposedly classless society. Educators had drawn graphs to show the relationship between income and formal schooling, and parents had sent their children to high school and college so they could escape the drudgery of farming, mining, or fishing. The result, said Coady, was that: "In our present educational procedure—which is essentially a skimming process—we are robbing our rural and industrial population of their natural leaders."[24]

The St. Francis Xavier Extension Department had no interest in contributing to the "skimming process." Unlike other such departments, it did not offer extramural courses that would earn credit toward a degree but, instead, took its lead from Tompkins's work in Canso. In shaking his parishioners out of their lethargy, grasping them by their lapels and urging them to read this or that pamphlet, organizing literacy classes and discussion groups, and persuading them that if they did not study the cause of their poverty they would never escape it, Tompkins pioneered the Antigonish kind of adult education. As he once said, "there is more adult education at the pit-heads, down in the mines, out among the fishermen's shacks, along the wharves, and wherever the farmers gather to sit and talk in the evenings, than you can get from one hundred thousand dollars worth of fossilized formal courses. . . . It springs from the hearts and pains of people. It is spontaneous."[25]

Tompkins never became officially connected with the Extension Department—he feared that with its systematic techniques it would become institutionalized—but in 1935 at the age of sixty-four, when he moved from Canso to Reserve Mines, he began at once to work with miners and steel workers on self-help projects. Coady had addressed public meetings and Alex MacIntyre had organized study clubs, but Tompkins set out to stir up his parishioners, identify their natural leaders, and create a library. Within a year a board of directors had created a People's Library, housed it in Tompkins's rectory, and spent $600 on books. To Tompkins a town library was a powerhouse of social action, a people's university, and a means of stimulating projects for land use, credit unions, and co-operatives. The example set by Reserve Mines led the indefatigable Tompkins to buttonhole members of the provincial government and the Carnegie corporation and ask them to support a system of regional libraries across Nova Scotia. With a matching grant of $50,000 by the Carnegie Corporation the project was launched.

Tompkins's other major contribution to Reserve Mines and through it to the movement generally was co-operative housing. And here again his genius translated an idea into actuality. A group of miners who lived on dreary streets in cold and damp company houses had formed a study club but had not yet decided what to study. With a little prompting from Tompkins and their leader, Joseph Laben, and after reading material from the People's Library, the group decided to analyze and discuss housing. When a co-operative housing expert from New York appeared in Reserve Mines, Tompkins immediately arranged for her to meet Joseph Laben and friends for an evening of conversation. In the event, Mary Arnold stayed for two years, meeting every Sunday evening with the ten miners and their wives, often with Tompkins as part of the group. When the miners decided to start building they employed one professional carpenter and did most of the construction work themselves, co-operatively. The project was finished by August 1938, and Angus L. MacDonald, premier of Nova Scotia, arrived to open the new community and name it Tompkinsville. It was the first housing co-operative in Canada. In 1941 Tompkins was honored again, this time with an honorary degree from Harvard.

The Antigonish Movement: Principles and Philosophy

Years earlier R. B. Bennett, yet to become prime minister of Canada, had visited Antigonish and after a ten-minute conversation with Tompkins angrily dismissed the outspoken little priest by saying, "It is in the Soviet Union that you belong, not in the priesthood of the Roman Catholic Church." This was a gratuitous insult, although Tompkins was clearly left of centre in his economic philosophy and resoundingly critical of the status quo. The movement itself was in step with the traditions of liberal Catholicism. In 1942, D. J. MacDonald, president of St. Francis Xavier, spoke critically of both extreme individualism and extreme collectivism and stated explicitly that the Antigonish Movement "aims at doing its share in combatting these false philosophies." Individualism creates an atmosphere favorable to ruthless capitalism and exploitation, and here President MacDonald quoted from the encyclical *Rerum Novarum,* which Pope Leo XIII had issued in 1891: "A small number of very rich men have been able to lay upon the masses of the poor a yoke little better than slavery itself."[26] In 1931, Pius XI in his *Quadragesimo Anno* directed his criticism to the abuses of monopoly capitalism under which giant corporations were able to control production, manipulate the market, and determine prices. "Immense power and despotic domination are concentrated in the hands of a few. . . . Free competition is dead; economic dictatorship has taken its place. . . . The whole economic life has become hard, cruel and relentless in a ghastly measure." When Coady quoted these strictures from the encyclical he was moved to add, "It takes a Pope to say things like that!"[27]

The popes were speaking of capitalism's abuses; Coady's criticism went deeper and, as he did so often, he made his point by using a vivid image. A group of men are building a smokestack 150 feet high. Some of the workmen are careless in laying the foundation and allow it to get out of plumb. At first the mistake is scarcely visible but when the stack is thirty feet high it can be seen to tilt a little, but it is firm and so the building goes on. When it has reached its full height it is a dizzily leaning tower. The builders hasten to prop it up. No props are long enough, so long heavy wires are attached to the stack and anchored to the ground. Now there is less danger of catastrophe but the smokestack is far from safe. It still leans dangerously, threatening all within range but beyond their power to repair it. It really needs to be rebuilt. Similarly, the economic smokestack that began with the Industrial Revolution has become a leaning menace and over the last 150 years the people have lost control of the means of production and consumption. As control of his economic destiny slipped out of his hands, man also lost his dignity and became the victim of forces he could not control. At this point Coady, while sympathetic, is not sentimental:

> This is a humiliating picture. It may be claimed that it is unkind to expose the plight of the unfortunate victim of circumstance and exploitation. But the victim is not entirely innocent and the sooner he realizes the fact the better. He is a delinquent and a defaulter. When the foundation of our faulty economic structure was laid, he failed to claim his rights, to say his say and play his part.[28]

Now was the time for rebuilding, and the leaders of the Antigonish Movement had a vision of a new structure, a new economic order in which co-operatives would be a significant factor. But private business would not be abolished; in fact, Coady regarded co-operatives as the "finest flower" of private enterprise. Groups of people form co-operatives with the intent of improving their economic status and "that is a profit motive in the real philosophical sense of that term, which basically means to make increase, as when a man plants one seed of corn and gets 27 in return."[29] The co-operative technique enables men to make increase by planting their own economic seed. Private business, by contrast, gets increase by taking a toll of other human beings.

Coady proposed an economy marked by four distinct kinds of ownership. Private ownership of farms, homes, and small businesses would continue and be extended to include more homes for the urban proletariat. Public ownership would embrace enterprises "that cannot be safely left in the hands of individuals or private corporations: money and banking, electric power, transportation, systems of communication, medical services, steel and chemical industries." A large proportion of the nation's business should remain in private hands, but ways must be found to check its excesses. In the past it had been assumed that competition would do this, but "competition is dead and economic dictatorship has taken its place." Co-operatives of all types—consumer, producer, industrial, medical, credit unions—would become the fourth method of ownership, their objective being to develop a co-operative network that would control 25 per cent of the Canadian economy. Coady frequently pointed to Sweden, where co-operatives controlled only about 12 per cent of that nation's business yet were successful in breaking the power of monopolies.

Thus the Antigonish Movement offered a criticism of the existing order and a vision of a new economic democracy. It was not a revolutionary vision that implied radical change of existing institutions, nor was it based on scholarly analysis. Coady used all his eloquence in making his case for co-operatives. His appeal was that of the idealist, not of the hard-headed economist.

> We now have the techniques by which people can, through co-operation, pipe down to themselves new wealth that they never had before. These techniques are applicable to the field of finance, business, marketing, and to the field of services. The techniques have been perfected beyond any possibility of failure.... There is no limit to the possibilities of new ownership that the people can gain for themselves by this type of group action. It is easy, it is safe, it is in harmony with our best democratic traditions ... and it gives

> the people new scope for initiative and creative thinking. It is a new and marvellous democratic runway from which the common people of the earth can take off to new levels of life heretofore undreamed of.[30]

Along with the visionary there were several other strands in the philosophy of the Antigonish Movement. For the clerical community at the university and in the parishes, the movement was a form of Christian social action. To Tompkins a program of adult education was a work of charity, because for him charity meant helping people to help themselves. To the president of St. Francis Xavier one goal of co-operation was a more just and Christian society.[31] To John R. MacDonald, a rural pastor and later Bishop of Antigonish, those co-operative enterprises that were promoting a more equitable distribution of wealth were fulfilling a basic Christian social principle.[32] Almost invariably, the link with Christian social action was related to the insistence of Coady and his colleagues that while the economic approach was basic, the movement had wider and deeper spiritual and cultural implications. These leaders emphasized that putting people on their feet economically was not an end in itself but a means to what Coady frequently referred to as the good and abundant life. Educators seriously interested in raising the cultural level of society should help to solve economic problems first so that men could stop worrying about bread and enjoy Brahms. Coady could popularize this idea even to the point of flippancy:

> When a man can't think of how he can make ends meet he won't care much about what Pirandello meant in his last play. So we said we are living in an economic world. We must go to people where we find them eking out their livelihood and show them first of all how they can make a decent living. Then when this is done they'll be ready for culture. We said Spinach before Spinoza. Some day we'll give them as much filosophy [sic] as they want, but right now we're going to tell them more about fertilizer.[33]

Behind this simplification lies Coady's basic conviction that co-operation is more than a business enterprise; it is a way of carrying on business grounded in spiritual values. It calls forth charity, encourages mercy, and generates a sense of brotherhood. To Coady these were religious values, and co-operation was the expression of religion in the economic order. But not sectarian religion. The Antigonish Movement was loyal to the Rochdale weavers, who began the co-operative movement in England in the mid-nineteenth century. To the Rochdale pioneers co-operation must be non-sectarian. While Catholic clerics in a Catholic university, and bishops and priests in a predominantly Catholic diocese initiated and led the Antigonish Movement, it soon crossed sectarian, ethnic, and language boundaries. Scots, Irish, English, and Acadians, whether Catholic or Protestant, became part of the movement. Tompkins had established this religious neutrality quite early with his much-quoted remark, "There's no Catholic or Protestant way of catching fish," and Coady had observed: "We cannot speak of Catholic co-operation or Protestant co-operation, of Buddhist, Mohammedan, Shinto or Hebrew economics any more than we can speak of Quaker chemistry or Mormon mathematics."[34]

There was also a strictly practical reason for a non-denominational stance: the provincial and federal governments and the Carnegie Corporation would never have supported a strictly sectarian movement. Such support was crucial: between 1929 and 1939 the federal Department of Fisheries contributed nearly $80,000 to the Extension Department, and the Carnegie Corporation made grants totalling $56,000. The most generous contributor was, however, St. Francis Xavier itself, which supported extension over this period in the amount of $83,000.

Neutrality in politics was another tenet of the movement and here again Coady was adamant in holding to Rochdale principles. The new left-of-centre party, the Canadian Commonwealth Federation, had shown its enthusiasm for co-operatives and probably would have welcomed affiliation with the Antigonish Movement, but Coady knew any such connection would bring his government and Carnegie grants to an abrupt end. In fact, when one of his staff, A. S. MacIntyre, was accused of political activity in an election in 1941, Coady made a thorough investigation and demonstrated that the accusation was false. He then assured the minister of fisheries in Ottawa that "It has been our policy from the very beginning to be neutral in politics. All our workers have been advised to this effect. They can vote as they please but they are not allowed to take part in any political activity." Coady also recognized the position of his Church. In the thirties the official teaching of the papacy had opposed socialism in any form, and the Catholic bishops of Canada warned the faithful against the C.C.F.'s socialism.[35]

But it was not these considerations alone that explain Coady's political neutrality. Again and again in letters and speeches he emphasized that the movement was educational and economic, not political. He was, in fact, dubious about workers, farmers, or fishermen engaging in direct political action unless they first prepared themselves through education:

> No political party can do the job that is to be done in Canada unless the people themselves are lifted to new intelligence and new economic efficiency. Political action to the organized workers looks like a quick remedy but there is nothing quick about it.[36]

Early in its development the movement welcomed the participation of women both as extension workers and members of study clubs. They were seen as crucial in stemming the flow of emigration, particularly if economic reconstruction could improve the quality and amenities of homes in rural areas. Women joined their husbands for discussion of problems related to production and marketing and ways of checking rural decline; and nutrition, health, and handicrafts became the central topics of hundreds of women's study clubs.

This brings us back to where the movement began and where Coady was always most comfortable, in the rural areas. He carried memories of the Margaree Valley all his life. His dream was to see men and women living the good and abundant life on the land, which would involve bringing all kinds of services—transportation, power, telephones, schools, medical services—to rural areas. The way to effect this transformation was "to build from the fringes in." Through knowledge and a critical awareness gained in the study clubs, and through self-help and local initiative, small co-operative enterprises would grow and join together to exert pressure on the economy and eventually affect the production and distribution of goods and services at the centre. Tompkins also believed in self-reliance and favored starting the movement in small communities because, as he once said, "the local people know where the ice is thin." In April 1939, Coady reported that the Extension Department had shown "more progress during the past year than in any previous year since its inception."

The regular fulltime staff of eleven had been supplemented by thirty workers supported by a grant from the Department of Fisheries. Using the same techniques and working under the supervision of the Extension Department, these workers brought the movement to the fishing villages of New Brunswick, Prince Edward Island, and hitherto "undeveloped" parts of Nova Scotia. Over 1,200 new study clubs were formed as a result of this infusion of funding and staff. The annual three-day Rural and Industrial Conference had attracted over 1,000 people. Following the conference, some 200 educators, social workers, and co-operators from thirty states and from every province in Canada toured eastern Nova Scotia to see the villages so dramatically and frequently described in the literature. Women's study clubs now numbered 350. Both in numbers and in influence this may have been the high point of the movement.

The Post-War Years

For Coady, the post-war years were the golden years during which he became the St. Paul of adult education in North America. He was honored by his church, but on the testimony of his secretary was not impressed when told in 1946 that he had been elevated to the rank of Monsignor. "Good God," he replied, "the sons of bitches can't *do* that to me!" In 1949 he became president of the Canadian Association for Adult Education and shared with E. A. Corbett the Henry Marshall Tory award for outstanding leadership in adult education. He crossed and recrossed the United States and Canada, making forty addresses in one year alone, including one to a United Nations conference on "Organizing Rural People for the Conservation of Natural Resources." His book, *Masters of Their Own Destiny,* which was translated into several languages including Japanese and Arabic, the wide distribution of the National Film Board's *The Rising Tide,* and a considerable amount of publicity in the popular press gave the Antigonish Movement an international following, particularly in the Third World. By 1950 Coady had himself become an international figure and was in such demand off campus that in its annual report the Extension Department had to remind itself that it was "the work here at home which is and must always remain our first care."

In 1951 at the age of seventy, Moses Coady retired as director of the Extension Department but stayed in his "old quarters" in the university which had been his home for forty-seven years. For the next several years he led an active life of retirement, making as he said, "the odd speech and lecture," doing some writing, and talking with visitors from abroad. In 1957 he wrote an autobiographical sketch used in a television interview. In this sketch, published by the Extension Department under the title, *My Story*, Coady also traces the progress of the movement, and his exuberance and confidence are as fresh as they were in mid-career. Again he tells the story of the village of Grand Etang, bringing its development up to date: "This small community spearheaded the movement in the spectacular regeneration of a people. They move in all fields of self-help through the Co-operative Movement." He goes on to speak of the fish processing plant, credit union, and co-operative store.

> They have paid their bills, painted their houses, and built new ones. They even have libraries and are, in a word, a joy to behold. It has always been our conviction at St. F.X. Extension that as long as we have a score or so of these successful communities which have scattered over the Maritime Provinces, there is little doubt about the ultimate success of our educational movement.

This was a far cry from capturing 25 per cent of the economy but Coady, at least on paper, remained buoyant. He continued to see eastern Nova Scotia as a great social laboratory big enough to be significant and small enough to be manageable in testing a program of self-help and economic democracy where the people who are descended "from the great races of Europe . . . are poor enough to want progress and smart enough to get it." In July 1959, Coady died of leukemia. Nearly 1,000 people attended his funeral and he was carried to his grave on a hillside overlooking St. Francis Xavier by two fishermen, two farmers, a miner, and a steelworker.

For the movement the post-war years 1945–59 were primarily a period of maintenance and consolidation, although there were some new developments. Radio was used effectively to stimulate discussion in small groups organized by the Extension Department and it was in this format that the People's School reappeared in 1946. The *Extension Bulletin*, which had been widely circulated since 1933 and had become a major factor in maintaining interest and morale among the study clubs evolved into the *Maritime Co-operator*, an independent journal of the co-operative movement. One historian of the movement reported in 1955 that "co-operation is now inseparably woven into the economic and social fabric of the Maritimes and bids fair to become a dominant feature of the life pattern of the people of these provinces."[37] Progress may be quantitatively summarized as follows: by 1959 there were in the Maritimes 438 credit unions; United Maritime Fishermen had a volume of business amounting to over $4 million; Maritime Co-operative Services had a volume of $15 million; and over 900 families were living in co-operatively built houses.

INFLUENCE AND RECOGNITION

By the late thirties the movement had taken root in the three Maritime Provinces, Newfoundland, and the Magdalen Islands. In 1939, by invitation of the University of British Columbia, St. Francis Xavier staff gave courses for west coast fishermen. Study groups grew out of these courses and in 1940 the Prince Rupert Fishermen's Credit Union was incorporated and chartered. Prince Rupert is one of many examples of the transfer of Antigonish principles to other parts of Canada and the United States. It is also a sign of the recognition the movement had begun to receive. The *Halifax Herald* was the first Canadian newspaper to show its support and enthusiasm, and in 1936 a correspondent of the *Times Literary Supplement* made this comment: "How many of the educated and intelligent people who read this Supplement have heard of Antigonish? Yet, amid a multitude of crowded experiences . . . nothing moved me so much as the extra-mural work of the University of St. Francis Xavier, Antigonish!"[38]

A report issued by the Carnegie Corporation in 1934 referred to the work conducted by the Extension Department as "some of the most original and promising experiments in adult education with which the Corporation is concerned." But the tone of other articles that appeared in magazines with national coverage in Canada and the United States was more florid, and Bertram Fowler's *The Lord Helps Those . . .* (1938) was scarcely this side of idolatry. For years, in fact, the movement suffered from an overenthusiastic and uncritical press. In 1953 *Maclean's Magazine,* in an article called "How FX Saved the Maritimes," claimed that "SFX has put new life into a dying fishing industry, restored idle farms and stamped out Communism in industrial Cape Breton, once a hot-bed of radical activity."[39] And in 1970 a Canadian journalist wrote, "Antigonish had a fantastic history of social action . . . it was here that Moses Michael Coady walked out of the Margaree Valley to found the co-op movement that spread throughout the world."[40] These showers of praise did not please the Extension Department and in an editorial titled "Exaggerations," the *Extension Bulletin* was sharply critical of the tendency to make premature judgments and underestimate the difficulties the movement was facing.

Recognition also came from other parts of the world. Visitors came to learn of the movement at first hand and in 1945 the university established a diploma program in social leadership together with a series of shorter courses lasting from one to three months. By 1959 more than 300 overseas candidates had enrolled in these courses. Also in 1945 the first staff member of the Extension Department answered an invitation to work abroad.

Joseph A. MacDonald taught summer school courses in adult education and the philosophy of co-operation at the University of Puerto Rico. In his fifteen return engagements there he encouraged the growth of co-operatives and arranged for a commission to visit Antigonish. In 1955 one of his former students was appointed minister of co-operation with cabinet rank. During the fifties, M. J. MacKinnon, Coady's successor as Director of Extension, joined a mission which studied the fisheries of Ceylon, and Alexander Laidlaw, Associate Director of Extension, was seconded for two years to the government of India to direct the training of some 20,000 leaders for a network of co-operatives. In 1955 George Topshee, then head of urban education in the Extension Department, gave a short course in Dominica on credit unions and co-operatives. He made connections with local leaders and in the next two decades some twenty people came from this small Caribbean island to Antigonish for training. Father Topshee also directed a project sponsored by Canada in Basutoland—development of an Extension Department and training of its staff.

Meanwhile, under a consultation program, teams of observers from a dozen or more countries came to Antigonish. These were usually government officials who wished to talk to staff and to make field trips to see the results of the Movement. To cope with teams of observers, operate a diploma course for social leadership, and send members of its staff abroad placed an intolerable burden on the Extension Department. There had been desultory discussion for years about the need for an international school or institute that would concentrate the experience of St. Francis Xavier and direct it toward the Third World. As early as 1939 Coady had revealed his vision of a people's institute international in scope and application. The emphasis would be on research and every co-operator in North America should be asked to "contribute his pence to the furtherance of research work on the baffling economic problems that confront us."[41]

In 1949 interest and pressure from abroad were sufficient for St. Francis Xavier to establish, in the United States, "The International Friends of the Antigonish Movement." The purpose of this organization was to raise funds "to build here an international centre of adult education and co-operative study."[42] The driving force in establishing such a centre was John R. MacDonald, now become Bishop of Antigonish and Chancellor of St. Francis Xavier. His enthusiasm for consolidating the connection with Third World countries was strengthened when, in a conversation in Rome, Pope John XXIII challenged him "to do something about Latin America." Largely through MacDonald's initiative, four months after Coady's death the Board of Governors resolved to respond to "the demands on the University for education in social leadership, based on the philosophy and techniques of the Antigonish Movement" by establishing the Coady International Institute.[43]

The Coady Institute

The first director of the Coady Institute was Francis J. Smyth, whose early career had followed the familiar pattern: St. Francis Xavier graduate, parish priest in Cape Breton, member of the university faculty with an assignment to the Extension Department. One of his first journeys as director was a visit to Cardinal Cushing in Boston during which he hoped to secure the cardinal's advice on fundraising; Smyth received not only advice but the cardinal's assurance that he would raise $200,000. This, together with grants from the Canadian government, a number of foundations, the "International Friends," and several church organizations made it possible to begin construction of the Macdonald Building, now one of two which accommodate students and staff. Meanwhile, Smyth was developing programs, selecting staff, and choosing students for the new eight-month diploma course, which began in 1960 with twenty-three students from twelve countries. In the next twenty-one years some 2,500 students from 111 countries came to the Coady for the diploma or other courses.

The Institute's program has two major divisions: diploma and certificate programs scheduled at the Institute; and regional workshops and consultation programs based overseas. A unique feature of the Coady is how a year is divided and used. From May to December staff and students are in residence; from January to May no students are in residence and the staff, in collaboration with former students, operate the overseas program in Third World countries. Thus the staff annually is brought face-to-face with Third World realities. There is, however, another reason for giving this structure to the Institute's year. For its first dozen years it followed the traditional academic year, but in 1972 it adopted a "climatic year," which in the words of a member of staff "spares the participants—practically all from the tropics—the rigor of a long northern winter and avoids the lethargy and low morale that usually come with February and March."[44]

The diploma program in social development, which normally has an enrolment of some fifty students, is the main course offered. All students are involved in the study of the Antigonish Movement, the principles and methods of adult education, and development economics; beyond this core there is a range of electives. Under the guidance of a faculty member each student completes a substantial written project relevant to his or her work at home. And through organized field trips to locations in eastern Nova Scotia both the triumphs and failures of the Antigonish Movement are examined. In 1981 the fifty-four students came from twenty-three countries, including seven blacks from South Africa. All had five or more years of work experience. There is ample evidence that Coady graduates have established training centres and extension agencies modelled on Coady lines in their own countries. Some fifty of them now operate in Asia and Latin America and a dozen or more are active in Africa. Through these centres and by maintaining the astonishingly strong ties developed between the Coady and its graduates the Institute's work has increasingly been transferred from Antigonish to the Third World.

Within the network of relationships the Coady Institute has created abroad there is an explicit assumption that both the philosophy and strategy of the Antigonish Movement are transferable, with modifications, to the Third World. The key word here is "modifications," which have occurred both at the Coady Institute in the interpretation given to the Antigonish Movement and in Third World countries where, in the last two decades, marked changes have been adopted in development policy. Broadly speaking, during its first ten or twelve years the Institute's training emphasis rested on the history of the Extension Department, the cultivation of adult education skills, and knowledge of the structure and function of co-operatives. The emphasis continues to be on adult education. However, according to A. A. MacDonald, the present director, it must be guided by a vision which recognizes the necessity of structural change in society as a condition for human development. For purposes of social change the disadvantaged must acquire organizational power. While co-operatives are regarded as one means through which power can be achieved, they are not the only organizational means, or necessarily the most effective means in Third World situations.[45]

Such a shift of emphasis to fundamental social change may be seen as a corrective to the appeal the movement made to some Third World countries in the post-war years. These were the countries that in moving toward independence were wary of capitalism and found the Antigonish stress on adult education, self-reliance, and local leadership compatible with their own political and economic policies. Furthermore, the methods and techniques appeared to be relatively straightforward and inexpensive, could be managed by poor people who had little education, and appeared to be aimed at meeting immediate needs. This was, of course, a basic misunderstanding, or at best a superficial view of the movement, but it was widely held and led to judging the success of Coady graduates simply by the number of credit unions and co-operatives they organized on their return home.

The other significant change is the adoption of a new development policy by the international agencies, such as the World Bank, and donor countries such as Canada. Interpretations of this change echoed through the auditoriums and corridors of St. Francis Xavier in October 1978, at the International Symposium Commemorating the Fiftieth Anniversary of the Antigonish Movement. Major figures from Canada and abroad, the "Development Establishment" one might say, were there. The late Barbara Ward, then too ill to attend, had prepared the keynote address in which she contrasted development strategy of the fifties and sixties with what she called "the conventional wisdom of the new economic thinking." Earlier, Third World countries had been urged to engage in central planning, accept foreign investment, adopt Western science and technology, increase economic growth through industrialization, and promote exports. There was wide optimism that the benefits of this strategy would "trickle down" to the poor. Instead, these strategies led to the uneven distribution of income, increases in the national debt and foreign exchange crises, particularly when oil was no longer two dollars a barrel, and "ghastly conurbations" in urban growth. The simple formula of producing more, selling more, and earning more did not work and poor countries grew poorer.

In the seventies a new orthodoxy developed that might be called the "self-reliance model." At the symposium it was espoused by all the major speakers, but perhaps articulated best by Sir Shridrath Ramphal, secretary-general of the Commonwealth Association:

> And it is important—indeed, it could be vital to the outcome of the dialogue between rich and poor—that self-reliance be made the underpinning of an action-oriented strategy of development within the Third World. Self-reliance rests on the conviction that development must come from within each society—conditioned by its history and its social, cultural and economic strengths, founded on its resources, including its human resources, and committed to the national well-being. Self-reliance development is based not on what the world can do for us, but on what we can do for ourselves. It strives to ensure the provision by national effort of the essentials of national subsistence—of food, of habitat, of health, of education. And it seeks fulfilment by exploring new frontiers of co-operation between developing countries themselves.[46]

In this concept of development, planning is decentralized and decisions are made at the local level using local resources, both human and natural. Development is not imposed from above, ready-made; it is started by the people themselves and proceeds slowly. Whether it is a change in agricultural method, digging a latrine, building a primary school, or starting a co-operative, the people should understand the significance of development and support it.

It was a surprise to no one that world leaders strongly supported self-reliance at the celebration marking the half-century of the Antigonish Movement. But in the midst of jubilation that development theory had finally caught up with Tompkins and Coady, the director of the Institute sounded a warning. A. A. MacDonald pointed out that the basic philosophy of the movement was to awaken, through education, man's critical awareness of his condition and then to work, through group action, toward achieving socio-economic reform. Moses Coady had spoken of shocking people out of their complacency so they would search for the truth and "every little blow of these co-operatives becomes a sledge-hammer lick in building the new social structure. The common people do not have to wait for the superman; by manipulating social forces they can do the apparently superhuman job for themselves."[47]

This is not a prospect that the governing elite of many developing countries welcome with enthusiasm. Once it becomes clear that the transfer of the Antigonish Movement and the adoption of the self-reliance model involves an adult education program that will give knowledge to the people, a knowledge that may point to the need for reform of basic social institutions, the question arises whether the control systems of developing countries will allow such a program to be introduced. In recognizing this problem, MacDonald stressed the need to invest more effort in creating understanding among the planning elite. "Without this 'conversion' of at least part of the policy makers, it is not likely that either of the two major programs associated with the Movement can be effectively implemented in developing countries."[48] In 1980 and 1981 the Institute addressed itself to this issue by offering a summer course on implementation of social policy for senior level administrators, legislators, and representatives of political parties. Strategies for achieving change are also discussed in the diploma course on social development and in workshops and seminars that are conducted throughout Asia, Africa, the Caribbean, and Latin America.

A visitor to the Coady while the diploma course is in session is struck by the open quality of class discussion, the easy camaraderie between staff and students, and the intellectual energy with which students engage in critical reflection and the analysis of data in preparing a substantial project. At the same time they appear to enjoy the ethos of a multicultural community, the like of which they may never experience again. To maintain the Institute and operate the campus and overseas courses, an annual budget of $1½ million is required. Nearly half this support has come in recent years from the Canadian International Development Agency (CIDA), the remainder from generous support by the university, the Roman Catholic Church, and a substantial number of non-governmental organizations. In November 1981, the Institute embarked on a campaign to raise $2.5 million. The small committee meeting that opened the campaign was chaired by the president of Gulf Oil Canada and held in the company's boardroom in Toronto. Several weeks later some fifty members of Canada's corporate elite met for dinner at the Toronto Club and heard that over a million dollars had already been pledged. In the midst of this array of corporate power the Honorable Allan MacEachen, Canada's deputy prime minister and a former economics professor at St. Francis Xavier, reportedly rose "to lightheartedly recall that the anti-establishment Dr. Coady would likely have found it 'pleasing and amusing, to say the least' to find such an audience, attending such a dinner in his honour, in such a club."[49]

The Movement in Retrospect

Coady's long-time friend and colleague, Alex Laidlaw, reported that Coady felt a keen sense of disappointment toward the end of his life.[50] Perhaps this is inevitable when a reformer and visionary faces the reality of how much there is still left to do. Or did he realize by 1959 that the movement had "matured" into its institutional stage and that the glory days of the thirties could never be recaptured? The adult education component of the movement had been largely transferred to the co-operatives, and with the relative prosperity of the post-war period there was less incentive to set economic goals "at the fringes." The Extension Department staff continued to criticize the economic status quo, to train leaders both for co-operatives and trade unions, and to operate the People's School, initiate programs of public housing and, in 1967, to provide the leadership which culminated in the provincial takeover of the Sydney Steel Plant.[51] Extension has become a substantial social force, but it is not the reform movement that Coady visualized in the thirties.

Is this the normal life-cycle of a social movement, the process by which the cause becomes buried in the institution? Tompkins was afraid of this development and warned that organizing and institutionalizing an idea or a cause tends to make it sterile. Or was the Antigonish Movement flawed by its own philosophy? Both Tompkins and Coady, in fact all the leaders of the movement, had enormous faith in education. It was almost a blind faith that education could be, in itself, an instrument of change and progress. Tompkins used the formula: people × resources × education = progress, and Coady believed that in western democracies "education is the main instrument of human progress," the key that unlocks life to any free people. Their emphasis was, of course, on a kind of education that would raise adult minds to new levels of critical awareness and from this would follow social and economic action. In the twenties and thirties this faith in adult education was little short of revolutionary. Thus Antigonish was the centre of an educational, not a political movement. There was no clearly defined strategy for changing the power structure of society and no affiliation with any political party. Instead, the affiliation was with a university and precisely because of this relationship one or two of the movement's shortcomings are surprising. There was no dearth of zeal, imagination, and ingenuity but there was much less critical and rigorous evaluation. As one study club leader wrote to Coady, "I realize that we must be charged with enthusiasm before we can tackle our problems in the right way," but objective analysis of socio-economic issues through research would have strengthened the movement's theoretical basis.

Coady recognized this problem and often spoke of the need for research, but the Extension Department budget never seemed large enough to employ experienced research workers. Alex Laidlaw has mentioned one other factor: "In the matter of careful research, there was, unfortunately, a subtle split between the University itself and Extension, and the full potential of the regular faculty for extra-mural activities and research studies was never used."[52] Zeal and enthusiasm frequently led to a tendency to overstate achievement and an almost compulsive concern to portray the movement as successful. Coady's ebullience was contagious, and through his exuberant articles in the *Extension Bulletin* and his vivid reports of the "transformation" of Cheticamp, Grand Etang, or Judique in his many addresses throughout North America he created a legend that the people of the Maritime Provinces were joining co-operatives in such numbers that they would, inevitably, change the economy. The fact is that in comparison with other parts of Canada the people of the Maritimes, generally speaking, have been slow to adopt co-operative ways.[53] The province of Saskatchewan, for example, with roughly the same population as Nova Scotia had, in 1979, three times as many credit union members and ten times the assets.[54]

Canada has developed a healthy co-operative movement. Nearly 40 per cent of Canadians are members of a credit union and more than two million Canadians belong to other forms of co-operatives. Western Canadian grain is almost entirely marketed co-operatively and some twelve large dairy co-operatives handle almost half of Canada's processed dairy products. But this growth has been largely confined to rural areas and in Canada as a whole consumer co-operatives account for less than 5 per cent of the country's total retail business. In order to survive, co-operatives have tended to become large and impersonal, operated locally and provincially in a businesslike way by well-trained managers. The executive director of the Co-Operative Union of Canada has said:

> The fact remains that co-operatives in Canada, despite their significant economic strength are seen as a clear alternative to other forms of business by only a relatively small proportion of the population. The commitment of many members to their co-operative appears to be based as much on convenience as on principle.[55]

While Coady's vision of co-operation as a philosophy and a way of life, a means of creating a new Canadian society, has not been realized, the Antigonish Movement amid the poverty and despair of the twenties and thirties gave the "little people" of eastern Nova Scotia a grand vision. They may not have built a New Jerusalem, but they found through self-reliance and local initiative a new confidence and a new dignity. It was an awakening to the conviction that if something was to be done it must start locally and the result was that in hundreds of families in rural communities, fishing villages, and mining towns co-operation became a way of life. One can point to the co-operative and low-cost housing projects of Sydney, which are probably more extensive than in any city of comparable size in Canada, the facts that practically all milk in Nova Scotia is now marketed through co-operatives and that a regional organization, Co-op Atlantic, united some 200 co-operatives which have a total membership throughout the Maritimes of 60,000 persons. But the intangibles may be more significant. The Antigonish Movement with its ecumenical attitude, emphasis on scientific agriculture, and stress on the participation of women may have raised new thresholds of tolerance and helped to create new attitudes. The movement was a pervasive influence but not one based on a clearly definable set of ideas or beliefs that people had been taught. As Gregory Baum has said, people do not change profoundly because new ideas have been put into their heads. What changes people is action.

> Consciousness is created by action. People get new ideas and acquire new intentions because they act co-operatively in a joint project of making a living. In adult education people analyze the reasons why they themselves, individually, cannot make a living and then engage themselves in a co-operative venture of production or distribution to beat the system and jointly make enough money to survive and live with dignity. This involvement changes their head.[56]

Beginning with Tompkins and Coady, Antigonish pioneered a new role for the university and a new kind of adult education. They were not the first to bring adults to the university and St. Francis Xavier did not invent the university extension department. In fact the movement borrowed freely, from co-operatives in England, the people's school and the study club in Scandinavia, the credit union in Quebec, and co-operative housing in the United States. Its originality lay more in taking the university to people where they lived and worked and using adult education as an instrument for identifying and solving social and economic problems. To do so effectively involved a new philosophy and new methods through which men and women would discover their own intelligence and their capacity for taking action. It is an approach to adult learning now also associated with the Brazilian adult educator, Paulo Freire, who uses the term "conscientization" and the concept of consciousness-raising in Third World countries. Another innovation, for Canada, was the study club and the emphasis on group learning through discussion led by a local leader who was not university-trained. Traditional adult education had stressed individual "enrichment" and personal development and satisfaction; the St. Francis Xavier program was oriented toward both the individual and the group, and there was the underlying assumption that the individual would find fulfilment not only in group discussion but in group action.

In other ways too the Extension Department broke new ground. It was not content to share in the initial enthusiasm caused by the papal encyclicals and then leave them on library shelves to gather dust. St. Francis Xavier clerics came out of their classrooms not simply to expound *Rerum Novarum* and *Quadragesimo Anno* but to use them for discussion of the rights of workers, the need for labor organizations, and the danger of economic power becoming increasingly concentrated in the hands of a few. Antigonish translated theory into action and applied papal teaching practically. The Extension Department sided with labor and supported the miners and steel workers of Cape Breton in their struggle to organize and bargain collectively. It went further by organizing labor education and co-operatives to the extent that the annual report of the Extension Department for 1934 stated that the greatest expansion of the extension program in that year was in the mining communities. The support of militant labor in the troubled thirties was not normal custom for the members of a department of a small denominational university. Throughout its fifty-five-year history the Extension Department has both supported and criticized organized labor, and has helped to train its leaders. Currently, one of the department's most successful programs is the Atlantic Region Labour Education Centre (ARLEC), which annually offers two-week residential courses in both English and French to young trade unionists with leadership potential.

Another radical departure from conventional university behavior is the Extension Department's continuing criticism of North American capitalism and the economic status quo. This too is not the stance university professors normally take in public, but it is arguably in keeping with a long-standing tradition of a university acting as a critic of society.

> The right—or better still, the responsibility of criticism might be claimed for the whole university community. The critical judgments expressed by official university bodies are necessary for the advancement of society, and are comparable to those of other institutions, such as the official opposition in a parliamentary regime or the various media for the free expression of opinion. . . . The public must understand that this is an essential part of the role of the university.[57]

One reason that a university is granted, and in some jurisdictions guaranteed, academic freedom and freedom of research is so that it may vigorously criticize the very society that supports it. Beginning with Tompkins and continuing for over half a century, the Antigonish

Movement has chosen this role. In November 1975, the staff of the Extension Department reaffirmed its position: "Today as well as yesterday, Extension is fundamentally opposed to the [economic] status quo. Today's society is morally unjust and ought to be changed."[58]

As St. Francis Xavier developed a new kind of extension department and a new philosophy and method of adult education it created a new relationship between the university and the people of the Maritime provinces. There are few universities in Canada that are closer to the men and women of their region, and probably fewer still that are so affectionately regarded. Fishermen, farmers, and trade unionists do not come to the Antigonish campus only to see a son or daughter graduate; they have been coming since the thirties for conferences or short courses, or more recently to one of the five offices of the Extension Department located in eastern Nova Scotia. For decades men and women active in the movement as adult educators, co-operators, or trade unionists have been awarded honorary degrees, and representatives of farmers, fishermen, and miners now sit on the board of governors. Since 1953 the constitution of St. Francis Xavier has stated that the university shall strive to attain its aims "by associating itself actively with the people in the solution of their problems." The Director of Extension is, ex officio, a member of the board of governors and also of the university council. Nevertheless, it would be nonsense to imply that St. Francis Xavier is a "people's university" (the term itself is meaningless), or that the university is dominated by its Extension Department. Behind the symbols of honorary degrees and board representation is the simple truth that average people grew to feel they had a special relationship with St. Francis Xavier; to some degree it was "theirs."

But this relationship may not be as strong now as it was in the Coady years, and through the Coady Institute the countries of the Third World may now be benefitting more from the movement than the people of the Maritimes. If so, this is more than the transfer of the movement abroad; it is a time-hallowed custom of Atlantic Canada: moving away.

FIVE

Kurt Hahn
1886–1974

Kurt Hahn: International Schools and Colleges

Kurt Hahn, reprinted with permission of the Gordonstoun School.

In 1902, as a boy of sixteen, Kurt Hahn and his uncle while on a walking tour in the Tyrol fell into conversation with three English boys. The two parties stayed together for several days, during which the boys shared their school experience. The English boys spoke enthusiastically of Abbotsholme, a new, progressive public school where they had been prefects. One of them later loaned Hahn a book written by a German educator, Hermann Lietz, who had spent a year teaching at Abbotsholme. The book, together with the zeal of his new friends, had a deep effect on the young Hahn and he later said that it was through this encounter that his fate cried out to him.[1] In 1904, he left his home in Berlin to enrol at Oxford, but he stayed only briefly because of a recurring illness. Soon after the First World War, however, he founded a new kind of British public school in Germany and later transplanted the basic principles of that school to Britain when forced to leave Hitler's Germany.

Over a forty-year period (1920–62) Hahn founded, or was involved with others in the founding of, seven enterprises. Two, Salem in southwest Germany and Gordonstoun in Scotland, are boarding schools; Outward Bound is a network of short-term residential schools that began in Wales and has now spread to five continents; the Duke of Edinburgh's Award Scheme is a voluntary, leisure-time program which gives young people a structure for personal achievement, community service, and adventure; and Atlantic College, one of six United

World Colleges, a two-year residential school committed to developing better understanding among an international and multiracial student body. Hahn's major contribution lay in challenging young people to discover new limits to their capacities of body, mind, and spirit through risk and adventure. The Gordonstoun coat of arms carries the motto "Plus est en Vous," which Hahn liked to translate colloquially as "You've got more in you than you think." Together with his emphasis on adventure in the development and unfolding of character, he stressed the nurturing of compassion through projects of service. The parable of the Good Samaritan, which he referred to often, was read by the Duke of Edinburgh at a memorial service at St. Martin's-in-the-Fields, London, on 11 February 1974.

Early Years

Kurt Hahn was born on 5 June 1886, into a well-to-do, cultivated family in Berlin. His paternal grandfather was a wealthy industrialist, owner of a rolling mill and textile factory and active in public affairs. Oskar Hahn, Kurt's father, entered the family business and travelled extensively. From many visits he developed a strong affection for England so there was no surprise within the family when Kurt was sent to study at Christ Church, Oxford. The Hahn home in pre-war Berlin had an atmosphere both German and cosmopolitan and was a warm and friendly salon for liberal scholars, politicians, and artists. Kurt attended the *Wilhelmsgymnasium,* but was only too glad to escape from its academic rigidities to the family summer home which Oskar Hahn had built on the lines of an English country house with broad lawns, rose garden, cricket fields, stables, and tennis courts. Here Kurt, the eldest of three sons, tutored the younger children and led them on expeditions. His passion for physical fitness and outdoor adventure was, however, accompanied by delicate health caused by a particular sensitivity to sunlight. It was this affliction that interrupted progress toward his *Arbitur* and gave him acute discomfort for many years.

Kurt's mother and maternal grandmother were major influences during his early years. His mother, Charlotte, a woman of great charm and beauty, married at eighteen, was a mother at nineteen yet continued to educate herself in philosophy and education and to become an accomplished pianist. His grandmother, a woman of intense vitality, had married at seventeen against the wishes of her parents and moved with her husband from her home in Poland to Germany. In her later years she lived as a matriarch in the Hahns' home in Berlin and so impressed the youthful Kurt that he recorded her conversational wit and aphorisms in his notebooks. Without any substantive evidence one can only speculate on the lasting influences of the Hahn household. His father may have given Kurt a sense of the world outside Berlin and a feeling for Britain in particular. His mother and grandmother may have appeared to him so vital and attractive that he never again found their equal and hence never married.

As mentioned above, Hahn went up to Oxford in 1904 but stayed only a year, during which he was ill most of the time. He returned to Germany and with the leisure and mobility reminiscent of a student in the Middle Ages spent the next several years at the universities of Berlin, Heidelberg, Freiburg, and Göttingen before returning to Oxford in 1910. By then he had written a short novel, *Frau Elses Verheissung*, in the tradition of Rousseau's *Emile* and Pestalozzi's *How Gertrude Teaches Her Children*. He dedicated it to his mother. With his tutor, J. H. Stewart, a Platonist, he discussed his ideas on education and at Christ Church he met men from the English public schools and formed a lasting respect for these schools, Eton particularly, and the training for leadership old Etonians had received. During his first Christmas vacation he stayed at the home of his student friend, William Calder, son of a farmer in the Findhorn valley close to Moray Firth. During later visits to northeast Scotland he rented a house in summer vacations and made lasting friendships among the fishermen and farmers of Morayshire; he was also welcomed by the Smith-Cumming family, who owned Gordonstoun House. It was Captain Smith-Cumming who in 1914 arranged for Sir Victor Horsley, a London neurosurgeon, to operate on Hahn and insert metal plates in his head and thus provide some relief from his sensitivity to light and heat. Later that year at the age of twenty-eight and without a degree, Hahn returned to Germany. He later revealed to an English audience that his one consuming ambition on leaving Oxford was to found a school in Germany modelled on an English public school.[2]

THE FIRST WORLD WAR

During the first year of the war a Cambridge undergraduate, Neville Butler, who had delayed too long his return to England, was released from an internment camp and allowed to live with the Hahn family in West Berlin.[3] He and Kurt became close friends and in Butler's journal of that year is this description of Hahn:

> Strongly built, with a fine head protected by a drooping broad-rimmed hat, walking with a slight stoop and a tread measured but capable of startling acceleration; a keen player of tennis and hockey, a sprinter and jumper (standing jump preferred) but keeping athletics well in its place, Hahn was an impressive figure.[4]

Hahn secured a position in the English section of the press centre of the German Foreign Office (he was exempt from military service on medical grounds), where his work involved reading and analyzing the British press and submitting reports and memoranda on political developments in Britain and the mood of the British people. In this position he gradually went well beyond matter-of-fact reporting and began to write critical memoranda. When Germany decided in January 1917 to proceed with unrestricted submarine warfare, that is, to torpedo civilian ships, Hahn opposed this policy in a memorandum that pointed out that the British government welcomed the decision because it would bring the United States into the war. For his audacity in criticizing the Foreign Office he was transferred to another position, that of adviser to Colonel (later General) von Haeften, the Supreme Command's liaison officer with the Foreign Office. This position gave Hahn more rather than less opportunity for backstage influence. Throughout the war he worked tirelessly to secure a declaration that Germany would guarantee restoration of Belgian sovereignty. This move, he felt, would divide public opinion in Britain and give support to those in the British government who were prepared to oppose Lloyd George and negotiate for peace.

In February 1917 Hahn first met Prince Max of Baden and a relationship began which would deeply affect the lives of both men. Close to the end of the war the prince became imperial chancellor, an appointment which in all probability originated in a suggestion from Hahn. He served at Versailles as private secretary to Dr. Carl Melchior, a Berlin banker who was an economic expert with the German delegation, and shared the task of drafting his delegation's reply to the proposals of the Allies. Hahn was in fact bitterly opposed to the Treaty of Versailles and thought that Wilson's peace program had been betrayed.

Hahn's participation in the First World War significantly affected his later career. His confidence in his political judgment had grown, and he now knew that in a face-to-face encounter or operating from behind the scenes—drafting memoranda, preparing speeches, giving advice—he could be powerfully persuasive. He also learned that he could find satisfaction in acting through others. When his recommendations were not initially accepted he fought passionately, often with success, for what he believed in. He acquired a blend of idealism and practicality, a quality that prompted Conrad Haussman, a member of the Cabinet, to write in 1917 of "Kurt Hahn, whose phenomenal intelligence and practical political idealism have been very active and useful to me in recent weeks."

Salem

Following the Treaty of Versailles, Hahn became secretary to Prince Max and moved to Schloss Salem, the prince's castle. In the prince's *Memoirs* both men were critical of Germany's political leaders during the war and expressed the belief that if a defeated Germany was to be regenerated better leadership must be developed through a new kind of education. This was the moment for Hahn to found his public school, but not, he was wise enough to know, by transplanting Eton. With Prince Max as its patron and his son one of the twenty pupils, Salem (located in southwest Germany) opened officially in April 1920.

The prince had made a wing of his castle available for a school and until his death in 1929 played an influential role in its development. The castle for 700 years had been a Cistercian monastery. The monks had worked in the fields, forests, and orchards and village craftsmen became lay brothers. Prince Max and Hahn wanted to continue this tradition of a community home in the new school. Thus from the beginning Salem was co-educational and open to both boarders and day pupils from a variety of classes and backgrounds. The aim of its founders was not, however, to serve only local interests. Prince Max's ambition was "to set in motion, by education, the cure of Germany's international and domestic troubles," and his message to the school staff (written by Hahn) was equally grand:

> Make use of the tragic lesson of the War. See to it that the world of action and the world of thought are no longer two divided camps. Build up the imagination of the boy of decision and the will-power of the dreamer so that in future wise men will have the nerve to lead the way they have shown, and men of action will have the vision to imagine the consequences of their decisions. Nurse the spirit of spontaneous discipline and cooperation, make a national brotherhood of your community, lay the foundation of class peace. Build bridges to the outer world and ultimately create a system of education which can be handed to the nation.[5]

From the beginning, Hahn was in charge of the residential side of the school, a teacher of English and history, and headmaster. With strong support from Prince Max he created a new kind of school for Germany, although he disclaimed originality and acknowledged the many sources from which he "cribbed and copied": Plato, Dr. Arnold of Rugby, Eton, Cecil Reddie of Abbotsholme, and Hermann Lietz and his country home schools. Prince Max also was wary of originality in education and is alleged to have told a visitor to Salem that in both education and medicine one must harvest the wisdom of a thousand years. A surgeon who wants to extract one's appendix in the most original manner possible is not to be trusted.[6]

Yet, despite these disclaimers, Hahn was innovative in how he combined others' ideas in a new way. He wanted his students to dwell in Plato's fair pasture, "a land of health amid fair sights and sounds," but at the same time to be of service to their community, as were the children of Leitz's schools. Also, like Plato, he wanted the child to discover his own unique powers but in a community richer in stimulation than the traditional English public school and more like Abbotsholme, where Cecil Reddie had emphasized modern languages, history, science, music, and crafts. Hahn followed Arnold's example in creating a climate of trust in the school community, but he realized that trust needed to be put into action. This he managed by creating a daily incentive, the training plan, through which students privately and confidentially checked off the many personal activities and responsibilities they were expected to undertake. From the Eton Society he developed the Salem Colour Bearers, a self-electing body of students from which the headmaster appointed "helpers" who shared with him the government of the school.

There is little doubt that Hahn expected Salem, under Prince Max's patronage, to train for leadership the children of the aristocracy and intelligentsia. Attached though he was to the public school ideal, Hahn refused to accept its emphasis on team games, and instituted instead at Salem a mid-morning break of fifty minutes designed to improve physical fitness through running, jumping, and throwing events. Following Reddie's lead, Salem broke with the Victorian tradition of school uniforms and adopted instead a loose-fitting pullover and shorts. It was also Reddie who inspired Hahn to make the morning run and cold shower compulsory.

Thus Salem was a public school with modifications borrowed from the new school movement in Britain and adapted to 1920s Germany. It did not, however, adopt the permissiveness of the more radical progressive schools or the discussion of sex that was frequently part of the open exchange between teachers and students. Throughout his life Hahn resisted Freud's influence and condemned what he felt to be "indiscreet inroads into the psychical inside of a boy." Strong as the British influence was, Salem recognized the realities of post-war Germany. Food was scarce and some children had lost their normal strength and vitality. The school developed its own farm and gardens in which older and stronger pupils worked for two afternoons each week. The athletic training during morning break was non-competitive, and with encouragement rather than pressure each student was expected gradually to improve his performance. This leisurely but regular program of exercise and training was designed to build not only health and fitness but also, in Hahn's words, to develop "resilience, stamina, and powers of concentration." The athletic break was more important than games, and it brought Salem to prominence in Britain in the thirties when its boys won the Challenge Cup for three successive years at the Public Schools Athletics Competition held at White City, London. Although Hahn had left Germany by then, he never tired of insisting that Salem did not coach its students for international competition—indeed, several members of the championship teams had started out as "physical duffers"—it was the daily athletic break that helped them "to defeat their own defeatism."

Each Christmas the school staged a nativity play, reviving a tradition that had started in the valley several hundred years earlier but had died out. Upwards of a thousand villagers attended. Hahn directed Shakespearian tragedies, *Hamlet* in particular, and in the early years of Irish independence *Cathleen ni Houlihan* was performed several times. When the ravages of inflation were over and it was possible for German youth to travel again, twenty Salem students toured the lakes of Finland in open boats. This expedition was the forerunner of the adventure-with-risk experience that became an essential part of the Hahn tradition.

His emphasis on service began in a thoroughly practical way when Salem boys formed a fire brigade to be used by the local community. By 1932 there were signs of a "Salem Movement." Four other schools had been founded under Salem auspices, two of which were junior or "feeder" schools for ten- to thirteen-year-olds. Total enrolment in the early thirties was 420 and Hahn by then was negotiating with education authorities in several cities to develop day schools on Salem principles. He also planned to transplant the athletic training and community service programs to the universities, but his first attempt, at Heidelberg, did not take root.

As a member of the Jewish middle-class intelligentsia, an Anglophile, an internationalist, and a liberal, it was inevitable that Hahn would sooner or later clash with Hitler and the Nazi movement. It was not, however, until 1932 that Hahn was fully convinced of the ultimate evil of Hitler and his party. Prior to that time he had seen Hitler as the leader of a national revival who was, unhappily, reckless and surrounded by undesirable elements—gangsters, adventurers, and former convicts. The event that persuaded Hahn to take a different view and a clear and courageous stand was the Potempa or Beuthen murder. In the autumn of 1932 five S.A. men trampled a young communist to death at Beuthen before the eyes of his mother. They were imprisoned, tried, and sentenced to death, but Hitler intervened and greeted them as "comrades" in a telegram of appreciation and praise. In response to this action, Hahn sent a letter to all former Salem boys and girls which said in part:

> By the telegram of Hitler to the "comrades" of Beuthen a fight has been initiated which goes far beyond politics. Germany is at stake, its Christian way of life, its reputation, the honour of its soldiers; Salem cannot remain neutral. I call upon the members of the Salem

Association who are engaged in S.A. or S.S. work to break their allegiance either to Hitler or to Salem.[7]

Some members of the Salem Association strongly disapproved of Hahn's letter, fearing that when Hitler came to power the school would feel his revenge. But Hahn had no regrets and followed up his letter with two public addresses elaborating his opposition to Hitler's degradation of human dignity and Christian compassion. In January 1933 Hitler was appointed chancellor by President Hindenburg and charged with forming a national government. Hahn knew that his stand had been noticed (he had already been labelled "a notorious Freemason and arch-Jew" in a Nazi newspaper) and following the Reichstag fire of 4 March he was arrested in a mass imprisonment of liberals, socialists, and communists. Through the intervention of the Margrave of Baden (Prince Max's son), Ramsay MacDonald, the British prime minister, and his private secretary, Neville Butler, and other friends and supporters, Hahn was released after five days in Uberlingen jail. In July he left Germany for England. In spite of harassment and intimidation Salem survived and was not taken over by the S.S. until 1944. Meantime, a number of Salem boys, both English and German, were transferred to Hahn's new school, Gordonstoun; one of these was Prince Philip of Greece, later to become the Duke of Edinburgh.

Gordonstoun

Hahn arrived in England depressed and dejected, a refugee with little money, but not without hope and several sources of support. Among his friends from Oxford days was Robin Barrington-Ward, then an assistant editor, later editor, of *The Times,* who assigned to Hahn one of his young colleagues to ensure that Hahn's projects and plans were given adequate publicity. British liberals admired the courage of his anti-Nazi stand and others, interested in the progressive school movement, were impressed with what Hahn had accomplished at Salem. They formed the Friends of Salem, among whom were such influential figures as William Temple (later Archbishop of Canterbury) and the novelist John Buchan, later Governor-General of Canada. Members of the New Education Fellowship invited Hahn to address their meetings and twice in 1934 he spoke over the

BBC. One observer has described Hahn and his effect on the audience at one of the N.E.F. meetings:

> His lectures made a considerable stir, less I think for what they said than for what he was. For whatever you may think of Hahn as an educator you could hardly deny that he had many of the attributes of a Great Man. He gave off personality in thick waves and the personality had a solid Germanic weight behind it.
>
> He had a full wide face with a small resolute chin, jutting firmly out from it. His pronouncements had a ring of both wisdom and authority; they were aphoristic and seemed to dig deep. I can't for the life of me remember any of them now, but I still remember the flavour of them and the aroma of personality with which he invested them. It was, I believe, partly the impression these lectures made that enabled him shortly afterwards to found Gordonstoun.[8]

When his friends asked Hahn to create a school in Britain on Salem lines he at first refused. He was now forty-seven and not in good health; in 1934 the prospects of raising money for a new school were not promising; and there was sharp competition for pupils among existing public schools. But a visit to Morayshire helped to change his mind. There he re-met the Smith-Cumming family, who were prepared to lease Gordonstoun House at the very low rental of £100 per year. Built originally in the seventeenth century and modified many times, the house by 1934 was suffering from years of neglect. In contrast with the founding of Salem, Hahn had no patron, no well-ordered estate or spacious buildings, and no capital except for a few modest gifts. He did, however, have the support of influential friends who had now formed British Salem Schools Limited. His first prospectus listed Lady Smith-Cumming as presiding over the household; a group of four "character training" instructors would take charge of seamanship, climbing, gardening, and craft work, and another five would form the academic staff. The thirty-two governors included the Archbishop of York, the Marchioness of Aberdeen, the Lord High Commissioner of the Church of Scotland, the Headmaster of Eton, and the Regius Professor of Modern History, Cambridge. The school opened on 10 May 1934 with an enrolment of thirteen boys. A year later there were forty-five.

When Hahn reported in 1935 to his board on the first year of Gordonstoun he revealed in direct and simple language and with a mixture of idealism and practicality a confidence that the school would succeed. The essence of both Hahn and Gordonstoun may be found in this first report,[9] which begins with a statement of the health of the boys and details of their losses and gains in weight. Hahn then gives his impressions of their well-being—clear skins, absence of slouchiness, and alertness in their bearing—which he attributes to the morning run and cold shower, athletics in the mid-morning break and later in the day. From health and fitness he moves on to character-building through the training plan, which he regards as a Protestant confession to oneself, not the Roman Catholic confession to a stranger. And he is encouraged that after only one year Gordonstoun boys appear to be responding to one of his basic tenets: that a school program of breadth and variety can arouse healthy passions that will absorb a boy's physical and emotional energies and thus help him to withstand the apathy and lassitude that so often afflict the adolescent.

These healthy passions were being nourished through sailing in the school's cutter on Moray Firth, building a stage for *Macbeth,* and accepting responsibility as color bearers or helpers for various aspects of self-government within the school. The school week was organized to give dignity and importance to a wide variety of individual projects so that each boy would be able to find and pursue his *grande passion,* a concept Hahn never abandoned.

In contrast to the traditional public school and following the custom of Salem, Gordonstoun dethroned organized games and gave relatively less emphasis to the academic program. Hahn and his colleagues adopted a modified version of the Dalton Plan, a system of individual assignments originating in the United States. They were convinced that, if motivation were strong, boys would not suffer from less time in class. From the beginning, Gordonstoun had an international flavor, and in its second year fourteen of the forty-five boys came from abroad. A system of grading fees according to the income of parents was soon introduced as a means of attracting boys of different backgrounds. On this matter Hahn was forthright:

> It is quite impossible to conquer the enervating sense of privilege, and to engender the spirit of joyous exertion, unless a considerable minority of our boys come from homes where life is not only simple, but even hard. I need inside Gordonstoun House, not only

> the brotherhood of nations, and of religions, I need the brotherhood of classes which is more difficult to achieve.[10]

Hahn also felt the need for close ties with Morayshire farmers and villagers. They had come to see the nativity play produced during the first year and plans were taking shape in Hahn's mind for a coast guard watch tower, but he also wanted local boys to attend Gordonstoun and fishermen and craftsmen of the district to serve as instructors. With old world courtesy he thanked the board for allowing him "to pitch his tent" in Morayshire. In his view: "Gordonstoun is situated in a peaceful and fertile land, but there is challenge on the horizon; to the north the challenge of the sea, and to the south the challenge of high hills."[11]

It was a vigorous and optimistic report given both with flair and formality in spite of an attendance of only nine of the thirty-two board members and the shadow of a bank overdraft of £2,000. Hahn's reputation for his work at Salem and his confidence and enthusiasm in the face of the difficulties of creating a new school in a remote area on a derelict estate must have inspired his board. They decided to raise £25,000 and thus enrol 100 boys over the next two to three years, and the chairman of the board commented that many educators had told him that no educational experiment in Britain was more important.

This initial confidence and optimism were harshly tested in the next ten years. At one point the chairman did not expect the school to survive, so severe were its financial troubles. There was no doubt in his mind that Gordonstoun could serve a useful purpose for a few years by demonstrating the Salem system, but that might be all that it could accomplish. With no endowment, the school had to rely on fees for its income. This meant enrolment must rise steadily, which in turn created a need for increased dormitory accommodation and a larger staff. To pay for these, still higher enrolment was required. Even the prestige of its headmaster and the innovations of its program were not sufficient to attract a substantial proportion of intellectually able boys. The common entrance examination normally required by the public schools was frequently waived, and boys who had failed to obtain entrance to the older schools or were obliged to leave such schools were accepted by Gordonstoun. This "comprehensive" aspect of the school had its merits; it meant that within the student body there would be "late bloomers," gifted rebels who could not tolerate the rigidities of traditional schools, and timid, sensitive, and imaginative youngsters who were happier in a setting which did not put major emphasis on games. But the fact that Gordonstoun attracted only a modest proportion of boys who were intellectually gifted affected its record on examination results, particularly for admission to Oxford and Cambridge; this in turn persuaded a good many parents of bright boys to enrol them elsewhere.

A traumatic event in the first ten years was the evacuation of the school to Wales. Although Hahn had become a naturalized British subject in 1938, there were lingering suspicions that he could be a spy. Some fifteen German boys and a dozen German adults were living on the school grounds at the outbreak of war in 1939 and there was a fear in the local community that this group might engage in fifth-column tactics. In 1940 Hahn negotiated with Lord Davies, parent of two Gordonstoun boys, to allow the school to move to his country home in central Wales. These negotiations were conducted in a style entirely typical of Hahn. He and his director of studies journeyed by taxi to Aviemore to meet Lord Davies in his train compartment and ordered the taxi to follow the train. At each station the director of studies slipped off the train, reported the state of negotiations to the taxi driver—now growing increasingly anxious about his rationed petrol—and persuaded him to go yet another station further.

Ten masters had left Gordonstoun to join the forces and five German teachers were interned as enemy aliens, so when the move to Wales took place enrolment dropped by one-third. A new financial crisis would have closed the school permanently had the governors not raised a £5,000 loan. Hahn reported wryly that in 1941 some of his staunchest friends came to offer their condolences and others arrived "manifestly measuring us for our coffin."

Three years later his tone had changed: the crisis was over, there was a financial surplus, and enrolment had increased appreciably.[12] Hahn reflects on the move to Wales and admits that for a time Gordonstoun-in-exile was not a happy ship. A number of boys lost their faith in the self-governing system of the school and some also lost their integrity. But then Hahn makes a very characteristic remark: "But the young have a power of recovery that astounds me ever again."[13] He also kept his faith in the public school system and in typical aphorisms list the qualities the schools seek to develop: "confidence in effort, modesty in success, grace in defeat, fairness in anger, clear judgment even in the bitterness of wounded pride and readiness for service at all times." But he fears that only the best in the public schools become men who can justify the privileges they enjoy. For an increasing number of boys who emerge from the schools, "it is not their inner life, but rather their gestures and intonation which are characteristic of the great institutions to which they belong. Ease and assurance remain impressive even if they are hollow."[14]

In looking to the future Hahn predicts a doubling of numbers when the school returned to Morayshire. In what is essentially a vision of a New Gordonstoun he reaffirms his long-held belief that a community of adolescent males can be kept spiritually healthy only if it refuses to become isolated. For Gordonstoun this would mean opening a day school which, together with the boarding school, would be the core of the "school city." Around these would be a number of vocational houses offering technical instruction in seamanship, agriculture, and forestry. All boys would dine together, and chapel services, the morning break, and expeditions would be common activities. Furthermore, boys from local villages would come to train on Gordonstoun playing fields. Clearly, Gordonstoun was not to serve only the sons of wealthy families. Hahn was, in fact, reaffirming the principles he had declared in his first annual report ten years before and still earlier at Salem.

In 1945 the school moved back to Morayshire and the formidable task of rebuilding began. Gordonstoun House, gutted by fire, had to be restored; Nissen huts scattered throughout the estate were converted into classrooms, workshops, and living quarters; and houses were bought or leased up to twenty miles away to accommodate the increased enrolment. In 1947, again with the help of a bank loan, the school bought Gordonstoun House and the estate of 300 acres from the Smith-Cumming family. Any hope of realizing Hahn's dream of a "school city" or "Greater Gordonstoun" had to be delayed, if not abandoned, in the face of the urgency of finding, renovating, or building facilities and accommodation for the core enterprise—the public school. The post-war years were difficult and frustrating until Antonin Besse, a French philanthropist, visited the school and saw both its potential and current needs. He agreed to donate £65,000 over five years. This was the turning point in the financial life of the school and from the date of the Besse bequest there has been steady progress in consolidating all buildings on the Gordonstoun estate.

In 1952 Hahn's old ailment returned and while in the United States he suffered a heat stroke. The effects of this stroke were so severe that he retired from Gordonstoun the following year. He was then sixty-seven. Two years later a surgeon in Freiburg operated so successfully that Hahn was again able to travel, lecture, and use his considerable energy to found and further several new projects. Under new leadership Gordonstoun continued to flourish and in the next two decades spent some £2 million on new buildings and the upkeep and improvement of existing structures. By 1977 the school was no longer in debt. As the school looked toward its fiftieth anniversary in 1984 the primary aim of the Golden Jubilee Appeal was to add substantially to the scholarship fund. Michael Mavor, who became headmaster in 1979, was determined to improve the academic performance of his school but at the same time keep the distinctive features that are a part of the Hahn legacy. The mid-morning "athletic break" had disappeared and the early morning run and cold shower were not quite the ritual they were in an earlier day. Enrolment had increased to 450, of which well over 100 were girls.

Traditions that began with Hahn are, however, still in evidence. Through the Seamanship Department all students learn to sail; the various rescue and community services are fully subscribed each year and bring the school into touch with the needs of local communities; students work half a day each week, often longer, on individual projects; and there is a high level of interest in music and theatre, the visual arts and various crafts. The training plan, Hahn's vehicle for demonstrating the value of trust in a school community, lives on. Student government is shared by students with different responsibilities and called color bearers and helpers, and a guardian, the head of the school, who in 1978–79 was for the first time a girl. Organized games are compulsory on two afternoons a week but with time needed for the services, projects, seamanship, and the arts there is no possibility that games will dominate extracurricular life. Among both staff and students Hahn is remembered with a respect that verges on awe and an affection that grows through the retelling of anecdotes that reveal his eccentricities. There are, however, few references in staff room conversations to "the enervating sense of privilege" or the *grandes passions*.

The Badge Schemes and Outward Bound

Within two years of the founding of Gordonstoun, Hahn was planning and publicizing a national scheme of tests and expeditions for British youth. As a model, Gordonstoun would become a part of the Moray community and open its athletic instruction and facilities to every boy in the district who wanted to use them. "The time is past," Hahn said, "when one can with an easy mind segregate boys and girls in beautiful houses and cut them off from the world. . . . Public schools should build themselves into strongholds of fitness for the districts in which they are placed."[15] Toward the end of 1936 Gordonstoun joined with Elgin Academy, a large day school nearby, in instituting the "Moray Badge." This was a scheme of tests in athletics and life-saving, and climbing, sailing, or riding expeditions. Gordonstoun already had ties with its community through H.M. Coastguard and its relations with local fishermen were cordial. But it was the fishermen's children who were Hahn's chief concern, particularly during their adolescence. Typically, he expressed his impressions forcefully: never had he known children of greater promise, but rarely had he encountered "more typical louts once they were half-way through puberty. . . . Who could witness this decline without feeling guilty that certain healing experiences were withheld from the underprivileged youth of the country?"[16]

As a means of announcing the badge plan Hahn wrote an open letter to *The Times*. (This letter was dated 1 November and printed on 3 November 1936, an indication that the editor made good his promise not to neglect Hahn's public appeals.) The letter gives details of the physical fitness program of Salem, reminds readers of the success of Salem boys at White City, and mentions the German sports badge as a forerunner to the Moray badge. Hahn's intent was to stimulate the voluntary organizations of Britain to co-operate in developing a nation-wide training scheme modelled on the Moray badge but modified according to regional opportunities. The letter ended with a plea to examination boards to recognize passes in fitness tests as the equivalent academic credits. Hahn received only one letter in reply. His attempts to gather support from the Board (later Ministry) of Education were equally disappointing. When he asked its president "What are you doing to molest the contentedly unfit?" the reply, according to Hahn, was "Nothing whatever."

By 1938 Hahn realized that residential summer schools were needed to demonstrate and test the Moray badge scheme. Three were organized, each for two weeks, one being based at Gordonstoun. These schools proved to Hahn and the others involved in their organization that in a two-week period the danger of overstrain was too great. Hahn's goal now was residential courses of one month for boys at work so that, as he said, "the twenty-third psalm was no longer suspended for the underprivileged youth of the country. Every youngster has a right to experience which restoreth his soul."[17]

During the first year of the war several prominent men, including Lord Dawson of Penn (the king's physician) and the Archbishop of Canterbury wrote letters to *The Times*, and Philip Noel-Baker spoke in the House of Commons urging the government to apply nationally the lessons learned from recent experiments in northern Scotland. A prestigious committee chaired by the Master of Balliol, A. D. (later Lord) Lindsay, was created to launch further experiments to test the training scheme and the name was changed from the Moray to the county badge. But there was still little evidence of nation-wide enthusiasm. Voluntary youth organizations were un-cooperative and only one local education authority, Hertfordshire, was prepared to launch a pilot program. The Board of Education was not ready to incorporate County badge activities into the national system of education and refused to award a grant toward the founding of a permanent short-term residential school. These disappointments did not deter Hahn, but rather persuaded him that letters and public appeals were going to have little effect. What was needed was a permanent "training home" or centre at which the Lindsay Committee could demonstrate the four aspects of the county badge scheme (project, expedition, athletics, and service) in one-month courses for young people from industry and the schools.

First the committee needed a full-time secretary and Hahn's choice, with full committee support, was J. M. Hogan, a secondary school teacher and a leader of youth groups. Hogan, himself a strong personality, had to stand up to Hahn whenever they had a difference of opinion. He had no reservations about Hahn's pioneering spirit and educational perception but he did have doubts about Hahn's tactics:

> On a number of occasions . . . we had our differences. . . . But opposing Hahn was a testing business. His exasperation could mount very quickly and when roused he would thunder at his critics, shaking

> his forefinger from his greatly superior height and flashing his eyes with righteous rage and indignation. . . . Without at least the outward appearance of independence I think I should have found it impossible to keep Hahn within what seemed to be the bounds of the reasonably practical.[18]

In the summer of 1940 Hahn organized a second experimental course, this time at Gordonstoun's new home in Wales. It was a three-week course for secondary school boys, Merchant Navy cadets, working boys, and twenty young army recruits sent by the War Office. Again the need for a year-round permanent centre for short-term residential courses was demonstrated. The evidence from the several summer schools together with the urgings of the County Badge Committee were, however, not persuasive enough. The necessary catalyst was war, particularly the war at sea. By 1941 the Merchant Navy was suffering heavy losses in the Atlantic. One shipowner most concerned about the loss of merchant seamen was Lawrence Holt, senior member of Alfred Holt and Company, owners of the Blue Funnel Line. He was sufficiently impressed by Hahn's work at Gordonstoun that he had enrolled one of his sons, and when Hahn decided that Gordonstoun's schooner, *Prince Louis,* should be sailed down from Scotland through the Caledonian Canal and despite war-time hazards along the west coast to Wales, it was men from Holt's company who were in command, with Gordonstoun boys serving as crew.

When *Prince Louis* finally arrived at Bangor after a three-week voyage, Hahn and Holt were among the welcoming party. Shortly afterward Hahn arranged a conversation between Holt and Hogan, who had agreed to become warden of a training centre if funds could be found. In this conversation Holt revealed that he had studied the accounts of survivors of enemy action in the Atlantic and had become convinced that the majority of merchant seamen whose ships were sunk were unprepared for the ordeals of managing small craft.

The merger of Holt's concerns with Hahn's county badge scheme was not difficult to arrange. Candidates for the county badge were required to pass physical tests involving swimming, running, jumping, and throwing; to complete a project demanding prolonged study or performance in some art or craft or skill; to go on an expedition requiring careful preparation and stamina; and to train for some form of service. Using the site Hahn had already chosen at Aberdovey on the west coast of Wales, small boat sailing and instruction in seamanship could form the basis of project work. Stamina in physical training together with technical skill could be developed and tested in expeditions at sea and in the hill country close by. As for service, lifeboat drills and the use of rocket apparatus could give training for rescue operations.

Lawrence Holt and his business colleagues saw these possibilities and in a meeting with Hogan in August 1941 agreed to buy the house Hahn had rented, to second trained personnel needed for seamanship instruction, and to subscribe £1,000 for equipment—all with one proviso, that the centre would open in five weeks' time. In spite of wartime shortages, difficulties in recruiting staff, and problems of accommodation, the "school" opened on schedule on 4 October 1941 with twenty-four boys enrolled. Gordonstoun loaned its director of physical training, Dr. Bernhard Zimmermann, like Hahn a refugee from Germany, and Holt and Company supplied all the staff for instruction in sailing and seamanship. In addition, they provided bunks, bedding, and household furniture from the company's stores in Liverpool. Lawrence Holt gave the school its name—the Outward Bound Sea School—and was chairman of the board for its first twelve years.

The Outward Bound Trust

In reflecting some years later on the beginning of Outward Bound, Hahn, with typical indirectness and his customary optimism, wrote: "Everyone who saw what can happen to boys in four weeks [at Aberdovey] as a result of certain 'healing' experiences felt convinced, as a friend put it, that we had the duty of multiplication."[19] The expansion of the Outward Bound idea became for Hahn a personal crusade. By 1944 some 1,000 boys in twenty courses had passed through Aberdovey; they came from the Merchant Service, the Royal Navy, business firms, industry, and secondary schools. Gordonstoun boys enrolled for the one-month course during term time and when the school returned to Scotland after the war Hahn lost no time in setting up the Moray Sea School in close association with Gordonstoun's own seamanship program. This was not, however, the pace of development that he would have liked. In the post-war years he publicly urged a network of residential county colleges, one for boys, another for girls, in each county, enrolling adolescents of fifteen to eighteen with courses modelled on Aberdovey and on sites near mountains or by the sea.[20] These colleges should offer ten courses a year, each for one month. But expansion was to come more slowly and under the auspices of a new organization, the Outward Bound Trust.

By 1946 Aberdovey had cost Alfred Holt and Company some £20,000 to establish and maintain; in addition, nautical staff and galley boys seconded to the school were a hidden subsidy. New sources of funding had to be found and an organizational structure created. On Hahn's suggestion a group of Gordonstoun and Aberdovey supporters early in 1946 met in Trinity College, Cambridge, under the auspices of the Master, George Trevelyan. Three members of the group had been founding governors of Gordonstoun in 1934. A decision was taken to establish the Outward Bound Trust, a foundation that would develop the Aberdovey experiment on a national scale. One of the Trust's first transactions was to receive from Alfred Holt and Company the gift of the Aberdovey buildings and their forty-acre site. As always, Hahn had chosen the members of the Trust for their capacity to arouse interest among benefactors and sponsors. Within a year of the founding the first executive officer of the Trust was making an extensive tour of factories and schools, and Seebohm Rowntree, President of the Trust, arranged for the Rowntree Village Trust to pay the salary and expenses of a full-time director. In 1948 Field-Marshall Montgomery launched an appeal for £100,000, and a year later the Duke of Edinburgh was guest of honor at a fund-raising dinner in the Mayfair Hotel.

The publicity given to this event was invaluable, and the next morning a supporter appeared and offered to lend £15,000 free of interest for starting a second school. The Trust then bought a spacious country house in the Lake District and renovated it into the Eskdale Outward Bound Mountain School. On Hahn's suggestion Arnold Adam-Brown, post-war chairman of the Gordonstoun Old Boys' Association, applied for the position of warden and following rigorous interviews, received the appointment. Eskdale opened its first course in March 1950, but the official opening ceremonies were held in June when George Tomlinson, Minister of Education, gave the chief address.

By the mid-fifties Outward Bound had become a movement. The Moray Sea School had been incorporated into the Trust and a new mountain school had opened at Ullswater. More than 700 firms were sponsoring their young employees (paying fees and continuing to pay wages or salary), and over seventy Education Authorities were sending boys to Outward Bound courses, usually in their final year of school. In all, over 20,000 boys had passed through Outward Bound by 1956. A course for girls had opened at Eskdale in 1951 with only slight modifications from the standard mountain school course. As a symbol of institutional respectability and well-being the Trust designed an old school tie—a yellow rope on a dark blue background.

Following the Eskdale course for girls a dozen similar courses were offered at existing schools until a girls' school, Rhowniar, was established in Wales a few miles from Aberdovey in 1963. The two schools have now merged to become Outward Bound Wales, and both programs are co-educational. The Trust has also encouraged wardens of the several schools to diversify their programs by initiating new courses designed for a wide range of ages and lasting for a varying number of weeks. This diversification began in the seventies and was largely a response to an economic crisis which arose when Local Education Authorities terminated their sponsorship because of budget stringencies. While the standard course for sixteen- to twenty-year-olds (now reduced to twenty-one days) is still basic to all programs, there are courses for ten- to thirteen- and fourteen- to sixteen-year-olds, a course designed for young people at the beginning of their working careers, two-week courses for business executives, and contract courses organized specifically for the employees of particular corporations. Perhaps the most radical departure from the earlier courses is "City Challenge," a program of voluntary service in urban settings. Outward Bound students, aged seventeen to twenty-five, work with handicapped children, homeless adults, or geriatric patients over a three-week period and discover not only the social and human problems of the city but also their own capacity for understanding and compassion. These courses, which began in Leeds in 1967 through the initiative and foresight of Captain J. F. Fuller, then warden of Aberdovey, have been held in several British cities.

Overseas Expansion

Throughout the fifties and sixties the Trust assisted in founding schools abroad. In post-war Germany, Hahn was active as early as the summer of 1945 in working with British, American, and German officials to establish schools on the Outward Bound model. With the aid of American funds Hahn arranged for a group of

German educators to visit Gordonstoun and the British Outward Bound Schools. Sir Spencer Summers, a founding member of Outward Bound Trust, travelled extensively in Germany to interpret Outward Bound principles. The result was the opening of a country home on the Baltic with its own lifeboat and fire brigade. Two other schools were later established, at Baad and Berchtesgaden, and both became mountaineering schools with expeditions, rescue exercises, and service to the community forming the central features of their work.

The Trust has also encouraged the development of schools in several Commonwealth countries. Between 1955 and 1981 Outward Bound schools opened in Australia, Canada, Hong Kong, Kenya, Lesotho, Malaysia, New Zealand, Rhodesia, Singapore, Tanzania, and Zambia. Six have been established in the United States. Usually these schools have grown out of experimental courses organized by a national committee or central organization in which graduates of Outward Bound frequently have played an active role. And it has not been unusual for the Trust to respond to requests for advice and counsel by sending a member abroad to meet with a national committee, arrange staff exchanges, and otherwise encourage the founding of new schools that maintain Outward Bound's principles, health and safety provisions, and standards of leadership. Procedurally, the Trust charters a national organization which in turn becomes responsible for founding schools permitted to operate under the name Outward Bound.

In 1950, at the instigation of Mrs. Lewis Douglas, the wife of the former United States ambassador to the Court of St. James, a young American teacher, Joshua Miner, was asked to make a six-week visit to Europe to learn about Hahn's work. He visited Salem, Gordonstoun, and Aberdovey and later, on Hahn's invitation, joined the Gordonstoun staff. Eighteen months later he returned to the United States determined, as he has said, "to insert as much as possible the philosophy and techniques of Kurt Hahn in the mainstream of American education."[21] He joined the teaching staff of one of the United States's oldest and most prestigious independent schools, Phillips Academy in Andover, Massachusetts (not exactly a mainstream institution), and was instrumental in incorporating the Gordonstoun athletic break and several aspects of Outward Bound into the Academy program. He was also largely responsible for creating the enthusiasm which led to the 1963 founding of Outward Bound Incorporated, the national organization for Outward Bound development in the United States. Earlier, however, and with the assistance of Captain J. F. Fuller, warden of Aberdovey, the first American school had opened in Colorado in 1961. In the early days of the Peace Corps, Fuller also was a consultant to Sargent Shriver, the first director, and conducted the initial training course for Peace Corps volunteers in an Outward Bound type of school in Puerto Rico. The schools that now operate under the auspices of Outward Bound Inc. are mountain schools in Colorado, New Mexico, and Oregon; wilderness area schools in Minnesota and North Carolina; and a sea school on an island off the coast of Maine.

Outward Bound activity in the United States is not confined to these schools. The parent organization has encouraged public and independent secondary schools, youth services, and other agencies to incorporate Outward Bound-like activity into their own programs. Outdoor education is now a recognized part of the curriculum in American schools. In Georgia, Colorado, and Massachusetts, Outward Bound programs for young offenders have been introduced, and experimental evidence has shown that the rate of recidivism has been reduced.[22] Variations of Outward Bound have been offered to minority group young people in the inner cities in an effort to give late adolescents a sense of their own potential and an outlet, other than violence, for their energy and initiative. These programs, variations or imitations of Outward Bound, number well over a hundred. In these ways Miner and his colleagues have inserted Hahn's philosophy into American education.

The first Outward Bound School in Canada opened in 1969 near Keremeos in British Columbia. It was a mountain school modelled on the British schools; the moving spirit in its founding, Arthur Rogers, had spent two years at Eskdale. Five years later Robert Pieh opened a wilderness school in Ontario, 100 miles north of Lake Superior. It was patterned on the American school which Pieh had started in 1964 in the maze of lakes and streams which form two million acres of wilderness on the Minnesota-Ontario border. In principle, the Canadian and American schools are in the Hahn tradition, but each has greater autonomy than the British schools. Few of their students, probably less than 10 per cent, are sent by their employers as part of their job training. And instead of using a country estate or manor house as a base, the North American schools tend to organize mobile programs in which young people, organized in brigades or watches, travel by canoe, sailboat, or on foot and sleep under canvas. Between 1962 and

1979 some 68,000 Americans alone had enrolled in Outward Bound.

Since 1941 Outward Bound has been exported, imitated, modified, and reshaped. When Geoffrey Winthrop Young, a founder of Gordonstoun and of the Outward Bound Trust, spoke at the opening of Eskdale, he dwelt at some length on the purpose of the school:

> Every individual should be given an adventure early in life, so that he may discover himself in the round, and may make a beginning with repairing the weakness, as well as of exercising the strength, of the self he discovers. Upon that basis alone can he begin effectively to know others as they are, and rightly direct his altruistic instinct, to serve his friends, his country and his kind. . . .
>
> We are not concerned here—and I wish to emphasize this—to turn boys into good or bad climbers. This is not a school of mountaineering. It is a Mountaineering School. Our concern is to bring the mountains to bear, as an incitement, an influence, a discipline, upon the characters of those attending our Courses. Many of us know from our own lives, that mountains can have this inspirational and educative power. They have given us our adventure, taught us discipline and friendship, awakened us to beauty and to the vitalizing feelings of awe and reverence. It is when physical strength and endurance have been tried to their utmost, that we become most sensitized to beauty, aware of deeper emotional possibilities in ourselves.[23]

This passage clearly implies that schools in different settings will have different programs and, to a degree, different purposes. Subsequent developments have confirmed this view. The Mountain School at Loitokitok in Kenya, at which the climax of the course is climbing Mount Kilimanjaro, has enrolled Africans, Asians, and Europeans and stressed the need for racial tolerance and co-operation. The Hurricane Island School of Maine ran a winter course within a state school for young offenders, and City Challenge courses in Britain provide students with entirely different environments and challenges. With considerable autonomy, the schools are run according to the visions of their wardens, the capabilities of their staff, and the opportunities offered by their "hinterland."

Early brochures carried the legend "Character-training through adventure and testing experience." As a former warden who did not like the term "character-training" remarked, "One pictures a group of boys arriving full of personal oddities and idiosyncracies, and leaving at the end of the month uniformly clean-limbed, keen-eyed and self-confident, 'the finished product'."[24] Recent attempts to attract wider sponsorship from business and industry have led another warden to use sociological jargon with tongue in cheek to interpret current objectives: "We are the agents of industrial trainers, concerned with attitudinal change in late adolescence by using stressful, task-related activities leading to peak experiences with resultant behavioural modification heightened by small-group interaction."[25] Behind the levity and the jargon and from evidence of Outward Bound experience over more than forty years on five continents it can be said that the essential features of the schools have not changed. Kurt Hahn's original concepts have taken many and varied institutional forms and have been adapted to many different settings. Some of the language he used in the early years on the values of Outward Bound—the brotherhood of adventure, healing experience, danger that cleanses and restores—may sound archaic, and wardens seldom speak now of "developing character," although they may believe that that is their function. Regardless of language, Hahn's contribution originally through the county badge scheme and in later years more indirectly and from behind the scenes through the Trust is a rich endowment. His basic belief that adolescents and young adults can achieve self-discovery through facing challenging experience in a group setting has remained at the heart of Outward Bound.

The Duke of Edinburgh's Award

Outward Bound had proved the merits of the county badge scheme but Hahn knew that one-month courses in a residential setting could not attract large numbers of young people. He returned, therefore, to the badge scheme and in the mid-fifties discussed it with the Duke of Edinburgh and Sir John Hunt, leader of the British expedition that had climbed Mount Everest in 1953. Hunt and Hahn had met during the war when Hunt was attached to an army unit in Wales not far from Gordonstoun's wartime home. He had visited Eskdale before and after the Everest victory to talk about the expedition. Before his retirement from Gordonstoun, Hahn had offered Hunt the post of provost. Although Hunt declined that offer Hahn continued to pursue him and invited him to become a member of the organizing committee then beginning to plan a new award scheme. Hunt has described their meeting and added his impressions of Hahn:

> In the autumn of 1954, when I was Assistant Commandant of the Army Staff College, I received a telephone call from Hahn; he wished to see me that same afternoon. It was typical of the man that his business would brook no delay. I remember his arrival at the portals of that distinguished building, presenting a somewhat cloak-and-dagger appearance to the doorman in his broad-rimmed black felt hat. On being ushered into my room his first act, before offering me a limp hand-shake, was to advance to the windows and throw them wide open; it was a cold November evening and the central heating was on. I think he tended to feel claustrophobic, but it made the interview a trifle unrelaxed. Perhaps it was all part of his technique. He sat hunched in a chair, his bald head slightly bent, his pale blue eyes transfixing me, but contriving to charm me with a singularly sweet smile. He told me in his soft, German-accented voice of his long cherished hopes of persuading his former pupil Prince Philip to give his name to a royal award, which would supersede the County Badge scheme; the Prince had at last consented. Hahn had arranged a small dinner party in Brown's Hotel for the following evening, at which a few people who had agreed to help work out the scheme would be present; would my wife and I join them? He wanted me to give advice on the conditions for adventurous journeys which would be a key feature of the award scheme.
>
> Hahn, a confirmed bachelor, was a skilful operator. He knew the value of enlisting the support of the woman in a family ménage, in order to secure the services of someone he needed. He made a lasting impression on my wife, clicking his heels as he bent over her hand. His forte was in choosing men, implanting his ideas in their minds and guiding them from the rear; that was his style of leadership. . . . Greatly as I admired Hahn, my contrary nature prompted me to resist the spell he cast on some; I think I was a disappointment to him. He appeared to exercise an influence upon some people which can best be described as mesmeric. I was conscious of its bearing on myself and, although I recognized the total integrity of the man and the basic truths behind his vision, I declined to succumb to that influence.[26]

Hunt may have believed that he could resist Hahn's spell, but he has since admitted that Hahn's visit was a turning point in his life and the beginning of the end of his career as a soldier.[27] His work on the committee so convinced him of the merits of Hahn's ideas that he suggested to Prince Philip that he administer the scheme. In accepting Hunt's offer, the prince confirmed Hahn's capacity to choose men and guide them from the rear.

In February 1956 the Duke of Edinburgh's Award Scheme was announced. Originally it was designed for boys between the age of fifteen, when the great majority then left school, and eighteen, the point at which they were called up for national service. During their spare time they could choose from a wide range of activities in four main areas: service, expeditions, pursuits, and fitness. Each boy would progress through three standards or levels of performance of increasing degrees of difficulty. The scheme began with enthusiastic support from most voluntary youth organizations, and before the first year was out there was strong pressure to lower the age of entry to fourteen, to begin a similar scheme for girls, and to find ways for local education authorities to be more actively involved. Throughout the first twenty-five years of the scheme, Prince Philip maintained his support and enthusiasm by chairing meetings of the board of trustees in Buckingham Palace, visiting various youth groups, and presenting awards in the United Kingdom and abroad.

In its first quarter century the scheme has shown its capacity to change and expand. With the demise of national service in 1958 there was no longer a good reason to retain the age limit of eighteen. Nor any reason to limit the scheme to boys. Young people from fourteen to twenty-five are now eligible, and close to two million in the United Kingdom and abroad have entered the scheme.[28] The activities are now designated as service, expeditions, skills, and physical recreation, and demanding levels of performance still lead to bronze, silver, and gold awards.

Handicapped youth are encouraged to enter the scheme and a special guidebook has been prepared for them. Young delinquents in custodial centres or on probation may also enrol but entry into the scheme must be voluntary. Youth leaders and social workers make vigorous efforts to attract disadvantaged youth to enter the scheme—with only modest success. "Problem" youngsters are not inclined to join social organizations, particularly those they associate with the establishment and royal patronage. Successful as the scheme may have been, it is not a panacea for urban crime or football hooliganism, and in any given year fewer than 10 per cent of the age group in Britain is actively involved in it. Nevetherless, by any measure—participation, diversity of program, quality of leadership, volunteer assistance, and support by local and national bodies—the scheme is the most successful youth program ever mounted in Britain.

It has also thrived when transplanted abroad. Thirty-eight countries or territories outside the United Kingdom had award programs in operation in 1980, all of which followed the essential philosophy and structure of the scheme. Most are members of the Commonwealth, but not all are prepared to follow the British practice of royal sponsorship. In Kenya and Sierra Leone, for example, the program is known as the President's Award Scheme. A similar scheme, but with no official connection, is the Congressional Award inaugurated in the United States in 1980 after receiving the blessing and enabling legislation from both Houses of Congress.

The scheme is not in itself a youth organization; indeed, its genius is to delegate responsibility to existing bodies, known as operating authorities, which are licensed to administer the program and grant awards on behalf of Prince Philip, or, as the case may be, the head of state. The authorities carrying the bulk of responsibility are national youth organizations and local education authorities. Within these the major "user units" are the youth service clubs and schools. Thus some 10,000 state-supported and independent schools, youth groups, industrial and commercial firms, police and fire services, and armed forces establishments have formed a network to work with young people either individually or in groups. Both professionals and interested amateurs provide adult leadership and instruction.

Hahn's influence is evident in the delineation of requirements, particularly those in the expeditions section. Expeditions may be undertaken on land or water for all three levels of award, and one option in the gold requirements is a four-day journey on foot of not less than fifty miles in wild country in groups of four to seven members. Such a journey must be planned with great care under the supervision of experienced adults, about which Hahn was adamant. Although he linked physical challenge with adventure training, he always insisted on the highest standard of safety measures, the need to know first aid and rescue techniques, and the use of proper equipment.

The Duke of Edinburgh's Award Scheme is thus a direct link with Hahn's Moray and county badges. It is more sophisticated and has a wider range of choices than its predecessors and is thus able to relate to young people of all abilities and backgrounds, in many parts of the world. While sensitive to their varied needs it can change in practice but hold to principle. Many factors have led to its success, not the least of which have been the continuing leadership of the Duke of Edinburgh and, in the early years, the contribution of Sir John Hunt. Kurt Hahn's indirect contribution has been assessed by Peter Carpenter:

> Although he was involved in the discussion which preceded the setting up of the Award in 1956, he has played no part in it since then. This is characteristic. . . . He is essentially a visionary whose prime concern is not with the implementation of his ideas. But he has an uncanny gift for finding people who will take up and develop his ideas, and of inspiring them to do what might well seem an impossibility. . . . Once having launched a project, his restless and fertile mind soon turns to other matters. Whatever they are . . . there can be little doubt that there is no more far-reaching medium through which Hahn has made his influence felt than the Duke of Edinburgh's Award.[29]

Atlantic College and the United World Colleges

According to Hahn, the plan for the Atlantic Colleges was born in Paris in 1955.[30] That year he met Air Marshall Lawrence Darvall and together they discussed Darvall's experience as Commandant of the NATO Defence College in Paris. Darvall spoke of his belief that among officers and diplomats who had attended the college, prejudices were reduced and tolerance increased. He asked Hahn whether these results would not be even more striking if a group of young men from the countries of the Atlantic community were brought together at their most impressionable age and given the opportunity to live in residential colleges. The initial proposal developed by Hahn and Darvall was ambitious: six colleges to be set up in six different countries—Canada, France, Great Britain, Greece, West Germany, and the United States. Carefully selected boys, aged sixteen to nineteen, from the fifteen NATO nations and other countries, eventually including those of the Soviet bloc, would enrol for a two-year course and prepare for university entrance through examinations recognized throughout the world. Each national group would be accompanied by a teacher of their own language, and boys would live in their own "national houses" equipped with furniture, pictures, and books to remind them of home. A rigorous academic curriculum would be combined with rescue training, life-saving techniques, and expeditions in mountains or on the sea.

By 1958 Hahn was speaking publicly of this plan at the Atlantic Community Conference at Bruges,[31] and he and Darvall asked Desmond Hoare, then on the staff of the admiralty and a volunteer youth worker in a working-class section of London, to leave the Navy and become the headmaster of the first college. Hoare agreed and, while not neglecting the Navy, joined Hahn in raising funds. Their record for results proportionate to time spent was £10,000 in twenty-five minutes.[32]

Hoare's other assignment was to find a site. When he found St. Donat's Castle on the south coast of Wales the search was over. Hahn immediately went to Antonin Besse, the benefactor of Gordonstoun, and secured a promise of £65,000 toward purchase of the castle. St. Donat's was the legendary treasure house of William Randolph Hearst, who had installed magnificent black marble bathrooms with chromium showers and had uprooted ancient structures elsewhere in Britain and packed them off to Wales to be set up on his lawns. The castle dates from the fourteenth century and at its centre is an Elizabethan courtyard. Hearst spent more than a quarter of a million pounds on it in the 1930s, and some of the elegant buildings he built on the 150-acre estate later became the dining hall, assembly hall, and library of the new college. With its terraced lawns and gardens sloping to the sea wall, heated swimming pool, and view of the Bristol Channel, it is possible for the college prospectus to claim without exaggeration that the beauty and facilities of the castle and estate are probably without equal in Britain.

The castle needed major renovations for use as a college and the customary inaugural dinner launched a campaign for £600,000 to build dormitory blocks, classrooms, and laboratories. Hahn and Darvall had now formed a promotional committee composed of well-known business leaders and industrialists, a bishop, two conservative M.P.'s, and a key figure in later years, A. D. C. Peterson, Director of the Institute of

Education at Oxford. When only a fraction of the objective had been raised Hahn proposed to open the college. Hoare demurred, but Hahn countered with characteristic optimism, "Once you have started the money will come rolling in." By the middle of 1960 *The Times Educational Supplement*[33] reported that the college, now well on its way to completion, would share some features of Gordonstoun, an emphasis on projects and rescue services for example, but would have higher academic standards. Boys would be drawn from all Atlantic countries and taught their national history and literature in their own language. Other subjects would be taught in English. In a front page statement in the same issue, *TES* commented: "Dr. Kurt Hahn has given education more promising new ideas than anyone else in his day. . . . This seems a venture exactly suited to our new kind of world and one would like to see it start in Britain."[34]

In September 1962 Atlantic College opened as a residential sixth-form college with an enrolment of fifty-six boys from twelve countries. Two years later its bankers gave formal notice that they could not continue the college's overdraft, and it was only the intervention of George (later Sir George) Schuster that saved the college from bankruptcy. Schuster, who had first met Hahn at Brown's Hotel in London, approached the governor of the Bank of England, who in turn was persuaded to make representation to the college's bank. At Hahn's request Schuster became chairman of a small action committee which took responsibility for the financial health of the college. The early history of Atlantic College was, in many respects, the story of Gordonstoun repeated. Capital was required to build accommodation for more students whose fees were necessary to increase operating income. Through what Schuster has described as "hard, slogging fund raising,"[35] the college was on safe ground by 1967.

The British government, in response to a direct appeal from Lord Mountbatten, had contributed £100,000 over a three-year period, and substantial other gifts had been pledged, one in particular from an American, Pompeo Moresi, which was designated for residential accommodation for girls. This donation not only precipitated heated discussion within the board of governors about the admission of girls, but also marked the beginning of continuing and substantial support by Moresi and his wife. As with earlier projects Hahn again was right: once a venture was started the money came rolling in. But as with the Duke of Edinburgh's Award Scheme he had chosen his men wisely and then withdrawn into the shadows. Hoare has recorded his gratitude for being able to work with his staff, without interference, in shaping the new college,[36] and Schuster served as an independent chairman of the board from 1965 to 1974. Hahn was the midwife; it was up to the parents to raise the child.

Under the second headmaster, David Sutcliffe, the college became in 1971 the first school in the world to abandon national examinations and adopt the International Baccalaureate, a university entrance qualification with international validity. As Professor Peterson was a director of the IB organzation it is not surprising that the college was involved in the detailed preparations and pilot projects which preceded IB's official appearance. Administered from Geneva as an independent foundation, under Swiss law the baccalaureate requires candidates for the full diploma to take examinations in six subjects, three at higher and three at a lower level. All candidates must study two languages (their own and one other), mathematics, one science, one of the humanities, and one elective, which may be art or music. Panels of examiners are chosen from several countries and the development of new courses of study is similarly an international enterprise. In its first decade students in some 150 affiliated schools followed the IB curriculum and gained entry into more than 450 universities. The adoption of the IB allowed Atlantic College to relinquish the English Certificate of Education Advanced Level (GCE A-level) examinations in favor of an internationally sponsored examination system. In turn, recognition of IB by Atlantic College undoubtedly gave the new courses and examinations academic status and respectability.

It is, however, in the non-academic side of the college program that the Hahn tradition is most visible. David Sutcliffe is a product of that tradition. He has studied and taught at both Salem and Gordonstoun, and has made a solo crossing of the Atlantic in a small sailboat. Thus it is not surprising that sections of the college prospectus ring with familiar echoes:

> Advancing material prosperity has brought evils in its train. Among these are a decline in physical fitness of young people, insufficient satisfaction of the youthful instinct for adventure and that decline of compassion which is reflected in the plain business of individual unhelpfulness to one another. . . .
>
> Our civilization has many roots. One is that sense of obligation to

> the community which overrides self interest when the issue is important. The instinct of helpfulness is present in every youth; it can either be fostered and flourish, or it can be neglected and fade away. . . . All students . . . will normally wish to give some time each week to one form or another of community service. Professional standards of training are adopted. Nothing binds individuals of different nations together more firmly than the shared experience of giving expert assistance to others in need.[37]

Community service occupies a student two afternoons or evenings a week and may take several forms.The social service unit places students with organizations which care for the sick, the elderly, or the handicapped, or students may devise service projects of their own. In one such project students taught canoeing skills to children in a school for the blind and ended the project in a three-day expedition on the River Wye. Rescue services have been an integral part of college life since its founding, and the inshore lifeboat, beach, and cliff rescue units have been given official responsibility for fifteen miles of Bristol Channel coastline. They operate with a high degree of professionalism and have been credited with over 150 rescues since 1962. (Hahn's enthusiasm for rescue training was once challenged by his close friend, Bishop Launcelot Fleming: "The Good Samaritan never had any rescue training did he?" "Ah, my friend," Hahn replied, "if the Priest and the Levite had been trained in the rescue services they would never have passed by on the other side.")

Other transplants from Gordonstoun and Outward Bound are expeditions and projects. One week in the middle of each term is given over to individual or group projects and both the sea and the hills are used. Staff and students have recognized, as did Hahn at Gordonstoun, the danger of becoming isolated. With support from the Welsh Arts Council, a community arts centre has been established, and the Extra-Mural Department, housed in what were Hearst's cavalry barracks, offers residential courses for delinquent or disadvantaged youth. The department is recognized by the courts as a centre to which young offenders aged fourteen to sixteen may be sent as an alternative to custody. Thus the Salem and Gordonstoun traditions of service and compassion continue, but there is no training plan or morning break, no helpers, and a more liberal attitude toward smoking and drinking.

In the early 1980s some sixty countries were represented in the college enrolment of 350, with boys and girls about equal in number. Almost all students are sponsored by their national committees, which raise scholarship funds from government and private sources. Once a student is selected for admission, on the basis of high academic and personal qualifications, his or her entry is assured, regardless of parental income. The international climate of the college may also be found in the staff, who offer instruction in seven languages. Atlantic College is now one of three United World Colleges—the other two are South East Asia College in Singapore (1971) and Pearson College in British Columbia, Canada (1974)—an organization which developed under the ten-year (1968–78) presidency of Lord Mountbatten. The second president of the International Council, a body whose members represent seventy-five countries, is H. R. H. the Prince of Wales. In recent years the council has helped found new colleges in India, Italy, and Venezuela.

Meanwhile, World Colleges have not been without their critics. There have been charges that they are over-intellectualized, elitist international Etons, or that in spite of the varied services they suffer from the traditional isolation of the public schools, or that they have little relevance to the Third World. Kurt Hahn and Lawrence Darvall believed that a healthy tolerance for diversity and an understanding of different cultures could be developed among young people when idealism is strong and the pressures of a specialized university course are not yet dominant. But whether such results can be achieved in a network of residential colleges that combine high-level academic instruction with activities requiring courage and compassion may not be known for many years. Indeed, the results may never be known with any precision. As is so often true in education, innovation calls for wisdom, commitment, and a leap of faith, not simply a set of measuring instruments.

Hahn as Educator

When Kurt Hahn died in December 1974, after several years of illness, he left a unique legacy, or more accurately, three legacies. At both Salem and Gordonstoun the pattern of the school day, the training plan, the system of school government—the very character and ethos of the schools—can be attributed to Hahn. And as we have seen, there were similarities to the schools in the design and structure of the early Outward Bound Schools, the Award Schemes, and Atlantic College. Hahn also has left a body of educational thought which, although it is neither systematic nor profound, reveals with clarity and eloquence the fundamental principles and beliefs that guided him as an educator. Third, he left the memory and legend of a wise, gentle, intuitive, forceful, swift-tempered, eccentric, overbearing, and passionately committed headmaster and educational pioneer. Much of his originality lay in his person rather than his ideas and in his enormous capacity to influence and persuade, to ignite enthusiasm in others, and through them to put ideas into practice.

Hahn and his supporters were not, of course, solely responsible for the success of his innovations. After the Second World War there was a climate of acceptance for new ideas in education, particularly in Great Britain. Fifteen- and sixteen-year-olds were attending secondary modern and later comprehensive schools, and there was need of a program that placed more stress on activity and participation, including risk and adventure in the outdoors. Local education authorities were funded sufficiently to send students to Outward Bound or to set up their own outdoor education centres. In these centres, which were by no means confined to Britain, several new trends converged: the "maturing" of physical education to embrace more than games and exercise, an emphasis on conservation, and the development of national concern for better health and fitness. The 1944 Education Act (England and Wales) embodied the philosophy that education must embrace mind, body, and spirit, not mind alone, and the "new" primary education stressed that what is learned best must be learned actively. A new network of youth agencies appeared as a part of the welfare state and developed programs in non-formal education. Industrial firms and business houses initiated training programs for employees, particularly apprentices, and industrial trainers (industrial training itself being a new career) used Outward Bound as a supplement to their own on-the-job training programs.

Hahn's educational beliefs can best be examined by using his own metaphors and analogies, many of which are medical. He speaks of the diseases of our society, the deformities of puberty, and the healing function of education, all within a framework of diagnosis and cure. The ills of society which concern him most are those which affect youth and which education has some power to cure: the loss of fitness, the decline of self-discipline, the weakened tradition of craftsmanship, and the decay of compassion. During puberty the child is susceptible to these social diseases which, together with the premature monopoly of sexual drives, can create the apathy and listlessness of early adolescence. Parents, psychologists, and educators have come to regard these "loutish years," as Hahn called them, as normal and inevitable, but he considered it his mission to unseat this dogma. A grave malady, yes, but one that can be avoided.

The contrast between childhood and adolescence calls forth both his deepest concerns and his most vivid language. The role of the educator is to preserve the child's strength, his eager curiosity, joy of movement, and powers of co-ordination. Children are forever dreaming, planning, building, discovering, asking, singing, and making believe. These qualities are the treasures of childhood and the central question the educator must ask himself is whether or not he has fulfilled the promise of the nursery by preserving the spiritual strength of childhood unbroken and undiluted throughout adolescence.

Under existing forms of education and the dogma of inevitable malaise, adolescence is usually a dim and cantankerous period when movements become awkward and the child loses his power of joy, grief, and anger; he grows lame and narrow in his love and his spirit of enterprise becomes tired. Sexual impulses insidiously seeking satisfaction make heavy claims on his vitality. Unless these are forestalled, they claim too large a share of an adolescent's physical and emotional strength. This was Hahn's gloomy analysis of the normal transition in Western society from the healthy joys of childhood to the deformities of adolescence. Given the diagnosis, was there a cure? Hahn was convinced that there was and that he had discovered it at Salem. It was, he believed, the major contribution that Salem made to education.

Hahn found that the one condition through which the joys and strengths of childhood could be saved was to kindle in the adolescent a *grande passion*. The potential was already there but the school had to provide a rich and stimulating environment of individual and group projects, expeditions on the sea or in the mountains, and community services. Both at Salem and Gordonstoun these activities were not added to an already crowded schedule but given a place of importance and dignity in the school program. The healthy passions could be kindled through the spirit of adventure, the zest for building, the love of painting or music, or devotion to a skill demanding care or patience. For Hahn these non-poisonous passions were the child's "guardian angels'' which, if allowed to develop, would protect him from dissipating his physical and emotional energy and falling into the ''loutish'' years. This was not simply a matter of suppressing sexual development, but rather of nurturing latent interests to the extent that they would capture the imagination of youth and withdraw emotional power from the sexual impulses which otherwise may gain a premature and unnatural monopoly in early puberty.

If not obsessed, Hahn was at least excessively concerned about the effect that the ''premature monopoly'' of the sex drive could have on his students. Former students have reported his violent anger and agitation over any evidence or suspicion of overt sexuality at Gordonstoun. Whether these strong feelings spring from a struggle in earlier years to control his own sexuality is not known, but his repeated references to ''poisonous passions'' that well up or are inflamed imply that for him adolescent sexuality was unhealthy. His belief that what he regarded as the deformities of puberty could be healed or cured by a *grande passion* had no grounding in psychological theory but was derived from his own observations and impressions of adolescent behavior, a moralistic view of the function of education, repression of his own sexuality, or a combination of these. In this connection the comments of an early progressive educator are interesting. William Curry, Headmaster of Dartington Hall from 1931 to 1957 and an influential member of the New Education Fellowship, attended a lecture given by Hahn soon after his arrival in England in 1933. A few days later Curry wrote to a friend:

> I have been thinking a good deal about the Hahn meeting last week. . . . I am . . . very much concerned about certain aspects of Hahn's policy, considered in relation to the amount of enthusiasm he is creating. . . . Take this punishment as expiation business. People like Hahn are so tormented themselves by their moral fanaticism that they set up a sense of guilt in any community in which they are important. Having created the sense of guilt, they then use it as an excuse for punishment. . . .
>
> Unless I am very profoundly mistaken . . . the education which Hahn advocates is incompatible with a really liberal civilization. It seems to me . . . to be the product of the tortured German soul. . . . I can understand that Hahn's views might seem liberal in Germany. What shocks me is that they are thought liberal in England. I grant

> that he is a man of immense power and vitality and of considerable intellectual ability. I also insist that his psychology has far more roots in his emotional nature than in the nature of other human beings. . . . [38]

Fortunately, Hahn's educational ideas survive independently of his deformity theory. It is not necessary to believe that the adolescent must be protected by summoning the non-poisonous passions to maintain the vitality and spontaneity of childhood. We can accept his stress on health and fitness, the emphasis on projects and expeditions, and the opportunity for rescue training and community service as valid in their own right without considering them as *grandes passions* that help youth to cope with adolescence. Hahn is on much surer ground when he criticizes modern society for blocking the development of adolescents by prolonging their dependence and preventing them from accepting responsibility and proving themselves. He believed they needed to be tested, encouraged to learn new skills and discover their limits, and offered ways to satisfy their Samaritan instinct. It was entirely appropriate for a nation with a maritime history such as Britain's to exploit the sea for educational purposes, and Hahn was always ready to quote his friend George Trevelyan when he christened the sailing ketch *Garibaldi* at Aberdovey in 1943: "The life of a Training Ship and the discipline of the sea give an education in the qualities of endurance, promptitude and love of adventure. Without the instinct for adventure in young men, any civilization, however enlightened, any state, however well-ordered, must wilt and wither."[39]

In an address[40] given in Liverpool Cathedral in December 1940, Hahn conceded that training in resilience and endurance on sea or in the hills, and laboring with precision and patience to master projects of art or science, could apply equally to the training of Hitler Youth. The qualities of responsibility and initiative are not unique to one country or culture, and they may be used for good or evil. Hitler Youth were hardy, disciplined, self-sacrificing, and moved to a great passion. But this was a passion of hatred inspired from their early years. What a Christian society must do is nourish love and compassion among the young through experience in service. Within young people there is a wish to be used, to give help where needed, an instinct that will effectively find release when service is combined with adventure and when high levels of skill and teamwork are required.

Another feature of Hahn's educational theory related to his emphasis on character development is the principle of "transfer." If a boy or girl is involved in activities of service during the adolescent years, this training, Hahn believed, would carry over into adulthood. That is to say, compassion, together with discipline and skill, learned in one's youth will be summoned as the need arises in later life. Similarly, the results of experience on the sea or in the mountains will resurface and sustain an adult faced with severe physical or emotional hardship. Hahn does not expand on this theme, and mentions it only briefly, but clearly he believed that character-building activities would have lasting effects.

It was, however, Hahn the man and not his educational writing that had the greatest influence. Through his very presence and remarkable eloquence he could reveal how deeply he believed in education as the liberation of dormant talents. With compelling conviction he could say to students that through experience at Gordonstoun, "You can grow into what you are." And with equal conviction he could persuade men and women of title and wealth to support his many schemes with their time, money, and influence. With a strong will and benign manner, or to use his own phrase, an "artful idealism," he arranged interviews and small meetings at which appointments were confirmed and money-raising strategy discussed. While in London, Hahn invariably stayed at Brown's Hotel and frequently held meetings over breakfast. (Desmond Hoare has recalled that he would have breakfast in Hahn's suite or in the dining room and that in either case Hahn would absent himself at frequent intervals. It took Hoare some years to realize that Hahn was conducting two meetings simultaneously.)

In spite of poor health for much of his life Hahn was a tireless and confident crusader. He spoke to audiences ranging from the Elgin Rotary Club to a congregation of notables at the opening of a new section of Liverpool Cathedral, travelled frequently to the Continent and the United States, and maintained connections both at home and abroad through an active correspondence and telephone conversations which allegedly gave Gordonstoun the highest charges in Scotland. Influential and respected as he was at Gordonstoun he was never fully confined to his school. He was away so often to deal with national and international concerns that on one occasion the editors of the school paper listed him among the previous week's visitors. These frequent absences worried him and after retirement he was candid enough to admit that his hopes for Gordonstoun had been only partially achieved: "It was through my fault that we did not succeed . . . intermittent and absentee headmasters cannot be reformers. You need a calm and watchful presence and an epic patience, which are out of tune with dramatic interventions."[41]

As a headmaster and an innovator Hahn combined idealism with practicality. Although he suffered periods of depression he was basically optimistic about the human condition. If you do not believe in a boy, he would say, then you have no right to educate him, and he placed a high degree of trust in his students. He had dreams and visions of a "Greater Gordonstoun" that would somehow take shape after the return from Wales. On the other hand he could be meticulously detailed and practical in devising the training plan or the final report to parents. In spite of frequent absences and his involvement in national enterprises he was deeply concerned for the physical and moral well-being of his boys. Godfrey Burchardt, who taught at Gordonstoun for over thirty years, has recalled one incident in which Hahn was speaking to a group of junior boys:

> They had been guilty of the form of bullying which consists in making the victim, too weak or simple to resist, perform humiliating acts. He talked to them quite quietly and in simple language about the dignity of the human being so movingly that one of them burst into tears then and there, saying, "Oh sir, I feel so ashamed of myself." I'm quite certain they all remembered those few minutes for the rest of their lives. It is as a great moral force that everyone in the school will remember him, I believe more than as an educational theorist.[42]

He inspired loyalties among his staff although he could be domineering and on occasion, ruthless. He recognized the strength of his own will and expected his staff to stand up to him. He once told his director of studies, "If I want to send a boy for health reasons into the hills for three weeks just before his examinations you must resist me."[43]

On both the national and international scene he achieved his success as a powerful personality who could exert an almost hypnotic effect on audiences and individuals, and as a figure behind-the-scenes or, to use the image he gave himself, as a midwife (in his later years "an ancient midwife"). He used his full energy and talent in presiding over the birth of his projects and then retired into the background, knowing full well that the parents could be trusted. He had after all, chosen them. Whether midwife, catalyst, or founder, Hahn has been the creative force behind extensive and substantial educational innovation. At the celebration of his eightieth birthday at Salem in June 1966, the headmasters and headmistresses of a dozen schools around the world founded the Round Square Conference "to cement the informal links that existed among the schools that had drawn their inspiration from Dr. Kurt Hahn." Representatives of these independent schools now meet once a year. Both independent and state-supported schools in many countries have adopted in varying degrees some of the aspects of Gordonstoun and Salem, and as we have seen, Outward Bound has spread throughout the world and has been imitated by voluntary agencies and adapted to school programs. Similarly, the Duke of Edinburgh's Award Scheme and the United World Colleges are international in scope.

In post-war years Hahn secured support for his ideas, but often only after a period of "hard slogging" and when his proposals were given royal patronage and endorsed by leading personages from the church, universities, and the armed services. His genius also lay in devising programs and projects that caught the imagination of young people themselves. From his own experience at Salem and Gordonstoun he found that adolescents wanted to be challenged, and in an increasingly impersonal society wished to escape from "the misery of unimportance" and learn skills they could use in helping others. He not only recognized these needs but set about abolishing the myth of the inevitable apathy of adolescence. He may have moralized outrageously about "poisonous passions," but he had the wisdom to invent or borrow ideas that adolescents accepted and the power of personality and organizational capacity to persuade their elders to transform those ideas into institutions.

SIX

Jennie Lee

Walter Perry

Harold Wilson, Jennie Lee, Peter Venables, and Walter Perry: The British Open University

Jennie Lee and Walter Perry, reprinted with permission of The Open University.

Forerunners and Harbingers

After church on Easter Sunday, 1963, in his cottage on the Scilly Isles, Harold Wilson sketched out his ideas for a university of the air. In September as leader of the Labour party, then in Opposition, he included his proposals in a speech at Glasgow to launch the pre-election campaign of the Scottish Labour party. (His addresses in Scotland usually included a review of Scottish problems and a statement of more lively interest to the whole of Britain.) Earlier in the year on a visit to the United States he had seen the teaching films made by *Encyclopaedia Britannica* under the presidency of his friend, Senator William Benton, for the use of television broadcasts by the Chicago College of the Air. On trips to the Soviet Union he had learned that more than half of all engineering students began their courses through correspondence work combined with tuition by radio. From this experience abroad and his awareness of similar developments in Britain, Wilson shaped his plan. The University of the Air would serve a wide diversity of part-time adult students working toward degrees. Its system of teaching would include television, radio, and nationally organized correspondence courses. Television broadcasts would be made over a new fourth channel or by pre-empting time on the existing three channels. By scheduling both radio and television broadcasts at appropriate times, hundreds of thousands of "eavesdroppers" could enrich their lives but would not necessarily enrol for credit.

This "new dynamic program" would be organized by an educational trust, a broadly representative body that would make arrangements with one or more of the established universities for examinations and the awarding of external degrees. Thus Wilson's initial proposal did not envisage a separate and autonomous university. The idea of a university of the air did not originate with Harold Wilson and his proposal did not closely resemble the Open University which was founded some years later. Nevertheless, he was the first powerful political figure to take seriously the provision of part-time university education for fully employed adults through a system that combined correspondence teaching and educational broadcasting. Astute and sensitive politician that he was, he knew that in 1963 the time was ripe for an idea that later would fire the imagination of the educational world and, in Wilson's words, become "one of the most important educational and social developments of this century."[1]

The use of radio and television in adult education was scarcely a startling proposal in Britain. In 1924 the evening program of the BBC included talks by eminent figures in science and public affairs. When the BBC, which had begun as a private company, was reconstituted by royal charter in 1927 as a public corporation, a series of twenty-five-minute talks on five evenings a week was supplemented by "Aids to Study" pamphlets. A year later in a graceful preface to his committee's report on the role of broadcasting in adult education Sir Henry Hadow wrote:

> We are in full sympathy with the use of broadcasting as entertainment—as "taking tired people to the islands of The Blest," but it also has other functions. Those of us who are specially engaged in education cannot refrain from giving our testimony to the encouragement . . . the BBC has accorded to educational work; not only directly in its program of lectures, but by raising the standard of judgment and appreciation throughout the country.[2]

Also during the twenties, the BBC's director of education, J. C. Stobart, drew up a plan for a "Wireless University" that would offer courses lasting two years, taught wholly or in part by radio. Stobart described his scheme as a Wellsian sketch of possibilities and in a reference to existing requirements for university entrance proposed that "no one need be prevented from learning science by inability to pass in Latin."[3] The BBC moved, however, in other directions, mainly in supplementing the work of voluntary and public agencies and, particularly in the thirties, informing listening groups, preparing pamphlets, and training leaders for a series of broadcasts on public affairs. Although 1,400 groups were recorded as listening to these broadcasts, there was an undercurrent of resistance to the use of peak listening time for adult education. "The indulgent listener is middle-aged. Around him fuming impatiently sit all the younger members of his family. They want to be amused. They do not want to be educated."[4] By the beginning of the Second World War the corporation had decided to continue its programs of talks but to withdraw grants for the organization of listening groups. In the post-war period the BBC strengthened its expertise and sophistication in educational broadcasting, but resisted proposals to set up separate television channels or radio networks designated as "educational" and did not develop links with existing universities.

With the support of the Ford Foundation, colleges and universities in the United States were experimenting with closed circuit television. Others, such as Chicago Television College, began in 1946 to integrate open circuit television, print materials, written assignments, and tutorials. In Japan radio and correspondence education were first linked in 1953. By the early sixties Brian Jackson was experimenting in Britain with a Dawn University using television only, and six-week courses in English and mathematics at secondary school level using television, correspondence, and a short-term residential school. Probably the first educator in Britain to use the term "Open University" was Michael Young, who was one of many then concerned over the increasingly large number of qualified school-leavers who were unable to find places in British universities.[5] Because of this shortage of places and because a substantial number of young people were obliged to study part-time and work full-time, enrolment in private correspondence schools was high, but results in the examinations for London University's External Degree were poor. Both Jackson and Young stressed the need for some system of *teaching*, not simply a succession of examinations. This system would involve correspondence courses that were carefully designed, television and radio broadcasts closely integrated with written assignments, and face-to-face tutorials whenever possible—in other words, teaching at a distance.

A second feature of the educational climate in Britain that alerted Wilson's political sensitivity was the increasing disquiet over provision of university places and the relatively low representation of working class children in university enrolments. It has taken Britain, England particularly, a long time to demonstrate officially a concern over elitism in higher education and to move toward greater equality of opportunity. The trend toward egalitarianism gained strength in the fifties and was reflected in the Crowther Report of 1959. (Throughout the twentieth century Britain has benefited enormously from the work of committees and commissions whose lucid and well-documented reports have informed public opinion and led to change in national policy. The chairmen of these committees have lent their names to the reports, and Hadow, Spens, Crowther, Robbins, Newsom, Plowden, and James are household words, at least to educators.) By using a sample of 7,275 National Service recruits, Crowther showed that among families of manual workers it was the exception for a child to stay at school after the then minimum leaving age of fifteen. This meant that the majority of children had no opportunity to attempt the sixth form course leading to the advanced ('A') Level of the General Certificate of Education, and, of course, no hope of ever entering a university. Furthermore, in another substantial sample of men entering the Army, over 40 per cent of those with the highest ability (as revealed in a battery of five tests) had left school before they were sixteen. The Crowther Committee argued that "the available resources . . . of high ability are not fully used by the present system" and that "there is hardly one amongst the advanced English-speaking countries who would profess itself content with so small a trickle as one in eighteen continuing in full-time education into the later teens."[6]

The Robbins Committee, appointed in 1961 to examine higher education, found that in Britain only 4½ per cent of the appropriate age group of young people entered full-time degree courses compared with France (7%), Sweden (10%) and the United States (20%). On the other hand, the proportion of the age group completing, as distinct from entering, degree courses in Britain compared quite favorably with western European countries, a finding which led the Robbins Committee to suspect that a comparative investigation would reveal that "the British university system is among the most efficient and economical in the world."[7] Nevertheless, the committee thought that the number of graduates from British universities was too small and one of the reasons was "the very large reserve of untapped ability." In examining the relationship between children's educational achievement and the occupation of their fathers the committee found that "the proportion of young people who enter full-time higher education is 45% for those whose fathers are in the 'higher professional' group compared with only 4% for those whose fathers are in skilled manual occupations. . . . the link is even more marked for girls than for boys."[8]

Robbins recommended a massive expansion in university places over the next two decades, in fact an increase of 165 per cent, on the principle that courses of higher education "should be available to all who are qualified by ability and attainment to pursue them and wish to do so."[9] This expansion was largely achieved, but it is nevertheless true that by 1971, the year the Open University admitted its first students, as many as a quarter of school-leavers with the normal qualifications of two A-level passes failed to secure a place in conventional British universities.

The Robbins Committee was, of course, primarily concerned with full-time higher education and the expansion of British universities was essentially a matter of increasing the number of places for school-leavers, not for adults. Robbins did, however, propose correspondence and evening courses as two temporary expedients to meet the crisis in university accommodation in the sixties. And the committee believed that television could have "considerable potential value as an ancillary both for part-time and correspondence study."[10] But even with these expedients, emphasis was on the education of recent school-leavers, not the working adult.

In British adult education the leading sponsoring agencies—the Workers' Educational Association, the extra-mural departments of universities, and Local Education Authorities—have traditionally offered non-credit courses. Few universities or polytechnics have scheduled part-time courses leading to a degree, and thus the men and women who left school at fifteen or sixteen had little in the way of a "second chance" for a university education, except, of course, the correspondence courses for a London University External Degree. This was recognized by a study group set up within the Labour party in 1962 under the chairmanship of Lord Taylor to consider the party's attitude toward higher education. The report of this group, issued in March 1963, drew attention to the very small representation of working-class families in higher education and reinforced the Robbins proposals for a major expansion of university places.

It went further by recommending that "as an experiment, the BBC sound radio and television and the Independent Television Authority should be required to cooperate in organizing a university of the air, for serious, planned adult education."[11] In April 1963 the Department of Education of Oxford University organized an Anglo-American conference to explore ways of meeting the needs of the home student in the United States and Britain. The conference learned of the problems facing the student at a distance, probably the most serious of which was loneliness. It was revealed that one of his greatest needs was contact with other students and tutors, the latter preferably with continuity over a period of years. Summer residential courses were also highly desirable, as Russian and Australian experience had proved, for two or three weeks each year. And this group of adult educators again emphasized the importance of co-ordinating television programs and correspondence courses as a means of enriching and diversifying teaching.

Harold Wilson and Jennie Lee

Within this context of reports and conferences, trends, and experiments Harold Wilson seized the moment to propose a university of the air. Press reaction to the Glasgow speech was mixed. The *Economist* was enthusiastic and regarded placing the University of the Air on Labour's program of action as one of the best things Wilson had done. Furthermore, Wilson should be commended for using the term "university" not just for degree purposes but also "to brighten up the notion of more learning for all that has become dusted over with the old-fashioned image and name of night school."[12] The *Economist* was one of the few daily or periodical papers to grasp that the name "University of the Air" was misleading: the sole or even predominant use of radio and television was not Wilson's intention. *The Times Educational Supplement* was highly sceptical. Wilson's proposal was a "heady prospect," but he defeated his object by the sheer magnitude of his dream. Where would the money and manpower come from? Would public money be squandered on students who started and then dropped out?

> The real trouble, however, with Mr. Wilson's plans is that they smack of a socialist idealism which is no longer necessary. . . . Many

> of his ideas would indeed be imaginative and adventurous in a country where physical difficulties hampered educational advance. But is it really necessary to extend education in Britain today as if we were living in the Australian outback? . . . Those who really want to advance their education have all sorts of chances to do so.[13]

This belief that existing facilities were entirely adequate and that the costs of imaginative leaps toward distance learning were more than the country could afford were also the initial reactions of the university and adult education communities. The BBC's experience of many years in educational broadcasting, the use of television and correspondence in other countries, and the experiments in Britain by daring young men were seen as interesting portents, but there was much scepticism not only in the universities and among adult educators but also in the Department of Education and Science.[14]

But Wilson was not to be deterred. He caught the mood of Labour's dissatisfaction with things as they were in his address to the annual conference of the party at Scarborough in October 1963. In a speech on labor and the scientific revolution he stressed the national need to adapt to scientific and technical demands and to produce more highly skilled manpower. He was cheered when he echoed Robbins's revelation that Britain was not making the most of her reserves of ability: "We simply cannot afford to cut off three-quarters or more of her children from virtually any chance of higher education. The Russians do not, the Germans do not, the Japanese do not, and we cannot afford to either."[15] In the same speech he referred to his proposal for a university of the air but made it clear that this new development would not become a substitute for the party's plans to increase the number of conventional universities and extend technological education. On the contrary:

> It is designed to provide an opportunity for those who, for one reason or another, have not been able to take advantage of higher education, now to do so, with all that TV and radio and the state-sponsored correspondence course, and the facilities of a university for setting and marking papers and conducting examinations, in awarding degrees, can provide. Nor, may I say, do we envisage this merely as a means of providing scientists and technologists. I believe a properly planned University of the Air could make an immeasur-

able contribution to the cultural life of our country, to the enrichment of our standard of living.[16]

In this speech, which was acknowleged to have strengthened Wilson's leadership, he used the term "our plans" for a university of the air and regarded them as firm. Nevertheless his proposal did not become a part of Labour's manifesto for the 1964 election and Wilson did not discuss it with the shadow cabinet. As he revealed later, "It certainly wasn't official Labour Party policy at this stage, except in the sense that I was running the party in a slightly dictatorial way; if I said something was going to happen I intended it to happen."[17]

The Labour party won the election of October 1964 and Wilson in forming his cabinet made a decision of crucial importance to his project. He appointed Jennie Lee, first as a parliamentary under-secretary with special responsibility for the arts in the Ministry of Public Buildings and Works; and several months later, as part of a cabinet reshuffle, he asked her to take responsibility not only for the arts but for the University of the Air as well. She accepted and both she and her ministry were transferred to the Department of Education and Science, on the clear understanding that she could work directly with the treasury and the prime minister. She has been described as "a politician of steely, imperious will, coupled with tenacity and charm,"[18] and these qualities were soon revealed. For the better part of two years senior officials of her department and the BBC had been designing a College of the Air using a combination of broadcasting and correspondence work for pre-university courses for adults. On her fourth day in the department Lee scrapped the college[19] and made it known that she wanted an independent university awarding its own degrees, comparable in quality with the other universities, and open to all without any entrance qualification.

This decision shook senior civil servants, who were poised to discuss their own proposals, and surprised members of the Wilson cabinet, who noticed that the principles on which Lee was insisting were not to be found in Wilson's speeches. Her determination to create an autonomous university of high academic respectability can be variously explained. She may have wanted to create a memorial to Aneurin Bevan, her husband who died in 1960, a member of the Labour cabinet and the minister responsible for creating Britain's National Health Service. He was a miner's son from South Wales who had left school at thirteen to go into the pits and at nineteen had won a Miners' Union scholarship to spend two years at the Central Labour College. He read everything from *Boys' Own* to Milton, was passionately fond of Keats, and delighted in imaginative talk.[20] He would have been a model candidate for an Open University degree. The explanation also may lie in Jennie Lee's long association with men and women who had been denied a chance to attend university. Here now was their chance and she was going to see that they would get the best education that the nation could provide. As she put it, the new university was not to be "Paddy the next-best-thing, a dawn patrol or a midnight parade, a patch on the working man's trousers."

Jennie Lee's father went to work in the coal pits of Fife at the age of twelve, and her grandfather was a miner for twenty-nine years before becoming an official of the Miners' Union. Leaders of the Independent Labour party visited her home and by the time she reached adolescence she was a confirmed socialist. With the help of a maintenance allowance from the Local Authority and a grant from the Carnegie Trust, she entered Edinburgh University and after four and a half years collected an M.A., a teacher's certificate, and a law degree. As a member of the Labour Club she spoke at open air meetings in parks and on street corners, though her life was not entirely wrapped up in politics:

> I went occasionally . . . to the theatre . . . and most magical of all to see Pavlova dance in the Usher Hall. We climbed the stone stairs to the "gods" and there, hanging like flies from the ceiling, devoured every movement, every sound. It was pure enchantment. Afterwards, taken completely out of ourselves, we did not so much walk home as float.[21]

She was graduated in 1926, the year of the General Strike, and from June to September threw herself into raising funds for the Scottish miners. At first hand she knew of the violence at the pits, and whenever there were signs of flagging morale she was one of those asked to address a meeting. This experience, together with an upbringing in a miner's home, gave her life its direction: "It was the struggle in the coal fields that shaped the whole of my after life, more than any other experience."[22]

In 1927 at the national conference of the Independent Labour party, Emmanuel Shinwell spoke in defence of Ramsay MacDonald, leader of the parliamentary Labour party, and Jennie Lee as an official delegate was called to reply. Fenner Brockway describes the occasion:

> A young dark girl took the rostrum, a puckish figure with a mop of thick black hair thrown impatiently aside, brown eyes flashing, body and arms moving in rapid gestures, words pouring from her mouth in Scottish accent and vigorous phrases, sometimes with a sarcasm which equalled Shinwell's. It was Jennie Lee making her first speech at an ILP conference. And what a speech it was! Shinwell was regarded as a Goliath in debate but he met his match in this girl David.[23]

It was not, then, any real surprise when she received a telegram asking if she would allow her name to stand as a parliamentary candidate in North Lanark. In a by-election in 1929 she ran under Independent Labour party auspices and won with a majority of 6,500, the youngest woman ever to be elected to the House of Commons. She won again in the general election later in 1929, but lost in 1931 when MacDonald and the Labour party joined Stanley Baldwin to form a national government, a decision which outraged Lee and her ILP supporters.

Her marriage to Aneurin Bevan in 1934 was a union of two forceful and exuberant Celts. In the election of 1945 she regained her seat in Parliament and held it until 1970. In Clement Atlee's Labour cabinet, Bevan, at forty-seven the youngest member, was made Minister of Health and was soon immersed in planning and shaping the National Health Service bill, which received royal assent in 1946. Jennie Lee was a member of Labour's national executive committee, the body that determined much party policy. During the Opposition years Harold Wilson as a member of Labour's shadow cabinet occasionally planned strategy in the Bevan home. Thus when he came to power he needed no one to tell him of Jennie Lee's depth of commitment to Labour, her talent in both writing and speaking, her no-nonsense practicality, and her capacity to get things done. She had served in the House for more than twenty years and knew the peculiar ways of Westminster. She had, in short, paid her dues.

As Minister for the Arts, Jennie Lee was initially a controversial figure. One of her first tasks was to produce a White Paper, *A Policy for the Arts,* which was presented to Parliament in 1965. It argued for a more coherent, generous, and imaginative approach in support of the arts, and also contained this statement: "Too many working people have been conditioned by their education and environment to consider the best in music, painting, sculpture and literature as outside their reach. . . . " To some people in the arts this sounded like a policy of "cultural welfare work" and one prominent musician ridiculed Lee's grants to local poetry festivals and other "worthy" enterprises by saying, "Why should such mediocre operations be *sponsored?* For God's sake—when did art become another word for *fair play?*"[24] But such comments from the cognoscenti did not daunt her and she frankly admitted that her intentions were "to break down the barriers between the insiders and the outsiders" and "to make things available" in all parts of Britain "to all kinds of people." She was an astute politician with a well-practised capacity for squeezing money out of the treasury. Without question, her direct line to Harold Wilson was of enormous benefit, but she could also work independently when necessary in dealing with Members of Parliament.

One M.P., William Mallalieu, has recalled her tactics: "I overheard her nobble a colleague in the corridors of the House of Commons. She didn't say: 'There's a scheme which is worth your support . . . ' or any formula of that kind. She said, 'Are you going to give me some money for the film school, you bastard?' "[25] In the four-year period 1963/64–1967/68 the government's grants to the Arts Council rose from £2,730,000 to £7,200,000. In the latter year the Labour government granted £14,000,000 for all kinds of support for the arts. One of Lee's closest allies and friends was Arnold (later Lord) Goodman, a London solicitor who became Chairman of the Arts Council. Her experience as Minister for the Arts and her collaboration with Lord Goodman, to say nothing of her years at the centre of Labour policy-making and intrigue, proved invaluable when she worked with civil servants, M.P.'s, and members of the Cabinet in creating a new kind of university.

Having scrapped the proposals for an experimental college of the air Lee made her second major decision: to refer the proposal for a University of the Air to the Cabinet Committee on Broadcasting. This committee, in turn, set up an advisory committee which, Jennie Lee insisted, must accept two stipulations: that she be its chairman and that its terms of reference be limited to considering "the educational functions and content of a University of the Air" as outlined by Wilson in Glasgow. At the first meeting one member rather shyly asked, "May I take it that we are looking at the project with an open mind?" "You are not," Jennie Lee snapped back. "If I had thought you had an open mind about it I should not have asked you to join this committee."[26] She made it clear that options such as an open college at a level below university or the extension of existing facilities for adult education would not be considered. The Advisory Committee met first in June 1965, and after six meetings finished its work in August that year, a short period for considering a major departure in higher education. One is tempted to believe that the committee was persuaded to accept the chairman's proposals. Its Report was not published separately but rather was embedded as paragraph 8 in a White Paper, *A University of the Air,* which the Secretary of State for Education and Science presented to Parliament in February 1966.[27]

This paper was itself the result of battles fought and won by Jennie Lee in the Cabinet. Both Anthony Crosland, Minister of Education, and Anthony Wedgewood Benn, Postmaster-General, were cool to the Wilson proposal. Only through a strong plea to the Cabinet and the National Executive Committee at a meeting at Chequers in early February did Lee win sufficient support to move forward. The White Paper sets forth the essential features that later marked the Open University. Through "an imaginative use of new teaching techniques and teacher/student relationships an open university providing degree courses as rigorous and demanding as those in existing universities can be established."[28] From the outset students were not to be offered "a makeshift project inferior in quality to other universities," but rather television and radio programs, correspondence courses "of a quality unsurpassed anywhere in the world," and residential courses and tutorials. A central headquarters would be required along with regional centres and local study centres. Funding should be provided directly by the Department of Education and Science rather than the University Grants committee; the university should confer its own degrees; and admission should be open to everyone "irrespective of educational qualifications." The discussion at Chequers had prepared the way not only for the White Paper but also for the inclusion of a statement in the Labour party Manifesto for the election of 1966. It was, in effect, a highly condensed version of the White Paper:

> We shall establish the University of the Air by using TV and radio and comparable facilities, high grade correspondence courses and new teaching techniques. This open university will obviously ex-

> tend the best teaching facilities and give everyone the opportunity of study for a full degree. It will mean genuine equality of opportunity for millions of people for the first time. Moreover for those who prefer not to take a full course it will bring the widest and best contribution possible to the general level of knowledge and breadths of interest.

Jennie Lee was enough of a realist to know that this commitment by the Labour party was not necessarily a government commitment. There was no date aimed at, and, as with the White Paper, no indication of cost. At the Chequers meeting she and Harold Wilson had the foresight to secure Cabinet approval to ask Lord Goodman to study costs, particularly those related to broadcasting. He accepted her invitation, conferred closely and cordially with Hugh Greene, Director-General of the BBC, and sent his report to the prime minister in May. He recommended that BBC2 should be used, starting with ten hours of television per week in the first year and increasing to thirty hours in the third and later years. He estimated the cost of the whole project at £3.5 million annually. Some eight years later, during a speech in the House of Lords, he admitted that he had greatly underestimated the cost: "When I see the figure I mentioned and the figure it is now costing I ought to blush with shame." But he refused to do so because the Open University "might not have been established except for my foolish miscalculation." Meanwhile in March 1966 the Labour party was returned with a substantial majority and Jennie Lee was reappointed to her position in Cabinet. Her task now was to secure a firm government commitment. This proved difficult, and it was not until September 1967 that she announced a government decision to move forward.

There were good reasons for this delay. Funding was not available during the financial crisis of 1966, and several influential cabinet members, including James Callaghan, chancellor of the exchequer, continued to be lukewarm about the project. Jennie Lee and Lord Goodman in an attempt to raise money from other sources began negotiations with McGeorge Bundy, president of the Ford Foundation, and a request went forward for funding an experimental project. However, critics were still vocal and the White Paper had been given a sceptical response by the press. *The Times* was worried about the probability of an initial large audience dwindling to a handful of students. "No one wants to throw cold water on good intentions. But a minimum of four years would be a long time to hold students to something as tenuous as a television course. The cost per degree could be fantastic."[29]

The Times Educational Supplement began on a patronizing note: "Mr. Wilson's pipe dream of a university of the air . . . as vague as it is unsubstantial, is just the sort of cosy scheme that shows the socialists at their most endearing but impractical worst."[30] The main theme of this leading article was an echo of the *Supplement*'s criticism of Wilson's Glasgow speech: Britain was already well endowed with a network of technical colleges, adult education classes, and the extramural departments of universities. Was there any evidence that something more was needed? Such concern was expressed in a letter to *The Times*[31] by Thomas Kelly, secretary of the Universities' Council for Adult Education. He believed the White Paper proposal was premature because so little was known about the numbers and needs of potential students. He referred to an inquiry then being conducted by the University of Manchester into home study for degrees and cautioned against mounting an expensive operation before knowing better what student response might be. *The New Statesman* summarized reactions from several sources: "The press was lukewarm, educators were doubtful about ends, broadcasters were doubtful about means, and the public was apparently unstirred. There are those who say that the Cabinet Ministers who disliked the whole project decided that the best way to kill it was to publish the plan."[32]

This kind of criticism did not, outwardly at least, dampen Jennie Lee's determination to secure a government commitment. Throughout the remaining months of 1966 and into the summer of 1967 she answered questions in Parliament as to whether the proposals for a University of the Air had been shelved, and if not when the university would be established. Such questions were asked monthly and on each occasion Lee replied confidently but vaguely that plans were going forward and estimates of both capital and operating costs would soon be available. Only once did she waver. She invited the vice-chancellor of Sussex University to have dinner with her in London and made a proposal that would have set up the new university in Brighton with degrees to be awarded by the University of Sussex.[33] The vice-chancellor was noncommittal and the proposal quietly died. Jennie continued to apply pressure, skilfully and relentlessly, on the cabinet. By July 1967 she was satisfied that she had sufficiently worn down the opposition to begin to choose members of a planning committee. She knew that if the cabinet appointed such a committee it would, by precedent, not reject the report produced. Hence the appointment of such a committee would commit the government to going forward. Throughout the summer Lee approached a number of individuals in the academic world and explored their willingness to become committee members. By September she had secured cabinet approval to name publicly the members she had selected. Another development at this period was the change, made quietly, from "University of the Air" to "Open University."

At a press conference on 18 September 1967, Jennie Lee announced the membership of the planning committee and reaffirmed the features of the new university as delineated in the White Paper. She gave Lord Goodman's estimates of costs and indicated that funding would be provided by direct grants from the Department of Education and Science. She emphasized that there would be no entrance qualifications but that the standard of the degree would be equivalent to that of any existing university. In her concern, almost obsession, for academic respectability and "parity of esteem," Jennie Lee had consulted more closely with the university community than with the world of adult education and as a result to some degree alienated university extramural departments, the Workers' Educational Association, and the local education authorities. To ease this resentment and gain the cooperation of these groups was one of the tasks of the first vice-chancellor.

Given her insistence on full university status Lee knew that the planning committee must have credibility in the academic community. For that reason it included five university vice-chancellors, plus representatives from local authorities, adult education, and broadcasting and educational technology, and a sprinkling of well-known academics. One other matter related to the planning committee can be attributed to Jennie Lee. When Anthony Crosland, Secretary of State for Education and Science, was finally persuaded to support an Open University, he proposed that the planning committee's terms of reference should include the option of linking the new institution to an existing university or group of universities. Through Lee's intervention he was overruled, and the final decision taken by the Cabinet gave the committee much more specific terms of reference: "To work out a comprehensive plan for an Open University as outlined in the White Paper of

February, 1966, *A University of the Air,* and to prepare a draft Charter and statutes."[34] By having the committee base their plan on the White Paper, the battle for an independent university awarding its own degrees was won.

With appointment of the Planning Committee, Jennie Lee had virtually completed her mission. She did, of course, keep in close touch with the committee and at the end of its report the committee paid her this compliment: "Throughout this year we have been unobtrusively but most effectively sustained by the enthusiasm of the Minister of State, the Rt. Hon. Miss Jennie Lee, M.P. and we are very glad to acknowledge her indispensable support of our work."[35] For the better part of four years she had poured her energy, enthusiasm, and political acumen into creation of an open university. In a period marked by trends toward greater egalitarianism in higher education she led the way toward a new kind of university, open yet thoroughly reputable. Without question, she had the enormous benefit of support from the prime minister, but there were hard times, particularly in 1966–67 when Wilson did not give her enough backing and support. As he admitted, "Maybe I left too much to her." While her contribution was primarily political, she was also influential in making educational decisions, particularly those of the advisory committee, which found their way into the White Paper. She could, if necessary, be ruthless, at other times charming; she knew from long experience where power and influence lay, but above all she was prepared to fight, and fight hard, for more equality of opportunity, and, as she had said, to break down the barriers.

Her political tactics were brilliant. She chaired the advisory committee and gave both it and the planning committee remarkably restricted terms of reference. She effectively dealt with opposition by adopting the strategy of "containment" by which the project was isolated from general debates on higher education policy.[36] When this strategy of separation aroused opposition within government she confidently used her own persuasion and Harold Wilson's support, and when groups in education, broadcasting, and municipal government were sceptical she relied on a prestigious planning committee to win widespread co-operation. In 1970 she was elevated to the House of Lords as Baroness Lee of Asheridge, and in 1974 Cambridge awarded her a Degree of Law *(honoris causa)*. The citation read, in part, "Did ever any married pair leave to posterity such an excellent pair of monuments . . . as our National Health Service and the Open University?"

Peter Venables and the Planning Committee

While the most crucial period of the political phase ended with appointment of the planning committee, specific decisions as to enrolment, program, staffing, teaching methods, structure, and other essential features of the university all had yet to be made. The White Paper had proposed a framework; the task now was to build the inner structure. Peter Venables, chairman of the committee, was the third influential personality in development of the Open University. In the university world he was highly regarded as the vice-chancellor of the University of Aston in Birmingham and the deputy chairman of the Committee of Vice-Chancellors and Principals. He had been a member of the Crowther Committee, and his views on widening the opportunities for higher education were well known. Furthermore, he was currently active on committees dealing with both adult education and broadcasting. As a condition of accepting the chairmanship of the planning committee he insisted that its membership be drawn from the world of education and broadcasting and that no politicians be appointed. Later he was adamant that the chancellor, vice-chancellor, and treasurer not be seen as political appointments, and he argued strenuously and successfully against Harold Wilson's proposal to announce the appointment of the first vice-chancellor in the House of Commons.

From the testimony of Planning Committee members Venables was a remarkably able chairman who had both biting wit and bubbling good humor. He and Walter Perry, the first vice-chancellor, worked effectively together to defend Open University interests when these were under attack from either Labour or Conservative governments. In 1969 the Labour chancellor of the exchequer, Roy Jenkins, proposed to the Department of Education and Science that the first entry of students ought to be revised downward from 25,000 to 5,000 or at most 10,000. Venables and Perry met with Edward Short, minister of state for education, and persuaded him, on the argument of economies of scale, to hold to the original figure. Venables again contributed significantly to the university by chairing a study of the university's role in non-degree continuing education. The report of this committee was published in 1976 and became the basis of policy for expanding what came to be known as the Continuing Education Programme. Sir Peter Venables's death in 1979 deprived the university of a strong supporter and influential friend.

The planning committee met first in October 1967 and submitted its report to Edward Short at the end of December 1968. As Jennie Lee's political instinct and experience led her to predict, he took the Cabinet's earlier decision to appoint a planning committee as reason enough to accept its report. In a crisp statement in the House of Commons the same day that the report was published Short said: "The Government fully accept the outlined plans for development set out in the Report. It will now be for the University authority, as an autonomous and completely independent institution, to carry the project forward, and in this it can count on the support of the government."[37] The response of the Conservative Opposition was less than enthusiastic. Through the Conservative party press, Sir Edward Boyle, Opposition spokesman on education, stated: "The Opposition cannot hold out any prospect at this time that funds of an annual rate of £3.7 million, as mentioned in the Report can be counted on for the future."[38] In the Commons, however, Sir Edward was more sympathetic and relatively mild in his remarks. Nevertheless, he did not give any guarantee of Conservative support, and the future of the university remained a matter for politicians to decide.

The Venables Report confirmed Britain's need for an Open University. "For long regarded as the privilege of the few, the opportunity to engage in higher education is at last becoming widely accepted as a basic individual right."[39] A modern society needed higher education, on the one hand to increase productivity and efficiency of management, and on the other to ensure the fulfilment of individual lives. With the opening of new universities and polytechnics, a larger proportion of school-leavers was now entering higher education but those born too soon to enjoy the benefits of increasing educational opportunity numbered around one million. There were also professional groups—the 250,000 certified non-graduate teachers, for example—who would form a pool of candidates for the new university. From studies commissioned by the committee using random samples of adults and from other countries' experience, there were strong grounds for believing that substantial numbers (estimates ranged between 34,000 and 150,000) would enrol. Such numbers would not be temporary; it could be assumed that large numbers of British children with the ability to cope with university work would continue to leave school early. And by no means all qualified sixth-form leavers would find a place in conventional universities; that number in 1966–67 was some 30,000. Furthermore, with the growth of technology the need would increase for updating skills and converting to new careers. And because of the traditional, long-standing denial of equal educational and occupational opportunities, a large number of women students could be expected.

From the moment that Harold Wilson used the term "University of the Air," a belief took root that radio and television, the latter particularly, would be the dominant feature of the new institution. Indeed, a good deal of the criticism and scepticism directed at the proposal was based on this misconception. Venables emphasized that it was neither "practically possible nor pedagogically sound to rely on broadcasting as the principal or exclusive means of instruction in an operation designed to provide disciplined courses of university level."[40] Evidence from Russia, Japan, Australia, the United States, the Federal Republic of Germany, and from British experiments at the University of Nottingham and the National Extension College in Cambridge, had revealed that broadcasting could be most effectively used as a part of a fully integrated system of teaching using specially written texts and directions for further reading, correspondence tuition, and face-to-face tutorials.

To achieve this integration would involve a unique administrative and academic structure. There should be no academic departments of the conventional kind and academic staff should be grouped into several "lines" of study roughly equivalent to faculties, each under the jurisdiction of a director of studies, who would be similar to a dean. These academic staff would be based at a central headquarters and initially it was thought that some sixteen to twenty subjects would be represented in the lines of study, with each subject or discipline needing four full-time staff. The committee also recognized that design of correspondence courses, production of radio and television programs, and assessment of student performance would demand a high degree of expertise in educational technology. Thus a director of research and educational technology and a multifaceted staff were provided for. The

White Paper proposal for regional offices, study centres, and a corps of part-time tutors was confirmed; in fact, the Report emphasized the need for adequate counselling services in the regions.

Another unique feature of the Open University was foreshadowed in the Venables Report—the course team. Members of the full-time academic staff, supplemented by academic specialists recruited part-time or for a short term, would work with various other specialists, including those in broadcasting and educational technology, in designing the courses, producing the appropriate content, and presenting it by various means. The initial contract with the BBC for both production and transmission services was negotiated by the planning committee. The BBC agreed to provide thirty hours of television each week and an equal amount of radio time. The television programs would be carried on the then new channel BBC2, between 5:30 and 7:30 on weekday evenings and during the day on weekends. Thus in the early years, Open University students had the benefit of television broadcasts twenty or thirty minutes in length at convenient times. This agreement was based on the principle of an educational partnership which extended over the whole range of relationships from the time the course was conceived to the final production of the broadcast programs. Each partner had a role to play. The university would prescribe the academic objectives and the general character of the broadcasts, while the BBC would provide the necessary presentation and production skills. It is in this "key relationship" between academics and production staff that the idea of the course team becomes evident.

The Venables Report was a lucid, succinct, and forthright statement that gave the new university its essential form and pattern, and at the same time a strong vote of confidence. Coming as it did from educators who commanded respect but who were known initially to have had deep reservations about the proposal, the Report did much to reassure the academic and adult education communities. The committee recognized the scepticism that existed but its support for the new venture was unequivocal.

> The whole concept of part-time higher education, of the acquisition of degrees by correspondence courses supplemented by broadcast teaching, was sufficiently revolutionary to have led to considerable scepticism in the academic world and among the lay public. As our investigations and discussions have continued, we have found little

> basis for such doubts. The evidence as it has accumulated has led us inescapably to the conclusion that the Open University is needed, and can function satisfactorily. To satisfy the need requires that the degrees of the Open University shall stand comparison with other universities. We are thus greatly concerned to ensure the quality of the staff and the standing of the graduates.[41]

The committee ranged widely and the scope of its decisions was remarkable. Not only did it confirm the credit system and a general degree, the introduction of foundation courses with an interdisciplinary emphasis, an academic year beginning in January, short-term residential summer courses, but as we have seen, it also established the administrative and academic staff structure, degree requirements, and the system of teaching. But then, thanks to Jennie Lee, its terms of reference did call for "a comprehensive plan." Working from its temporary offices in Belgrave Square ("If your social status in insecure you need a good address," said Lee), the committee fixed on a site for permanent headquarters at Milton Keynes, submitted to the Privy Council a draft charter, and drew up a budget for both capital development and recurrent costs. The committee was, clearly, more than its name implied; it acted as an executive committee that made all the necessary academic and administrative decisions up to the first meeting of the Congregation of the University. It was at this meeting, an elegant ceremony on 23 July 1969, in the new premises of the Royal Society, that Lord Crowther was installed as chancellor and the charter was awarded. On the eve of the ceremony, *The Times* in a more mellow mood than three years earlier reported that "one of the bravest and most controversial adventures in British higher education this century" would start on the morrow and that when he addressed the Congregation Mr. Harold Wilson could be forgiven if he reflected on the occasion with satisfaction. The Open University was now being watched across the world as "a bold and imaginative experiment, unmatched elsewhere."[42]

Walter Perry

Over a year earlier, the planning committee had advertised, short-listed, and filled the position of vice-chancellor. The candidate chosen from among more than 100 applicants was Walter

Perry, then forty-six, professor of pharmacology and vice-principal of Edinburgh University. Almost from the day his appointment was announced in June 1968, he began to work with the planning committee, and for the next twelve years he profoundly influenced development of the university. Perry was a Scot educated at St. Andrews and Edinburgh and he shared Jennie Lee's respect for academic credibility; he also supported her proposal to transplant the credit system and the ordinary degree from Scotland to England. His professional background was in medical research and teaching and by his own admission he had no qualifications directly related to his new post: he had never been interested in adult education and knew nothing of educational technology or the use of broadcasting for educational purposes. Nor had he been active in national politics or driven by an urge to make educational opportunity more equal. He was, however, attracted by the challenge of facing the enormous difficulties of teaching effectively at a distance and of designing courses through teamwork. In his application for the vice-chancellorship he was asked to state what he considered to be the significance and scope of the work of the Open University:

> I believe that the established academic world has, in expressing scepticism [about the Open University] assumed that the common educational pattern in the established universities is both inevitable and inherently desirable. It is this assumption that I would challenge. . . . If the Open University were successful, even in a limited sense, its impact upon development [in other institutions of higher education] could be profound, and, as a new institution, it can experiment with new patterns of teaching with a freedom that would be impossible to achieve in established universities.[43]

From the time he officially took office on 1 January 1969, Perry literally did almost everything. He wrote the prospectus virtually singlehanded, chaired the admissions committee, acted as director of public relations, recruited and selected staff, and visited the University of South Africa in Pretoria, which then had one of the world's largest programs of correspondence teaching. He never turned down an invitation to speak about the new university, particularly to university audiences, and between mid-1968 and the end of 1970 he spoke at twenty-two British universities. Through these appearances he worked tirelessly to win the respect of his academic peers and, in turn, attract academic staff. One of his major problems lay in the uncertainties surrounding enrolment.

An open university was obliged to admit those who applied, but their numbers could be 5,000 or 25,000 and the level of enrolment would determine the number of courses and the size of staff, to say nothing of the number of buildings to add to Walton Hall, the rather small country house on seventy acres in Buckinghamshire chosen as the permanent headquarters. Perry simply had to guess about all kinds of issues and courted the danger of becoming too deeply immersed in practicalities. In these years he had no choice other than to make decisions alone, which was both a necessity and a preference. He is alleged to have said that his concept of democracy was to give everyone a full opportunity to express his views, after which he could then make up his mind. In 1969 "everyone" meant an ever-growing number of staff, but there was no formal academic structure. The Senate did not meet until September 1969, and Perry made decisions and submitted them later to the Senate for ratification.

A senior member of the academic staff observed:

> Walter Perry is a man of vision and drive, and it was this combination which rocketed the University off the ground and into the air. He has the capacity to be firm in practice while remaining . . . amiable in manner. He is informal and the last man to stand on dignity. He is a masterly administrator with an obsessive command of detail. . . . He trusts his own judgement, and in the early days delegated too little. . . . Fortunately his judgement is usually good. . . . All in all, it is hard to think of anyone who could have achieved more than a fraction of what he has brought to the Open University.[44]

In 1969 and 1970 Perry worked eighteen hours a day, seven days a week, ending up in December 1970 with a coronary thrombosis which forced him to delegate responsibility for three months at the very time the first students were beginning their courses. Fortunately for his morale, enrolment was substantial. He made a complete recovery and said later that it was the price he had to pay for leading the team that brought the Open University into being.

OPEN UNIVERSITY STUDENTS

How open an open university could or should be was a question the admissions committee struggled with. The White Paper and the planning committee had decided that no educational qualifications would be required, and it was understood that the minimum age of students would be twenty-one. It was, however, conceivable that there would be more applications than the number of places agreed on—25,000 for the first entry in January 1971. In that event the admissions committee decided on the principle of first come, first served. Candidates not admitted in one year's quote would have priority the following year. It was a useful decision, as over 40,000 students applied in the first year, and in every succeeding year the number of places has been oversubscribed. There were, however, two further constraints on admission. New students were required to take an interdisciplinary foundation course in the first year of study. To avoid imbalances, a quota was imposed: 55 per cent of entering students enrolled in the arts or social sciences course and 45 per cent in the mathematics, science, or technology courses. Furthermore, there has been an attempt to allocate places as fairly as possible among heavily and sparsely populated regions and among England, Wales, Scotland, and Northern Ireland.

In the "class of 1971" a substantial proportion, over one-third, were teachers. This was to be expected since a large percentage of British teachers had attended colleges which awarded certificates but did not grant degrees. Teachers knew that a degree could lead to salary increases and better promotion prospects. When the Open University announced that it would grant exemption from some parts of its degree requirements for work completed earlier at training colleges, the attraction for teachers was strong indeed. Gradually, however, the proportion of teachers has decreased and among the applicants for entry in 1981 it stood at 16 per cent. By contrast, the proportion of women in the total number of applicants has risen—from 27 per cent for entry in 1971 to 45 per cent in 1981. And close to 60 per cent of all applicants in the first ten years were in the twenty-six to forty age group.

Largely because of the policy of offering credit exemptions to teachers and others who had taken post-secondary courses leading to diplomas and certificates, some 800 students had completed their degrees at the end of 1972. A graduation ceremony was held in the Great

Hall of Alexandra Palace. Honorary degrees were awarded to, among others, Jennie Lee, Peter Venables, Hugh Greene of the BBC, and Paolo Freire, the Brazilian adult educator and author of *Pedagogy of the Oppressed.* As the names of graduating students were called they came in their blue gowns to sit on the large platform. It was all very traditional except for the ending: the officers of the university, followed by honorary and ordinary graduates, left the platform as trumpets played Copeland's "Fanfare for the Common Man." The ceremony was televised, and nearly every local newspaper in the country carried a picture and story of one or two graduates.

There was a marked increase in the number of applications the next year. By 1976, twelve separate graduation ceremonies were necessary and it could then be predicted with reasonable certainty that half those enrolled in the Open University would complete their degrees.[45] For the "class of 1981" 43,000 students submitted applications for the 21,000 available places. At a news conference in January 1981, Mark Carlisle, minister of state for education and science in the Conservative government, defended the 46 per cent fee increase imposed by his department by pointing out that student fees would still account for only 13 per cent of the cost of an Open University education. He also mentioned that the 1980 grant to the university by the Thatcher government was in excess of £45 million. At this press conference the new vice-chancellor, Dr. John Horlock, made his first public appearance.

A discussion of Open University students seldom omits some reference to the "working-class issue," that is, the proportion of manual workers in the total enrolment. In applying for admission, students are asked to identify their occupation within a code of occupation groups based on categories used for statistical purposes by the registrar general of Great Britain. (See Table 5.)[46] When it was revealed that fewer than 5 per cent of applicants for the first (1971) entry were in categories eight, nine, and ten, usually referred to as working-class occupations, there was substantial criticism in the national and periodical press. Critics[47] recalled the early emphasis on the theme of the "second chance," and quoted Harold Wilson, who had predicted that the new university would offer opportunity to "those who, for one reason or another, have not been able to take advantage of higher education," and Lord Crowther, who said in his inaugural address that the first and most urgent task was to cater to the many thousands capable of a higher education but who had not got it. Surely, it was argued, these

Table 5
Applications by Occupation for Entry in 1971 and 1981

Code	Occupation Group	Applications for 1971	1981	Percentage of U.K. Population in 1970
01	housewives	9.2	16.7	26
02	armed forces	1.7	2.7	1
03	administrators and managers	6.9	2.4	2
04	education	35.9	16.4	1
05	professions and the arts	11.9	12.1	3
06	scientists & engineers	8.0	3.1	1
07	technical personnel	7.5	11.1	1
08	skilled trades	1.8	4.8	8
09	farming, mining, & other manufacturing	2.8	6.4	23
10	communications & transport			
11	clerical & office staff	8.2	12.1	9
12	sales, personal services	3.4	6.3	13
13	not working	2.5	4.2	12
14	in institutions			

were references to those who had left school at fifteen and were now manual workers in skilled or semi-skilled jobs. But they were not responding to the lure of a second chance, and some who had entered the Open University were finding it difficult to cope, particularly in mathematics and science. This evidence led critics to two conclusions: that the intentions of the Labour party to mitigate social inequality by opening higher education to disadvantaged members of British society had turned out to be fraudulent; and that if the intent had been to create greater equality the decision to found a university was a mistake. What disadvantaged adults in the working class needed was an open school or college that would place the second chance at the secondary school level and thus remedy academic shortcomings and prepare such adults for university courses later or, alternatively, give them a different option entirely through a curriculum directly related to their needs and problems. In place of a study of the traditional academic disciplines they should probe the problems of poverty, housing, and rundown neighborhoods and learn self-help strategies.[48]

Jennie Lee, Walter Perry, members of the planning committee, and the academic staff vigorously entered the debate. They replied that while there needed to be greater egalitarianism in higher education, the major objective of the new university was not to redress the balance of educational opportunity toward the working class. Jennie Lee made her own position quite explicit. She believed in the need for greater equality of opportunity, particularly for able adults who had grown up in the mining and agricultural villages and left school at fourteen or fifteen, but she was emphatically against a working man's university.[49] She never wavered in her determination to begin at the university level and then use the credibility gained through founding a first-rate institution to offer other courses and programs. She rejected the alternative: "the way not to start was from the bottom up."[50]

Walter Perry supported Lee's position:

> She showed no signs of wavering from this stance, and with hindsight, it seemed to me that she was right. Had she given way, had she attempted to start with a scheme of offering education through the media to adults, at school or pre-university level, I think the concept would have disappeared. Its costs would have been no less, its status would have been much less, it would have had no glamour. It was the glamour of a university in name and actuality that enabled her to win her way.[51]

Perry and his colleagues were, nevertheless, anxious to attract more working-class students. He felt that one reason for the small number was lack of information. This was confirmed in a study undertaken by the university in 1972, which revealed that while 78 per cent of the middle and upper classes had some knowledge about the Open University, only 22 per cent of the working class had heard of it. To correct this failure in communication, Perry commissioned a more vigorous advertising campaign in the mass circulation dailies. (One consultant recommended two national newspapers of different political bias with good football coverage.) Perry knew that other universities placed their students in socio-economic classifications by their parents' occupations. As a means of making comparisons and countering the adverse publicity, he asked his staff to investigate the parental occupations of their students. This study confirmed Perry's hunch: about 65 per cent of Open University students had working-class fathers,[52] but a good proportion had moved up the social and occupational ladder into the middle class. One student commented: "I'm a police inspector. You might think therefore I was middle-class. But I'm not. I'm working class born and bred. I left school at 15. I worked my way up from the beat by sheer hard work. And I want the education commensurate with the job I'm doing."[53]

In the debate over enrolment, can it be said that the Open University is failing to meet its obligations because a relatively small proportion of its students falls into working-class occupational categories? Or is it meeting its obligations very well indeed because on the basis of the father's occupation it has a larger proportion of working-class students than any university in Britain? And the proportion of students who are themselves in working-class occupations has more than doubled in ten years. (See Table 5.) In 1979, 40 per cent of students who were educationally unqualified (fewer than two A-levels) had graduated, thus confounding the sceptics, who had predicted a one-in-ten survival rate for all students. The basic irony in the "working-class debate" nevertheless remains: the expectation that disadvantaged students who have less previous schooling, less time off, and less money can thrive in a degree program that is, as Walter Perry was fond of saying, one of the most difficult that the wit of man has yet devised.

The B.A. Degree Program

There is only one undergraduate degree at the Open University, the Bachelor of Arts, and it is awarded to all students whether they have taken arts or science courses, or a combination of both. All courses are nine months long, from February to October. On average, students find that a full-credit course requires twelve to fifteen hours of study each week, a half-credit course the same amount of time spread over two weeks. Six full credits are required for the degree and eight for an Honours B.A. Most students take one full or two half-credit courses a year and thus complete their degree in six years. It is not a highly structured degree. The only restrictions on the choice of courses are that study for the degree must include two foundation courses, one of which must be taken in the first year. These interdisciplinary courses are offered by each faculty, except educational studies, and are designed to be not only a foundation for further study but an introduction to the concepts and principles, issues, and problems found in the arts, social sciences, science, mathematics, and technology. In setting out the nature of these courses the faculties have attempted to reassure the beginning student and at the same time guarantee a good measure of intellectual challenge. Here are three excerpts from course descriptions given in the 1982 *Guide for Applicants:*

> *A Science Foundations Course* (S101)j
> The course is designed both for students who do not expect to study science beyond foundation level, and for those who intend to go on to higher-level science courses. It will be within your reach even if you have no previous formal education in science and no mathematical knowledge beyond simple arithmetic. However, the treatment of science in the course, although essentially non-mathematical, is not superficial or trivial or at an elementary level, and it will present you with considerable intellectual challenge even if you have previous qualifications in science.
>
> *Social Sciences: a Foundation Course* (D102)
> We are aiming in this course to introduce you to some of the main issues which have concerned social scientists over the past two centuries. The primary focus is modern Britain, but the questions addressed are perennial:
>
> To what extent does the individual create his society or is himself constrained and moulded by it? How is it that societies hold together as they (usually) do, and how do they change over time? How do social conflicts arise and what sorts of forces either allow them to be contained or promote open insurrection? Why do people consent to be governed, and what control do we have over government policies?

> *An Arts Foundation Course* (A101)
> [Among the several aims of the course are:]
> To introduce you to the separate purposes and methods of the different individual disciplines in the Arts. . . .
>
> In the last part of the course you will make an integrated study of the arts, philosophy and history. You will consider various aspects of the movement in art, music and literature known as Romanticism, and its relationship with the changing material world produced by industrialization. In particular, you explore ideas of work, nature and preservation of the past with a view to discovering their significance in mid-nineteenth century Britain.
>
> This section includes study of paintings by Constable and Turner, Charlotte Brontë's novel *Jane Eyre,* some philosophical writings of Marx and J. S. Mill, and the music of Liszt.

Besides the foundation courses there is a wide selection of full-credit and half-credit courses. In mathematics, science, and technology many courses have recommended, but not required, prerequisites and students may secure advice on the choice of second- and third-level courses from tutors and counsellors at study centres.

When intending students have completed their applications, chosen a foundation course, applied for credit exemptions if any, they can expect to hear by September whether they are among the 45 per cent offered a place in the first year of application. If admitted, they receive the first three or four course units (an early decision was not to send out all the paperback booklets at once for fear of overwhelming the student), the list of set texts and booksellers who stock them, notes on radio and television programs and broadcast times, and advice on success as a student. This wealth of material, together with the ongoing correspondence after the courses begin in February, on average accounts for the thirty-five tons of mail that leave Milton Keynes each week.

The System of Teaching

The two most innovative features of the Open University are its "openness" and its system of teaching at a distance. As mentioned earlier, all the separate elements of distant teaching and learning—correspondence courses, radio and television broadcasts, assignments, tutorials, and summer schools—had been used for years, but it was not until the Open University was founded that top levels of talent and creativity and substantial resources were used to produce, maintain, and use highly sophisticated teaching materials. The creation of courses by the first course teams, ranging from nine to sixteen members, was a new experience for practically every member. It would have been surprising if tensions had not arisen; some academics were not convinced of the need for educational technologists, and professionally trained BBC producers were reluctant to give up control of the content of their broadcasts.

Initially, eighteen months was allocated for a course to be conceived, designed, written, and produced, but it was soon found this was not long enough. Drafts of course units were individually written and circulated to all members of the team for comment and discussion. A draft was then sent to a group of students for their comments, and the final draft was "vetted" by an external assessor. In recent years some course teams have grown large—thirty-two staff and twelve consultants in one instance—and gestation periods of three years were not unusual. Course teams may include editors, librarians, designers, and illustrators, but all team members do not attend all meetings, and much writing is assigned to individuals. The development of courses has accounted for the major share of academic staff time, in fact in some instances for all of it, to the detriment of research.

By 1982 a total of thirty-nine full-credit and ninety-two half-credit courses were available, and it was generally agreed that this number would not grow. Some courses will need to be replaced, others revised, and all updated. But the task of creating new courses is largely over and, given budget stringencies, course teams in the future will likely be smaller and more frugal with their time. Originally, a course was expected to continue for four years with minor revisions made each year by a small "maintenance" group. For reasons of economy this period has been lengthened and it is now not unusual for courses to last for six years. To Walter Perry the concept of the course team was "the most important single contribution of the Open University to teaching practice at the tertiary level."[54]

On the other hand, there are iconoclasts who have said that "the course team is a menace to the academic output and reputation of the Open University" and that "where good courses have been produced and maintained this has been in spite of, rather than because of it."[55]

This particular critic does not dispute the basic idea of the course team; it is, in his judgment, simply too difficult for academics to make it work. They are happy to engage in the early phases of discussion—discovering and articulating problems—but reluctant to make decisions or reach solutions. In large teams the members are obliged to comment on material about which they have no expertise, and the team setting gives the more articulate and domineering members undue influence.

But other academic staff members feel strongly about the value of team experience: "We owe much of our intellectual development and enthusiasm for experiment to the stimulus provided by collaboration, self-criticism, and exchange of ideas fostered within course teams. Some of the courses we have produced would have been unthinkable in the more hierarchical, departmentalized set-up typical of conventional teaching institutions."[56] Another vindication of the course team may lie in the fact that its products are open to the world. This aspect of the Open University means that a team's course units, readers, and broadcasts can be read, seen, and heard by scholarly critics, teachers, students, politicians, and the general public. Knowing this, a team is likely to take more pains to prepare a course than an individual academic who lectures in a closed-door classroom.

A further innovation in correspondence tuition is the unremitting attention given to teaching strategy. The arts faculty, for example, has attempted to make its course units into "tutorials in print," which is to say the staff tries to recreate an informal and reassuring relationship using a person-to-person approach and frequently asking students the kind of questions they would get in a face-to-face tutorial. This is particularly evident in the course units for the arts foundation course. Here are two illustrative paragraphs from Arnold Kettle's *Introduction to Literature,* which includes Units 6–8, page 12:

> You have probably wondered why I have started the unit this way, plunging almost straight into a rather complex piece of poetry, rather than beginning with some straightforward, reassuring "facts" about *A Midsummer Night's Dream* and its background, plot, stage history etc. I have, I'm aware, risked putting you off. But if you've got as far as this without being hopelessly put off you have probably realized what I'm up to.

Page 19
Did Shakespeare believe in magic? How would you answer the question? Have a go and compare your answer with mine, but don't *accept* mine unless you really think it's better than yours.

Open University course materials have been widely used both in Britain and in universities abroad. Requests to purchase these materials grew so demanding that in 1977 the university set up Open University Educational Enterprises Limited (OUEE). It markets the course texts, tapes of radio and television programs, and other teaching and learning aids in the United Kingdom and through a network of distributors in eighty other countries. Foreign-language editions are available in Spanish, Italian, Japanese, and Portuguese. Sales by OUEE have amounted to over £1 million a year. The quality of these materials lies primarily in their content, but in their format and design as well. A group of over 100 editors, designers, and illustrators has worked with academic staff to create what world universities apparently regard as a revolution in the quality of correspondence tuition. Together with the printed material and the broadcasts, some courses, particularly in science and technology, have developed home experimental kits. The kit for the foundation course in science arrives by post in two large cartons and a student finds inside some 270 items ranging from chemicals and test tubes to an analytical balance and a microscope. There are some fifty kits related to various courses which are loaned to students on payment of a returnable deposit.

The interest of national governments, international agencies, and universities overseas, together with the flow of visitors and the stream of enquiries, made it necessary to set up a Consultancy Service in Milton Keynes in 1973. Through it, contracts for staff consultation were negotiated on a fee-paying basis for more than seventy projects. In 1977 the Consultancy Service became the Centre for International Co-operation and Services (CICS), with a small full-time staff and a mandate to expand co-operation with governments and institutions in various parts of the world, not only through contractual projects but also through a program of conferences, seminars, and research. But the Centre was soon in trouble. The British government was not prepared to have any portion of its grant to the Open University diverted to overseas aid; such aid is the function of the Foreign Office. On the other hand, the new Centre found it impossible to be fully self-supporting. To sustain itself it would have been obliged to charge £200 a day a person for consultancies, which Third World countries found well beyond their means. With no immediate prospect of resolving this dilemma, the Centre closed in March 1980, on the understanding that, in the words of a review body on the future of the centre, "the university must retain a capability of effective response to approaches from overseas."

BROADCASTING

One of the few battles Jennie Lee lost was over broadcasting. She had her mind set on a new television channel given over exclusively or predominantly to the use of the Open University. It was only when the cost of a fourth channel was revealed (some £60 million for capital and operating costs) that she compromised and agreed to use BBC2, which was then, in the mid-sixties, in the development stage but would be available to audiences in almost all of Britain by the end of the decade. She and other members of Cabinet were confident that BBC2 would allocate 6:00–9:00 p.m. five days a week. It was, of course, wildly optimistic to expect to capture such a large amount of prime time. Nevertheless, agreements with the BBC allowed Open University television programs to be scheduled throughout most of the first decade 5:00–7:00 p.m. on week days and the whole of Saturday and Sunday mornings. In the early eighties the BBC insisted on scheduling more programs in the early morning and late at night and reducing the total number of hours of broadcast time.

The value of broadcasting has never been seriously questioned. A survey of some 10,000 students made in 1974 showed that on average students watched about two-thirds of the television programs and listened to about half the radio programs. To the beginning student television and radio can be a vital and interesting bridge from the familiar to the unfamiliar; perhaps this is why some 90 per cent of students in the foundation courses watch each program. The broadcasts also serve a very practical purpose. Traditionally, correspondence students have started a course at any time and continued at their own pace. Open University courses are different; they all start and stop at a given time and assignments are due on stated dates. Because the broadcasts are integrated with the course units, they serve as a pacing mechanism. A student is more apt to keep his reading and writing up-to-date when stimulated by the broadcast and thus more likely to struggle out of bed to see a scene from *A Midsummer Night's Dream* if there is an assignment on the play to be completed that week.

The broadcasts may also lessen the loneliness of the distance learner and give him a sense that others too are coping with a particular course. This feeling is reinforced when programs recognize the difficulties students may be having. There is a good deal of intentional informality in the broadcasts: colleagues address each other by first names, dress is casual, and pompous language and academic jargon are avoided. Faculty members recognize that television appearances are one way of establishing ties with students, thus creating a semblance of personal relationships. The broadcasts also bring to students leading authorities in the various disciplines and nationally known figures from government, business, and labor. Depending on the time of transmission, the broadcasts have thousands of "eavesdroppers," people not enrolled in a course but interested enough to watch and listen. This is another aspect of "openness," a chance for members of the general public to follow a course without enrolling for credit and for the university to attract new students.

In recruiting broadcasting staff, particularly the seventy specially trained BBC/OU producers who head a staff of 300, emphasis was placed on a strong academic background and, preferably, some teaching experience. There was, in short, a tendency to select an academic and train him or her in broadcasting rather than the reverse. Thus, BBC producers have worked at parity with academic staff and jointly have adapted broadcasting to the pedagogic requirements of particular faculties. In general, the science faculty has used television to demonstrate experiments that would be too costly or complex to be performed in students' homes. Mathematics has used animated graphic material to illustrate key concepts. Social science, technology, and educational studies have sent television crews to many parts of the world to film "real-life" case studies, and arts has created programs that have demonstrated interdisciplinary approaches to history, literature, music, and the visual arts.

Some early programs could only be described as dreary: a dull script read in a monotone by a lecturer who lacked both style and enthusiasm. Most programs however, are comparable in quality to the education and information programs made for BBC mainstream television.

According to one well-known critic, a program on the Managua earthquake and the lack of preparedness for it which was made for the technology faculty course, "Systems Performance: Human Factors and Systems Failures," was a program that could have been mistaken for an episode of Panorama, a prestigious BBC weekly production.

As this is written, the future of broadcasting within the Open University is uncertain. In 1982 the BBC removed all programs from early evening hours and scheduled them on week-day mornings and Saturdays and Sundays. The total number of hours was reduced from thirty-five to thirty-one. As a consequence, the university supplemented public transmission by distributing video cassette recorders to almost all the study centres. It is likely that the number of television broadcasts per course will be reduced, and some courses may have no broadcasts at all. Experiments will be made with the new Cyclops project, which uses TV screens and telephone lines for two-way audiovisual communication between tutors and students for group tutorials. With the use of a "pen," which is really a light-sensitive camera, a seminar can be conducted with both students and tutor able to draw diagrams and graphs and write on their screens while conversing by telephone. Television will continue to be used in courses where the course team can demonstrate it is essential, and there may be a greater use of television prior to the academic year and during summer schools. The use of "open" radio may give way to a greater use of audio cassettes. In developing new patterns of broadcasting and using new technologies there will be no dearth of expertise or facilities. With respect to the latter, in the autumn of 1981 the BBC/OU group moved from Alexandra Palace to a new and magnificently outfitted Production Centre on the Walton Hall campus at Milton Keynes.

TUTORING, COUNSELLING, AND ASSESSMENT

An Open University student divides the time he spends on a course as follows:[57]

Systematic reading	65%
Viewing and listening to TV and radio broadcasts	10%

Contact with tutors and counsellors; attending study centres; meeting other students; attending summer schools	15%
Doing practical work on projects; doing written work; taking examinations	10%

On average, a student through preference or necessity devotes a relatively small proportion of time to visiting study centres and engaging in face-to-face tutorials. The essential features of the system are independent learning and tutorial assistance given primarily through correspondence. Nevertheless, regional offices and study centres are indispensable in maintaining personal contact with students at the local level. In fact, one of the most innovative features of the Open University is the opportunity it gives a student to secure individual counselling on any matter. Counselling includes both the academic dialogue between tutor and student, with the tutor critically yet constructively commenting on written assignments, as well as face-to-face conversations in a study centre concerning academic and personal problems. When a student first registers he is assigned a tutor-counsellor to grade and comment on his assignments in the first-year foundation course, confer with him individually or in group tutorials, or talk to him by telephone. If, however, he is not interested in establishing these relationships or cannot conveniently get to a study centre he is under no obligation. There are, however, some students who feel there are subtle pressures placed on them to take advantage of these services:

> Throughout my long career as an OU student I have noticed the continuing efforts to make the OU more like a *real* university with emphasis on direct tuition—summer schools, tutorials, weekend schools, telephone tutorials, meetings in the pub. . . . The trouble is that while we appreciate this, the very reason we entered the OU is because we *want* distance teaching.
>
> I rather like communicating by the written word. . . . No waking in the night with the feeling, "If only I'd said that," or the crushing clincher of an argument that only occurs to you on the bus home. We can just re-write the last paragraph.
>
> No, it is the staff who really need all these day schools and tutorials. They just cannot believe that the written word really

> works. They have a distressing lack of faith in the power of print.
>
> Can't someone think of something? Perhaps OUSA [students' association] could set up "Rent-a-Student" while the rest of us get back to that fascinating book propped against the sauce bottle.[58]

Following the foundation course the student will have different course tutors for each course and when a course enrolment is small the tutor may live at a considerable distance. Comments on the assignment scripts, a telephone call, a postal exchange of an audio cassette, or an occasional telephone tutorial involving several students and a tutor are then the usual means of communication. Some students take the initiative in forming self-help groups. The original tutor-counsellor continues in a counselling capacity with the students "assigned" to him in their first year, a relationship that continues throughout the student's association with the university. The more than 5,000 tutor-counsellors and course tutors are employed part-time by the university and are usually based full-time at other universities, polytechnics, and colleges of higher education. Many have had previous experience in the field of adult education.

The 260 study centres are located in all manner of premises. They are usually open in the evenings and on occasional Saturdays throughout the teaching year, and may cater for as few as fifty or as many as 1,000 students. Their facilities and services vary a good deal. Larger ones may offer a library, computer terminal, common room, and cafeteria, but all provide rooms for watching television broadcasts, listening to radio programs, holding discussions, and meeting tutors. These study centres offer support and service of the kind that many students need, but for a variety of reasons—distance and travel problems, family and job commitments, or the simple fact of wanting to work alone—only about half the students use the centres regularly.

The regional offices are an integral part of the administrative and teaching system. Through these thirteen offices, strategically located in England, Wales, Scotland, and Northern Ireland, student services are provided in each region and a close liaison maintained with Walton Hall. A corps of academic staff known as staff tutors appoint and supervise the course tutors in each region and also serve as members of faculties and course teams. They are intermediaries and mediators between academics at headquarters and students and course tutors in the field. Similarly, a group of full-time senior counsellors set up the counselling and support services for students in their region and are responsible for the operation of the study centres. Student records are kept at both regional offices and Walton Hall and, through a computer network, data from student records can be shared for counselling purposes. The regional office staff negotiate the rental of space for study centres and keep relationships with local education authorities, further education colleges, local W.E.A. offices, and universities in good repair. Without the continuing co-operation of these bodies in providing part-time tutors, counsellors, examiners, and consultants and in making their facilities available, the Open University simply could not have its present decentralized system of tutoring and counselling.

A further aspect of the teaching system which is also organized on a regional basis is the summer school. From all the evidence available, ranging from carefully designed surveys to anecdotal reports, summer schools have been an exhilarating success for both students and staff. They offer Milton Keynes academics the only face-to-face encounter with students and they give students the intellectual and social "shot in the arm" that many need to stay the course. Again, as with study centres, there are students who are perfectly happy to work alone throughout the year, but for others summer school brings new ideas, intense discussion, and growing confidence that university-level work is not beyond them. Students in foundation courses and in most science and technology courses are required to attend the one-week summer schools held on university campuses all over Britain. Tutors come from other universities as well as from the Open University staff. One from the University of East Anglia has described his students as a mix of "company directors and city councillors, pilots and priests, housewives and hairdressers, pregnant mothers and men from the Prudential, social workers and salesmen, journalists and Justices of the Peace . . . and one lady who would rather not say."[59] He found that intelligence varied ("not a few first-class brains"), but what did not vary was the friendliness, tolerance, eagerness to learn, determination to participate positively in all the week's activities, responsiveness, sense of fun, and stamina.

Assessing and examining a student's work creates enormous problems for a university whose thousands of students are scattered throughout the country. The problem is compounded when the university adopts a credit system which demands assessment in each course, where assessment is regarded as an integral part of learning, and the university is determined, through assignments and examinations, to establish standards comparable to those of the more conventional universities. To satisfy all these requirements the university combines a system of continuous assessment, that is periodic assignments, with a three-hour final examination.

Assignments are of two kinds, those marked by tutors (TMA's) and those processed by the computer (CMA's). TMA's, usually eight for a full-credit course, are essay questions devised by the course team and marked by tutors. CMA's consist of multiple choice questions, also developed by the course team, that pose problems calling for the analysis and comprehension of material included in the course. A student normally receives a marked TMA within three weeks and a CMA grade within one week of its receipt by the university. Thus these assignments serve two purposes: they tell the student how well or badly he is progressing and, because there are deadlines to be met in submitting the assignments, they also are a pacing device.

The Open University realized that valuable as continuous assessment may be, there was no way to ensure academic integrity without a final examination. Students could secure the help of friends or spouses in doing assignments (and possibly learn a good deal in the process), but the only known way of testing the student's knowledge, judgment, and comprehension was the traditional essay question examination. The logistical problems of administering examinations for some 60,000 students in nearly 150 centres throughout Great Britain and Northern Ireland are daunting, to say nothing of setting and marking the examinations in order to maintain appropriate standards. Each course has its own examination and assessment board, composed of the chairman of the course team, academic staff, and external examiners appointed from other universities. This board monitors the whole apparatus of assessment: its members receive a selection of marked TMA's throughout the year; they scrutinize, comment upon, and approve the final examination; and read a sample of marked examination papers. They must also approve the appointment of markers, who are normally selected from the course teams and course tutors. In determining the pass list, the board, with the help of the computer, normally uses the best 75 per cent of a student's assignments and gives equal weighting to the final examination. In the first ten years more than 65 per cent of registered students obtained credit in their courses, an unusually high survival and pass rate for students in distance learning at the undergraduate level.

The First Decade

It is well-nigh impossible to judge accurately the performance of an institution as complex as a university, let alone one that at least in its own country is unique. But if we employ the usual criteria, the Open University was an astonishing success in its first decade. Sceptics' forebodings proved to be wrong, as highly qualified staff were engaged, student applications poured in, the drop-out rate was lower than predicted, student and staff morale was high, course materials were widely sought after, and missions from dozens of countries made their pilgrimage to Milton Keynes. Labour and Conservative governments provided adequate, if not generous, support. Frustrations were many and frequent, but were accepted with a spirit customary among pioneers as the price one pays for being a part of a new idea. It was, on the whole, a euphoric decade.

It is tempting to argue that the time was ripe for such a development in higher education in Britain and that Harold Wilson, Jennie Lee, Peter Venables, and Walter Perry were the right people who appeared at precisely the right time. That time was marked by technological and cultural developments indispensable to teaching and learning at a distance. Britain was blessed with BBC radio and television, both available in all parts of the realm, served by a highly competent staff, and committed to serving minority interests in a spirit of public service. Britain also had a large population living in a relatively small area, a good system of roads with generally short distances to study centres, a postal service that by international standards was fast and dependable, and a telephone network. It also enjoyed a high rate of literacy in one language. Computers and data processing made it possible to cope with large amounts of information connected with applications, student records, and assessments. As well, the late sixties was a period of relative affluence that enabled governments to found new universities; and wage and salary levels permitted young and early middle-age adults to pay Open University fees, buy television, and radio sets, own cars in which to drive to study centres and attend summer school.

One Ministry of Science and Education serves all of England and

Wales (Scotland has its own department) and thus a national enterprise can be planned in ways fundamentally different from those of, say, Canada or the United States where education is a matter of provincial or state jurisdiction. In spite of a good deal of pluralism, British universities, through external examiners and assessors, award degrees with similar standards. Hence a new university that aspires to academic respectability can engage in common discourse with any other university. In fact, all British universities founded in the past three decades have been monitored by academic advisory committees of senior academics drawn from other universities. A respected and extensive network of adult education programs, including further education colleges and informal evening courses, provided the Open University with tutors and counsellors.

To these characteristics of British education and British society add the shortage of university places in the face of a strong trend toward egalitarianism and the case for an open university would appear to be very strong. But innovation is regarded as a mixed blessing in Britain, although there have been notable examples such as the National Health Service and other aspects of social welfare. R. H. Tawney was probably right when he said: "A precipitate enthusiasm for audacious novelties is not among the characteristic weaknesses of our fellow-countrymen." Major new departures in higher education have been few, and a publicly planned university is rare. The birth and early nurture of the Open University (by Harold Wilson out of Jennie Lee) were essentially political, and it is tempting to believe that with the support of a shrewd prime minister and a determined Scot the new university was an irresistible idea whose time had come. In politics, however, there are few irresistibles. Wilson frequently had to negotiate with members of his cabinet, Callaghan and Jenkins particularly, trading cuts in one or another ministry to protect his infant. In these negotiations Jenkins as chancellor of the exchequer usually began by proposing that the Open University be abandoned, Wilson would vigorously disagree, and a compromise would result.[60] Edward Short, himself an external degree graduate and an enthusiastic Wilson supporter, likely accepted the Venables Report without debate in order to avoid opposition within the cabinet. The election of a Conservative government made the future even more precarious. At any time between the election of the new government in the summer of 1970 and the beginning of courses in 1971 the university could have been abolished. The Conservative chancellor was Iain Macleod. It has been reported, but never confirmed, that on his desk the night he died on 20 July 1970, was a paper recommending abolition of the Open University.[61] Abolition did not come; instead the Heath government cut the university's budget by £1 million over the next three years.

But after a decade of success what of the future? Higher fees and an ailing economy may affect the number of new students, but it would be surprising if total enrolment fell below 60,000. A leaner budget is almost inevitable, and ways will have to be found to create and maintain courses more cheaply. Course teams will be smaller, the one-man course team is not beyond imagining, and academic staff will increasingly share responsibility for tutoring. Course teams may have to demonstrate convincingly that television broadcasts are necessary, particularly for third- and fourth-level courses, which are usually low in registration.Thus with minor adjustments the university should be able to maintain a stable undergraduate program.

The frontier lies in a different direction but one that has already been penetrated. Among the objects listed in the Open University charter is one that is nothing if not broad-ranging: "to promote the educational well-being of the community generally." This, said the Committee on Continuing Education chaired by Peter Venables, clearly requires the university to provide more than degree-level courses. Writing in the fall of 1980 just prior to his retirement as vice-chancellor, Walter Perry thought that now the university had established its reputation through a degree program there was a new priority: "I believe that the future of the OU in the next decade depends, more than many people think, on its successfully developing programs of continuing education."[62] In the context of the Open University the term *continuing education* embraces "all learning opportunities which are taken up after full-time compulsory schooling has ceased. They can be full or part-time and will include both vocational and non-vocational study." Non-credit courses have, in fact, been offered for some years and short courses (eight weeks) with such titles as "The First Years of Life," "The Pre-School Child," and "Childhood 5–10" attracted 15,000 parents in 1981. Employing specially qualified staff and using the experience gained in creating the undergraduate courses, the Community Education Section has developed these and other courses (consumer decisions and health choices, also with a family emphasis), each of which includes a "learning package" of handbooks, leaflets, and exercises and television and radio broadcasts. Computer-marked assignments are part of these courses but tutorials are normally not arranged.

Enrolment in the continuing education program offers a still wider range of options: degree-level courses, professional in-service training for teachers and social workers, and courses for managers and engineers who need to keep abreast of new technologies. Perry has estimated that by 1990 there will be some 110,000 students, other than those in the undergraduate degree program, taking continuing education courses developed by the university through collaboration with all sorts of voluntary, professional, and governmental organizations. With a substantial staff at Walton Hall and in the regions, and an estimated budget of £9 million, the Continuing Education Centre would become a major enterprise and could well challenge the priority given to the undergraduate program in the first decade.

Inevitably, this development will create friction with the academic staff, whose backgrounds and loyalties are strongly attached to the undergraduate program. But if, as is probable, the public need for an expanded program of continuing education becomes evident, and the only purpose for which new government grants can be used, it would be surprising if the Open University did not respond. To accept undergraduate and continuing education jointly as top priorities, each competing on equal terms for academic and technological services, could become a punishing test of survival, punishing because it will mean creating courses and programs that do not have the prestige of university status and degree credit, and because there will be renewed political battles to secure support for "adult education." On the other hand, it may bring a resurgence of the energy, creativity, and idealism of the first decade.

SEVEN

The Dynamics of Innovation

I have examined six innovations in Europe and North America over a period of 150 years. Their founders possessed unique abilities and beliefs and addressed these to unique social, economic, and political situations, thus making a strong case that any major innovation in education is a remarkable and singular event. Jennie Lee and Mary Lyon held entirely different views on the basic purposes of education, and the condition of Horace Mann's 1837 Massachusetts called for different leadership and solutions from those of Kurt Hahn's 1920 Germany. And while Grundtvig, Coady, and Tompkins occupied more common ground, the privately operated but state supported folk schools of rural Denmark never made their way to Nova Scotia. The Antigonish Movement was based on the Extension Department of a vibrant university. To what extent, then, is innovation in education a unique combination of the founder's talent and power, the faith and loyalty of his followers, and their combined capacity to face and deal effectively with stress or crisis? If every innovation is unique, can we find any valid generalizations among the six educational movements and their founders?

There are certain concepts in the development of social movements and in the characteristics of leadership which may apply to movements in education and to educational leadership. A social movement seems to go through a "career," a typical pattern of unfolding and development, a "regular sequence of stages through which each . . . movement typically passes as it matures and becomes more institutionalized."[1] As we have seen, there is a period of heightened stress based on such dynamics as deprivation, economic depression, feelings of injustice, or political and social strain (the loss of Schleswig and Holstein, the decay of common schools in Massachusetts, the price of fish in Nova Scotia, the shortage of university places in Great Britain). Such stress may lead to social unrest and agitation or to collective behavior designed to establish a new institution or movement. Attempts to heal this cultural "distortion" may attract leaders to strengthen morale, create an esprit de corps, develop an ideology, and devise a set of tactics (Grundtvig's outdoor addresses, Tompkins's meetings in Canso, and Hahn's reports to his board of governors and members of the British establishment). The leader and a small corps of followers then espouse the ideology defining the causes of strain and prescribe a solution. A movement is organized and its ideas are spread through established channels of communication.

Increasingly, during this organizational phase, there is a determined effort to implement prescribed solutions (Mount Holyoke Seminary, Christian Flor's folk high school, Gordonstoun). If the time is ripe (constitutional reform in Denmark, post-Second World War prosperity in Britain), a society allows the movement to succeed. Finally, there is a period of "routinization," an increasing emphasis on matters of organization, creation of a bureaucracy, and development of an institution which are accepted as means of reducing the strain (such as the American women's colleges and the co-operatives organized by the Extension Department of St. Francis Xavier University).

Causes of stress vary. Grundtvig and Tompkins and Coady lived in societies in deep economic stress. Hahn attempted to moderate the effects of an industrial society on its youth; Lyon and the Open University group worked to improve the education of young women in the United States and adults in Britain. Mann revived an existing institution, demonstrated its weaknesses, and transformed it into a system of public schools.

In exploring the growth of a movement it becomes clear that both the characteristics of the leader and the demands of the individual situation must be examined simultaneously. "The controversy between those who view leadership as a personal trait and those who view it as determined by the situation can be laid to rest by emphasizing the need for congruence between personality and situation."[2] In fact, the leader identifies and interprets a given situation, for his people do not see it clearly, recognize its causes, or envisage possible solutions. Coady analyzed the depression in the Maritime Provinces and the causes of the capitalist economy's failure. To make such an analysis requires experience and reflection and all the founders had time in which to be detached, brood, and experiment before they became committed and involved.

All founders had the capacity to speak persuasively in public. There are first-hand accounts of Hahn's magnetism, Perry's conviction, Mann's eloquence, and Coady's ability to shatter complacency. Grundtvig could cast a spell over thousands at an open air meeting, but appears to have been equally effective with Kold sitting at his feet. Mann, Coady, and Lee were similarly able to hold large audiences, but Mary Lyon and Tompkins were more comfortable and effective in small and informal settings. However, they all used a variety of methods; Hahn privately printed his speeches and through radio, correspondence, *The Times,* and annual reports found ways of getting through both to the public and to his disciples and supporters.

In their personal lives there were similarities and differences among all these founders. Evidence abounds of individualism in their dress and bearing. They would immediately attract your attention: Hahn with his wide-brimmed hat; Mann who looked like an orator even in repose; and Grundtvig, who seemed to be a patriarch for most of his life. Childhood was a time of both trouble and great joy in their lives, and they later mentioned the strong influence of their mothers. Only Hahn came from a wealthy home. Mary Lyon taught all her life. Coady, interestingly, was the only one professionally trained in education. A basic motive behind their careers (with the exception of the Open University Group) was religious conviction, usually rooted in a Christian denomination. For Mary Lyon fulfilment of that conviction was nothing less than the salvation of her students. In Coady and Tompkins and Hahn and Mann religious beliefs also ran deep. Grundtvig's religious feelings were linked to his concern for a Danish renaissance; Jennie Lee's mission was a better life for the common man. Frequently these leaders' sense of mission allowed them to carry into their work tremendous bursts of energy, though on occasion this zeal deserted them and they were the victims of deep depression.

Together with the inner intensity and vitality through which they pursued their mission there was also a search for new ideas and concern for the practicalities of building a movement or institution. Every member of the group, except for Mary Lyon, who did not have the time or money, travelled abroad looking at recent developments in his field. Coady and Tompkins explored university extension in Britain and the United States, Mann made an extended trip to European schools, and Grundtvig studied the influence of industrialization in England and enjoyed the intellectual atmosphere of Trinity College, Cambridge. Each brought home new ideas and communicated them. They were confident and optimistic in their belief in education. They had no doubt that education could awaken individuals and change the course of society. Their goals were clear and quite specific and while on occasion they were disappointed with results, their basic belief did not falter: they believed education *could* make a difference. This belief drove them sometimes to the point of exhaustion, in planning, persuading, fund-raising, organizing, and administering a movement or institution. They could weather disappointment and criticism, work through difficulties, and face indifference and remain resilient and optimistic, at least to their followers.

This kind of charismatic leadership rejects old customs and beliefs and calls for new ways of living and thinking. The leader defies the past and demands new obligations, particularly of a small circle of disciples. They are not technically trained officials in the usual sense, but rather a communal group whose members are intensely loyal to the leader and prepared to serve him, if need be, without rank or salary. This inner circle may establish a church, party, or institution requiring a body of theory or legal regulations. For Mary Lyon these were her benevolent gentlemen, and her Holyoke staff and alumnae. Hahn had the loyalty of Gordonstoun graduates and the enthusiastic support of influential members of the university, church, and business communities. Members of the rural clergy were among Coady's disciples and prepared the way for his mass meetings. A group of friends and colleagues did the same for Horace Mann as he rode the circuit for five years throughout Massachusetts.

All leaders discussed were, in effect, self-appointed to the crusades they initiated. To be sure, they held other appointments, but these positions did not determine the nature or direction of their crusade. Coady as director of extension and Mann as secretary of the board of education were not obliged to choose a given set of priorities. Nevertheless, they and others benefited from the prestige and influence office gave them: Tompkins as a priest and Jennie Lee as a cabinet minister.

Each founder fulfilled another requisite of charismatic leadership:

evidence of success. For Grundtvig and his followers—Flor, Kold, and Schroeder—this meant expansion of folk high schools and their continuing support; for Lyon, Hahn, and Perry enrolment figures were significant. Coady was sensitive to study club attendance and the growth of co-operatives, and Mann gained credibility and prestige through passage of new legislation and the defeat of his enemies through pamphlet warfare.

All these leaders used the spoken and written word, and in several cases their writings are a valuable legacy. Tompkins's *Knowledge for the People,* Coady's *Masters of Their Own Destiny,* and Mann's *Annual Reports* are historic documents of high quality. But it was not through a body of written work that these men achieved their authority as leaders. It was rather through the spoken, the "living word." All had new, indeed original ideas to impart, all were in some degree challenging the status quo, and all wanted to appeal to their constituencies. Their appeal was largely emotional and expressed through personality or charisma.

One of the most cogent formulations of this kind of leadership was made by Max Weber (1864–1920), the German political scientist, social historian, and sociologist. Of Weber's three types of authority—the bureaucratic/legal, the traditional, and the charismatic—it is the charismatic that is useful here. The idea of charismatic leadership came originally from religion. The root meaning of charisma is a gift of grace, an endowment of extraordinary powers direct from the gods. Weber generalized this concept to include leaders in fields other than religion. His most well-known definition is as follows:

> The term "charisma" will be applied to a certain quality of an individual personality by virtue of which he is set apart from ordinary men and treated as endowed with supernatural, superhuman, or at least specifically exceptional powers or qualities. These are such as are not accessible to the ordinary person, but are regarded as of divine origin or as exemplary, and on the basis of them the individual concerned is treated as a leader.[3]

Weber uses the term charisma without reference to ethical, aesthetic, or other judgments and thus he includes founders of religions, prophets, warrior heroes, and demagogues who may be good or evil. Such leaders are usually self-appointed and emerge in times of strain and trouble. When multiple stresses converge and the distress reaches a crisis a state of "charismatic hunger" may develop, as was perhaps the case in post-World War I Germany, in India of Ghandi's time, and in the new African states. To retain his authority a leader must "prove" himself through success; if he fails to do so he will lose his charismatic claim and authority.

Both the institutions and the influences of the founders surveyed in this book live on. Gordonstoun and Outward Bound graduates lovingly tell anecdotes about Hahn, alumnae quietly gather at Mary Lyon's grave in the centre of the Holyoke campus, and Coady is still an almost palpable presence in eastern Nova Scotia. Inevitably, the fire and excitement have subsided and charismatic authority which, as Weber noted, exists only in "the process of originating," has given way to organizational structure or bureaucratic hierarchy. Ideas have become institutions, but in the process ideas have not died. In fact, the well-known axiom to the effect that the only way to preserve an idea is to institutionalize it and in the process the idea dies, is scarcely relevant here.

There has been, indeed, an infusion of new ideas to modify and supplement the founders' contribution. The folk high schools, women's colleges, Outward Bound, and the Antigonish Movement have modified their programs to meet changing times. The American elementary school has not only survived bureaucratization but has also weathered swings in the educational theory pendulum. The Open University is enrolling both degree and continuing education students, and some ten other universities based on distance teaching now thrive in various parts of the world. Thus we have a paradox: in a period when faith in the power of education has been partially shattered, here are diverse institutions and movements, founded by men and women who had a consummate belief in education, that are in sound health. Maybe the founders built better than they knew: their ideas have been transformed into adaptable and resilient institutions that have attracted a high quality of leadership. In recent years Walter Perry, A. A. MacDonald, David Sutcliffe, Ebbe Lungaard, and Joshua Miner have brought creativity and flexibility to their administrative roles. These latter-day leaders refused to cast their founders' ideas into a mold and instead have struck off in new directions. Yet they have kept the faith.

These, then, are some reflections on innovation in education. The original founders continue to be relevant in our time. Their problems are not our problems and their lives do not speak directly to our condition, but those committed to education need to know the nature of these innovations, the context of the struggles, what preceded and what followed them, and the intensity of their founders' passion. It is good to know that a leader with a committed group of disciples can cut his way through or around an educational bureaucracy and build something vital to his time. But their real contribution was their vision and the fire and passion that moved them to bring a new idea to birth. The Outward Bounders, Mary Lyon's young ladies, Danish farmers, Nova Scotia fishermen, the children of Massachusetts, and the Open University's police inspector are the results of original ideas hurled at the status quo by founders with passionate and unwavering conviction.

NOTES

CHAPTER 1: N. F. S. GRUNDTVIG

1. Kaj Thaning, *N. F. S. Grundtvig,* trans. David Hohnen (Copenhagen, 1972), p. 11.
2. Poul Georg Lindhardt, *Grundtvig: An Introduction* (London, 1951), p. 13.
3. Jindra Kulich, "N. F. S. Grundtvig and the Folk High Schools," *Dalhousie Review,* XLIII (1963), 68.
4. Olive Campbell, *The Danish Folk School: Its Influence in the Life of Denmark and the North* (New York: Macmillan, 1928), p. 62.
5. Thomas Rørdam, *The Danish Folk High Schools,* trans. Alison Borch-Johansen (Copenhagen: Danish Institute, 1965), p. 11.
6. Ragnar Lund, *Scandinavian Adult Education* (Copenhagen: Danish Institute, 1952), p. 20.
7. Peter Manniche, *Rural Development and the Changing Countries of the World* (London: Pergamon Press, 1969), p. 92.
8. Johannes Knudsen, ed., *Selected Writings of N. F. S. Grundtvig* (Philadelphia: Fortress Press, 1976), pp. 169–70.
9. Georgina Noëlle Davies, *Education for Life: A Danish Pioneer* (London: Williams and Norgate, 1931), p. 75.
10. Ibid., p. 78.
11. Knudsen, *Selected Writings of N. F. S. Grundtvig,* p. 164.
12. Davies, *Education for Life,* pp. 109–10.
13. Holger Begtrup, Hans Lund, and Peter Manniche, *The Folk High Schools of Denmark and the Development of a Farming Community* (4th ed., London: Oxford University Press, 1949), pp. 52–53.
14. Manniche, *Rural Development,* pp. 82–83.
15. Begtrup et al., *The Folk High Schools,* p. 31.
16. Campbell, *The Danish Folk School,* pp. 103–4.
17. Ibid., p. 101.
18. Rørdam, *The Danish Folk High Schools* (2nd ed., Copenhagen: 1980), p. 89.
19. Ibid., pp. 74, 86, 104.

20. Ibid., p. 76.
21. Rørdam, *The Danish Folk High Schools,* pp. 88–89.
22. Victor Andersen, "How Danes Earn Their Living," *Denmark Today* (Copenhagen: Ministry of Foreign Affairs, 1979), p. 34.
23. Central Co-operative Committee of Denmark, *The Co-operative Movement in Denmark* (Copenhagen, 1966), p. 3.
24. Christopher Follett, "Waves of Woe Are Breaking," *The Times,* "Special Report on the Nordic Economies," 21 May 1980, p. ii.
25. Lisbeth Larsen, "A Large and Varied Choice in Education," *Denmark Today* (Copenhagen: Ministry of Foreign Affairs, 1979), p. 23.
26. Kolding High School, *Statement of Objectives,* n.d.
27. P. A. Godecke, principal of Östergötland Folk High School, 1873, in Rørdam, *The Danish Folk High Schools,* pp. 174–75.
28. Fridlev Skrubbeltrang, *The Danish Folk High Schools* (Copenhagen: Danish Institute, 1947), p. 80.

CHAPTER 2: HORACE MANN

1. Horace Mann, *Journal,* 18 May 1837, in Mary Mann, *Life of Horace Mann* (Boston, 1888), p. 70.
2. Ibid., 27 May 1837, p. 72.
3. Ibid., 14 June 1837, p. 76.
4. Ibid., 29 June 1837, p. 80.
5. Ibid., 30 June 1837, pp. 80–81.
6. Horace Mann, *Lectures on Education* (Boston, 1855; reprint, Arno Press and the New York *Times,* 1969), pp. 11–59.
7. Ibid., p. 19.
8. Ibid., p. 21.
9. *Journal,* 10 Nov. 1837, p. 91.
10. Mary Mann, *Life of Horace Mann,* pp. 10–11.
11. Ibid., p. 17.
12. Mann to Charlotte Messer, 9 June 1830.
13. Ibid., 8 July 1829.
14. *Journal,* 31 July 1837, in Jonathan Messerli, *Horace Mann* (New York: Alfred Knopf, 1972), p. 160.
15. Mann to Mary Peabody, 26 Aug. 1833.
16. Ibid., 2 July 1837.
17. Mann to Lydia Mann, 27 Nov. 1837.
18. *Journal,* 3 Nov. 1837, in Mary Mann, *Life of Horace Mann,* p. 90.
19. Horace Mann, "First Annual Report," *Lectures and Annual Reports* (Cambridge, MA, 1867), p. 387.
20. Ibid., p. 394.
21. Ibid., p. 403.
22. Ibid., p. 407.
23. Ibid., p. 410.
24. Ibid., p. 412.

25. Ibid., p. 422.
26. Horace Mann, "Special Preparation: A Pre-requisite to Teaching," *Lectures,* p. 71.
27. Messerli, *Horace Mann,* p. 293.
28. *Journal,* 18 Jan. 1838, p. 99.
29. *Common School Journal,* I, 6 (15 Mar. 1839), 96.
30. *Common School Journal,* III, 10 (15 May 1841), 156.
31. Ibid.
32. Ibid., p. 157.
33. Messerli, *Horace Mann,* p. 373.
34. Horace Mann, "Tenth Annual Report," *Common School Journal,* IX, 8 (15 Apr. 1847), 127.
35. Mann to Henry Barnard, 4 May 1839.
36. Michael B. Katz, *The Irony of Early School Reform* (Cambridge, MA: Harvard University Press, 1968), p. 7.
37. Frank Tracy Carlton, *Economic Influences upon Educational Progress in the United States, 1820–1850* (New York: Teachers College Press, Columbia University, 1965), p. 32.
38. David B. Tyack, *The One Best System: A History of American Urban Education* (Cambridge, MA: Harvard University Press, 1974), p. 30.
39. Carlton, *Economic Influences upon Educational Progress,* p. 32.
40. Rush Welter, *Popular Education and Democratic Thought in America* (New York: Columbia University Press, 1962), p. 46.
41. Merle Curti, *The Social Ideas of American Educators* (Totawa, NJ: Littlefield Adams, 1968), p. 89.
42. Horace Mann, *Twelfth Annual Report,* in Lawrence A. Cremin, *The Republic and the School* (New York: Teachers College Press, Columbia University, 1957), p. 87.
43. Curti, *Social Ideas of American Educators,* p. 77.
44. Curti, ibid., p. 78.
45. *Common School Journal,* IX, 22 (15 Nov. 1847), 339.
46. Curti, *Social Ideas of American Educators,* pp. 86–87.
47. *Journal,* 11 June 1837, in Mary Mann, *Life of Horace Mann,* p. 74.
48. In Cremin, *The Republic and the School,* p. 78.
49. Ibid., p. 7.
50. Raymond B. Culver, *Horace Mann and Religion in the Massachusetts Public Schools* (New Haven: Yale University Press, 1929; reprint, Arno Press/New York Times, 1969), p. 217.
51. In Cremin, *The Republic and the School,* p. 102.
52. Neil G. McCluskey, *Public Schools and Moral Education: The Influence of Horace Mann, William Torrey Harris and John Dewey* (New York: Columbia University Press, 1958), p. 92.
53. Ibid., p. 273.
54. In Cremin, *The Republic and the School,* p. 63.
55. *Common School Journal,* I, 24 (16 Dec. 1839), 381–82.
56. In Cremin, *The Republic and the School,* pp. 77–78.

57. John D. Davies, *Phrenology: Fad and Science* (New Haven: Yale University Press, 1955), pp. 3–4.
58. E. I. F. Williams, *Horace Mann: Educational Statesman* (New York: Macmillan, 1937), p. 232.
59. Mann to George Combe, 11 Feb. 1839.
60. Mann to Lydia Mann, 9 Nov. 1838.
61. Davies, *Phrenology*, p. 100.
62. Messerli, *Horace Mann*, p. 383.
63. "Seventh Annual Report," *Common School Journal*, VI, 6 (15 Mar. 1844), 103.
64. Ibid., p. 152.
65. Ibid., p. 171.
66. Ibid., pp. 191, 194.
67. Mann to William B. Fowle, 17 Apr. 1848.
68. Charles Sumner to Mann, 24 May, 21, 25 June 1848, in Messerli, *Horace Mann*, p. 466.
69. Horace Mann, *Slavery: Letters and Speeches* (Boston, 1851; reprinted, Arno Press and the New York *Times*, 1969), p. 72.
70. Messerli, *Horace Mann*, p. 533.
71. Mann to the Rev. E. Fay, 13 May 1852.
72. Horace Mann, "Baccalaureate Address," in Messerli, *Horace Mann*, p. 583.
73. Ibid., p. 584, Mann's italics.
74. Mann to Richard Henry Dana Jr., 17 Sept. 1847.
75. Robert B. Downs, *Horace Mann* (New York: Twayne Publishers, 1974), pp. 150–51; George Henry Martin, *The Evolution of the Massachusetts Public School System* (Appleton, 1894), p. 174.
76. Lawrence A. Cremin, *Transformation of the School* (New York: Knopf, 1961), p. 13.

CHAPTER 3: MARY LYON

1. Mary Lyon to her mother, 13 May 1821.
2. Marion Lansing, ed., *Mary Lyon through Her Letters* (Boston: Books Inc., 1937), p. 36.
3. Thomas Woody, *A History of Women's Education in the United States*, Vol. I (New York: Octagon Books, 1966), pp. 302–3.
4. Willystine Goodsell, ed., *Pioneers of Women's Education in the United States* (New York: AMS Press, 1970), p. 196.
5. Ibid., p. 173.
6. Joan N. Burstyn, "Catharine Beecher and the Education of American Women," *New England Quarterly*, XLVII (1974), 386–403.
7. Mary Lyon to Amanda White, 20 Feb. 1826.
8. Mary Lyon to Zilpah Grant, 28 Feb. 1827.
9. Edward Hitchcock, *The Power of Christian Benevolence Illustrated in the Life and Labors of Mary Lyon* (Northampton, MA, 1851), p. 138.

10. Mary Lyon to Zilpah Grant, 4 Feb. 1833.
11. Mary Lyon, "New England Female Seminary for Teachers," in Hitchcock, *The Power of Christian Benevolence,* pp. 164–67.
12. Mary Lyon to Zilpah Grant, 6 Apr. 1833.
13. Mary Lyon to Hannah White, 26 Feb. 1834.
14. Mary Lyon to Zilpah Grant, 1 Mar. 1833.
15. Mary Lyon to her mother, 12 May 1834.
16. Elizabeth Green, *Mary Lyon and Mount Holyoke: Opening the Gates* (Hanover, NH: University Press of New England, 1979), pp. 141–45.
17. Mary Lyon to her mother and sister, 23 July 1835.
18. Hitchcock, *The Power of Christian Benevolence,* pp. 244–45.
19. Mary Lyon to Zilpah Grant, 9 Oct. 1836.
20. Mary Lyon, *General View of the Principles and Design of Mount Holyoke Female Seminary* (Boston: Perkins and Marvin, 1837), p. 21.
21. Edward N. Kirk, "Commemorative Address," *Twenty-fifth Anniversary Memorial of Mount Holyoke Female Seminary* (South Hadley, MA, 1862), p. 26.
22. Lansing, *Mary Lyon through Her Letters,* p. 264.
23. Mary Lyon to Zilpah Grant Banister, December 1842, n.d.
24. Mary Lyon to Zilpah Grant Banister, 8 March 1843.
25. Ibid.
26. Mabel Loomis Todd, *Letters of Emily Dickinson* (New York: Harper and Bros., 1931), p. 25.
27. Green, *Mary Lyon and Mount Holyoke,* p. 221.
28. Hitchcock, *The Power of Christian Benevolence,* p. 453.
29. *Springfield Republican,* 8 Aug. 1846.
30. Mary Lyon to Zilpah Grant, 8 Mar. 1841.
31. Sarah Locke Stow, *History of Mount Holyoke Seminary* (South Hadley, MA: Holyoke Seminary, 1887), p. 287.
32. Green, *Mary Lyon and Mount Holyoke,* p. 344.
33. Ibid., p. 383n7.
34. Stow, *History of Mount Holyoke Seminary,* p. 267.
35. Ibid., pp. 327–47.
36. Ibid., pp. 318, 323.
37. Ibid., p. 224.
38. Arthur C. Cole, *A Hundred Years of Mount Holyoke College* (New Haven, CT: Yale University Press, 1940), p. 201.
39. Woody, *A History of Women's Education in the United States,* Vol. II, p. 140.
40. Mabel Newcomer, *A Century of Higher Education for American Women* (New York: Harper and Bros., 1959), p. 17.
41. Ibid.
42. Woody, *A History of Women's Education in the United States,* Vol. II, p. 185.
43. Willis Rudy and John Brubacher, *Higher Education in Transition, 1636–1956* (New York: Harper and Bros., 1958), p. 67.

44. Edward H. Clarke, *Sex in Education or a Fair Chance for the Girls* (Boston, 1873), pp. 40, 62–63.
45. Roberta Frankfurt, *Collegiate Women: Domesticity and Career in Turn-of-the-Century America* (New York: New York University Press, 1977), p. 41.
46. Barbara M. Cross, ed., *The Educated Woman in America: Selected Writings of Catharine Beecher, Margaret Fuller and M. Carey Thomas* (New York: Teachers College Press, 1965), p. 36.
47. Frankfurt, *Collegiate Women*, p. 52.
48. Ibid., p. 33.
49. Mary Woolley, "Inaugural Address," *The Mount Holyoke Inauguration Number* (1901), pp. 8–15.
50. Ibid.
51. Frankfurt, *Collegiate Women*, p. 99.
52. Mount Holyoke Alumni Association, *One Hundred Year Biographical Directory, 1837–1937*, ed. Mary C. J. Higley (South Hadley, MA: Mount Holyoke College, 1937), pp. 708–9.
53. Frankfurt, *Collegiate Women*, p. 99.
54. Mount Holyoke College, *The Seventy-Fifth Anniversary, 1912* (South Hadley, MA: Mount Holyoke College, 1913), pp. 56–57.
55. Mount Holyoke, *One Hundred Year Biographical Directory*, p. 707.
56. Liva Baker, *I'm Radcliffe! Fly Me!: The Seven Sisters and the Failure of Women's Education* (New York: Macmillan, 1976), pp. 10–11.
57. Woody, *A History of Women's Education in the United States*, Vol. II, pp. 416–19.
58. Baker, *I'm Radcliffe!*, p. 193.
59. Catharine Stimpson, "Women at Bryn Mawr," in *Women on Campus: The Unfinished Liberation* (New Rochelle, NY: Change Magazine, 1975), pp. 174–94.
60. Baker, *I'm Radcliffe!*, pp. 188–89.
61. Caroline Bird, "Women's Lib and the Women's Colleges," in *Women on Campus*, pp. 220–35.
62. David Truman, "The Women's Movement and the Women's College," in *Women in Higher Education*, eds. W. Todd Furness and Patricia Graham (Washington: American Council on Education, 1974), pp. 56–60.
63. Gale Stubbs McClung, "What Is This Thing Called Co-education?," *Mount Holyoke Alumnae Quarterly*, LV, 6 (Winter 1972), 241–52.
64. Ibid., LXV, 3 (Fall 1981), pp. 14–17.
65. Baker, *I'm Radcliffe!*, p. 149 and *Mount Holyoke Alumnae Quarterly*, LXV, 3 (Fall 1981), 14–17.
66. "Directory of Basic College Data," *Peterson's Annual Guide to Undergraduate Study* (Princeton, NJ: Peterson's Guides, 1982), pp. 2–39.
67. *Mount Holyoke Alumnae Quarterly*, LV, 3 (Fall 1971), special insert.
68. Mount Holyoke College, *For Women: A Challenge to Excel* (1981), p. 11.
69. Mount Holyoke College, *Why a College for Women*, n.d.
70. M. Elizabeth Tidball and Vera Kistiakowsky, "Baccalaureate origins of

American Scientists and Scholars," *Science*, Vol. 193, No. 4254 (20 Aug. 1976), 646–52.

71. M. Elizabeth Tidball, "Educating the New Majority: Women and Achievement," *Mount Holyoke Alumnae Quarterly*, LXV, 3 (Fall 1981), 10–13.
72. Matina S. Horner, "Fail: Bright Women," *Psychology Today*, III, 6 (Nov. 1969), 36–38, 62.
73. *Mount Holyoke Now*, No. 3 (Nov. 1971), 3.
74. Norma Rosen, "Mount Holyoke Forever Will Be for Women Only," *New York Times Magazine*, 9 Apr. 1972, p. 63.
75. Ibid., p. 56.
76. Gene Maeroff, "Perspective for the '80s: Patterns, Problems and Expectations in Higher Education," *Mount Holyoke Alumnae Quarterly*, LXIII, 4 (Winter 1980), 2–7. See also Alexander Astin, *Four Critical Years: Effects of College on Beliefs, Attitudes and Knowledge* (San Francisco: Joss-Bass, 1978).
77. *Seattle Post-Intelligencer*, 19 Nov. 1980, p. A11.
78. *Mount Holyoke Now*, LXXX, 5 (1980), 1.

CHAPTER 4: JAMES TOMPKINS AND MOSES COADY

1. Daniel W. MacInnes, "Clerics, Fishermen, Farmers and Workers: The Antigonish Movement and Identity in Eastern Nova Scotia, 1928–1939" (Ph.D. dissertation, McMaster University, 1978), p. 140.
2. J. J. Tompkins, *Knowledge for the People: A Call to St. Francis Xavier's College* (privately printed, 1921), p. 5.
3. Ibid., p. 26.
4. William S. Learned and Kenneth C. M. Sills, *Education in the Maritime Provinces of Canada* (New York: Carnegie Foundation for the Advancement of Teaching, 1922).
5. J. L. MacDougall, *History of Inverness County, Nova Scotia*, Appendix II, "A Report on the Proposed Federation of the Maritime Universities" (privately published, 1922; reprint, Mika Publishing Co., Belleville, Ontario, 1972), pp. 644–90.
6. Ibid., p. 679.
7. Ibid., pp. 680–81.
8. D. C. Harvey, "Scottish Immigration to Cape Breton," in Don MacGillivray and Brian Tennyson, eds., *Cape Breton Historical Essays* (Sydney, NS: College of Cape Breton Press, 1980), p. 31.
9. D. C. Harvey, "The Age of Faith in Nova Scotia," *Proceedings and Transactions of the Royal Society of Canada* Third Series, XL (May 1946), Section II, p. 10.
10. Ibid., p. 12.
11. Brian Tennyson, "Economic Nationalism and Confederation: A Case Study in Cape Breton," in *Cape Breton Historical Essays*, p. 55.
12. *The Maritime Provinces in Their Relation to the National Economy of*

Canada: A Statistical Study of Their Social and Economic Condition (Ottawa: Dominion Bureau of Statistics, 1948), pp. 7–8.

13. J. J. Tompkins to Morse A. Cartwright, 9 Dec. 1924. Quoted in George Boyle, *Father Tompkins of Nova Scotia* (New York: P. J. Kennedy, 1953), p. 127.
14. Minutes of the 1924 Diocesan Clergy Conference, Diocese of Antigonish.
15. Alexander K. MacLean, *Report of the Royal Commission Investigating the Fisheries of the Maritime Provinces and the Magdalen Islands* (Ottawa: King's Printer, 1928).
16. M. M. Coady, "My Story," text of an interview for CBC-TV, 8 July 1957. Transcribed by St. Francis Xavier Extension Department. Mimeo. 11 pp.
17. Ibid., p. 1.
18. United Maritime Fishermen, *The Cornerstone of the Co-op Fisheries Movement* (Moncton, NB, 1975), p. 12.
19. R. J. MacSween, "The Little University of the World," *The Universities Review*, XXV, 2 (Feb. 1953), 19.
20. Letter from M. M. Coady to R. J. MacSween, 24 Mar. 1953.
21. Extension Department, St. Francis Xavier University, "Annual report" (1932), mimeo, p. 1.
22. Extension Department, St. Francis Xavier University, "Extension Activities, 1932–1939," mimeo, p. 1.
23. Malcolm MacLellan, *Education for Social Needs* (Antigonish: St. Francis Xavier University, 1938), p. 4.
24. M. M. Coady, *The Social Significance of the Co-operative Movement* (Antigonish: Extension Department, St. Francis Xavier University, 1949), pp. 9–10.
25. J. J. Tompkins, "The Future of the Antigonish Movement," n.d. Mimeo, p. 2.
26. D. J. MacDonald, *The Philosophy of the Antigonish Movement* (Antigonish: St. Francis Xavier University, 1942), p. 12.
27. M. M. Coady "Put These Encyclicals to Work," *The Canadian Register*, 12 May 1956.
28. M. M. Coady, *Masters of Their Own Destiny* (New York: Harper and Row, 1961), p. 24.
29. M. M. Coady, *Socialism and Economic Co-operation* (Antigonish: St. Francis Xavier University, Extension Department, 1951), p. 1.
30. M. M. Coady, "Indirect Action: Role of Adult Educator," address to the American Association for Adult Education, 1950. Mimeo, p. 5.
31. MacDonald, *Philosophy of the Antigonish Movement*, p. 18.
32. J. R. MacDonald, *Christian Principles Underlying the Antigonish Movement*, address delivered to the Social Leadership Seminar, St. Francis Xavier University, Feb. 1948. Mimeo, p. 6.
33. M. M. Coady, "Spinach before Spinoza," *Extension Bulletin*, III, 6 (10 Jan. 1936), 1, 4.
34. Coady, *Masters of Their Own Destiny*, p. 141.
35. Gregory Baum, "The Relevance of the Antigonish Movement Today"

(Coady-Tompkins Seminar, Scarborough, Ont.: Foreign Mission Society, 1978), mimeo, p. 15.

36. Francis J. Mifflen, "The Antigonish Movement: A Revitalization Movement in Eastern Nova Scotia," Ph.D. dissertation, Boston College, 1974, p. 96.
37. Alexander F. Laidlaw, *A Factual Outline of the Antigonish Movement* (Antigonish: Extension Department, St. Francis Xavier, rev. ed., 1955), pp. 14–15.
38. *Times Library Supplement,* 1 Aug. 1936.
39. David MacDonald, "How St. F.X. Saved the Maritimes," *Maclean's,* 1 June 1953, p. 25.
40. Margaret Daly, *The Revolution Game* (Toronto: New Press, 1970), p. 44.
41. Coady, *Masters of Their Own Destiny,* p. 164.
42. Extension Department, St. Francis Xavier University, *Annual Report 1949–50,* p. 4.
43. Summary of a resolution adopted by the Board of Governors, 3 Dec. 1959.
44. A. Queinnac, "The Coady International Training Programs" (Antigonish: Coady International Institute, 1974), mimeo, p. 11.
45. A. A. MacDonald and F. J. Mifflen, "Some Considerations on the Transfer of a Social Movement: A Case Study of the Antigonish Movement (Antigonish: Coady International Institute, 1980), mimeo, pp. 13–14.
46. S. S. Ramphal, "Human Development: Defining the Problem," *Human Development through Social Change* (Antigonish: Formac Publishing Co., 1979), p. 38.
47. Coady, *Masters of Their Own Destiny,* p. 135.
48. A. A. MacDonald, "Report on the Role of the Coady Institute," in *Human Development through Social Change,* p. 159.
49. Harold T. Shea, "Helping to Build a World of Peace," *Halifax Chronicle-Herald,* 28 Nov. 1981.
50. Alexander F. Laidlaw, ed., *The Man from Margaree: Writings and-Speeches of M. M. Coady* (Toronto: McClelland and Stewart, 1971), p. 19.
51. Mifflen, "The Antigonish Movement," p. 127.
52. Alexander F. Laidlaw, "The Coady-Tompkins Experience," address given at the Coady-Tompkins Seminar, Scarborough, Ont., Mar. 1978, mimeo, p. 14.
53. Alexander F. Laidlaw, "The Antigonish Movement: A Retrospective Analysis" (Antigonish: Coady International Institute, 1978), mimeo, p. 6.
54. *Co-operatives Canada '81* (Ottawa: Co-operative Union of Canada, 1981), p. 18.
55. Bruce Thordarson, "The Public Image of Co-operatives," *Atlantic Co-operator* (July/Aug. 1981), 4.
56. Baum, *Relevance of the Antigonish Movement Today,* p. 7.
57. René Hurtubise and Donald C. Rowat, *The University, Society and Government: The Report of the Commission on The Relations between Universities and Governments* (Ottawa: University of Ottawa Press, 1970), pp. 44, 204.

58. *The Antigonish Movement, Yesterday and Today* (Antigonish: Extension Department, St. Francis Xavier University, 1976), p. 40.

CHAPTER 5: KURT HAHN

1. W. A. C. Stewart, *The Educational Innovators*, Vol. II, *Progressive Schools: 1881–1967* (London: Macmillan, 1968), p. 69.
2. Kurt Hahn, *Aims and Obstacles: An Address Broadcast on BBC, October 22, 1950* (privately printed).
3. For this section I am indebted largely to Golo Mann, "Kurt Hahn's Political Activities," in Hermann Röhrs and H. Tunstall-Behrens, eds., *Kurt Hahn* (London: Routledge and Kegan Paul, 1970).
4. Neville Butler, "A Glimpse of Kurt Hahn and Family in Berlin: August 1914–September 1915," in D. A. Byatt, *Kurt Hahn: An Appreciation of His Life and Work* (Gordonstoun School, 1976), p. 74.
5. Kurt Hahn, "A German Public School," *The Listener*, XI (17 Jan. 1934), 90.
6. Kurt Hahn, *Address to the London Committee of the Friends of Gordonstoun, November 21, 1957* (privately printed), p. 6.
7. Stewart, *Educational Innovators*, p. 187.
8. T. C. Worsley, *Flannelled Fool: A Slice of Life in the Thirties* (London: Alan Ross, 1967), pp. 182–83.
9. British Salem Schools Ltd., *Report on the Progress of Gordonstoun School, 1934–35* (privately printed).
10. Ibid., p. 16.
11. British Salem Schools Ltd., *Report on the Progress of Gordonstoun School, 1934–35* (privately printed), p. 17.
12. Kurt Hahn, *Ten Years of Gordonstoun: An Account and an Appeal, 1944* (privately printed).
13. Ibid., p. 23.
14. Ibid., p. 3.
15. Kurt Hahn, "Origins of the Outward Bound Trust," in David James, ed., *Outward Bound* (London: Routledge and Kegan Paul, 1957), p. 3.
16. Ibid., p. 4.
17. Kurt Hahn, "Outward Bound," in G. Z. F. Bereday and J. A. Lauwerys, eds., *Yearbook of Education, 1957* (London: Institute of Education, University of London), p. 440.
18. J. M. Hogan, *Impelled into Experiences: The Story of the Outward Bound Schools* (London: Educational Productions, 1968), p. 24.
19. Hahn, in *Yearbook of Education, 1957*, p. 448.
20. Kurt Hahn, *The Loyalties by Which We Live* (privately printed, 1949), pp. 6–7.
21. Joshua Miner, "Outward Bound in America," in Byatt, *Kurt Hahn: An Appreciation*, p. 51.
22. Joshua Miner, "Outward Bound in the U.S.A.," in Röhrs and Tunstall-Behrens, *Kurt Hahn*, p. 207.

23. Adam Arnold-Brown, *Unfolding Character: The Impact of Gordonstoun* (London: Routledge and Kegan Paul, 1962), p. 166.
24. Tom Price, *Outdoor Education: Some Reflections on Outward Bound's Contributions* (London: Outward Bound Trust, n.d.), p. 4.
25. Wendy Johnson, "Personal and Tutorial Skills," in Byatt, *Report of Training Conference, January 1980* (London: Outward Bound Trust), p. 21.
26. John Hunt, *Life Is Meeting* (London: Hodder and Stoughton, 1978), p. 130.
27. John Hunt, "The Duke of Edinburgh's Award Scheme," in Byatt, *Kurt Hahn: An Appreciation,* p. 56.
28. *The Duke of Edinburgh's Award Annual Report, 1980* (London), p. 1.
29. Peter Carpenter, "The Duke of Edinburgh's Award Scheme," in Röhrs and Tunstall-Behrens, *Kurt Hahn,* p. 104.
30. Kurt Hahn, "The Atlantic Colleges," *Time and Tide,* XXXIX (8 Feb. 1958), 154–55.
31. Ibid.
32. Desmond Hoare, "The Atlantic College—St. Donat's Castle," in Byatt, *Kurt Hahn: An Appreciation,* p. 59.
33. "Bid for St. Donat's Castle," *The Times Educational Supplement,* 29 July 1960, p. 152.
34. Ibid., p. 141.
35. George Schuster, *Private Work and Public Causes* (Cowbridge, Glamorgan: D. Brown and Sons, 1979), p. 171.
36. Hoare, "The Atlantic College," p. 60.
37. *Student Prospectus 1980,* United World College of the Atlantic (Llantwit Major, Glamorgan), p. 4.
38. Athur Marwick, *Clifford Allen: The Open Conspirator* (London: Oliver and Boyd, 1964), p. 143.
39. Kurt Hahn, "Origins of the Outward Bound Trust," in James, *Outward Bound,* p. 14.
40. Kurt Hahn, *First Lecture in New Portion of Liverpool Cathedral, Dec. 22, 1940* (privately printed).
41. Kurt Hahn, *Hopes and Fears* (privately printed, 1954), p. 3.
42. Godfrey Burchardt, "Personal Recollections," in Byatt, *Kurt Hahn: An Appreciation,* pp. 84–85.
43. Henry Brereton, *Gordonstoun: Ancient Estate and Modern School* (London: W. R. Chambers, 1968), p. 129.

CHAPTER 6: HAROLD WILSON, JENNIE LEE, PETER VENABLES, AND WALTER PERRY

1. Walter Perry, *Open University: A Personal Account by the First Vice-Chancellor,* introduction by Harold Wilson (Milton Keynes: Open University Press, 1976), p. xi.
2. Asa Briggs, *The Golden Age of Wireless,* Vol. II, *The History of Broadcasting in the United Kingdom* (London: Oxford University Press, 1961), p. 188.

3. *New Ventures in Broadcasting: A Study in Adult Education* (London: British Broadcasting Corporation, 1928), pp. xi–xii.
4. *Daily Mirror,* 10 Jan. 1927.
5. Michael Young, "Is Your Child in the Unlucky Generation?," *Where?,* X (Autumn, 1962), 3–5.
6. Ministry of Education, *A Report to the Central Advisory Council for Education (England),* Vol. I, *15–18* (London: H.M. Stationery Office, 1959), p. 316.
7. Prime Minister's Committee on Higher Education, *Higher Education,* Appendix I, Cmnd. 2154 (London: H.M. Stationery Office, 1963), p. 44.
8. Ibid., p. 51.
9. Ibid., p. 8.
10. Ibid., p. 262.
11. Report of the Study Group on Higher Education, *The Years of Crisis* (London: Labour Party, 1963), p. 34.
12. "Teleducation: University of the Air," *Economist,* CCVIII (14 Sept. 1963), 891–92.
13. *Times Educational Supplement,* 13 Sept. 1963.
14. Brian MacArthur, "An Interim History of the Open University," in Jeremy Tunstall, ed., *The Open University Opens* (London: Routledge and Kegan Paul, 1974), p. 5.
15. Harold Wilson, "Labour and the Scientific Revolution," *Report of the 62nd Annual Conference* (London: Labour Party, 1963), p. 136.
16. Ibid.
17. Harold Wilson, "In the Beginning," *The First Ten Years,* special edition of *Sesame,* the Open University newspaper (1979) p. 3.
18. MacArthur, "An Interim History of the Open University," p. 5.
19. Ibid., p. 6.
20. Jennie Lee, "A Warrior Can Fight Just So Many Battles," *Observer,* 10 Dec. 1972, pp. 44–56.
21. Jennie Lee, *My Life with Nye* (London: Jonathan Cape, 1980), p. 41.
22. Ibid., p. 50.
23. Fenner Brockway, *Inside the Left* (London: George Allen and Unwin, 1942).
24. Pat Williams, "The Queen of Arts," *Sunday Times Magazine,* 19 Nov. 1967, p. 52.
25. Ibid.
26. John Scupham, "The Original Brief for the Open University," *Teaching at a Distance,* II (Feb. 1975), 67.
27. Department of Education and Science, *A University of the Air,* Cmnd. 2922 (London: H.M. Stationery Office, 1966).
28. Ibid., p. 3.
29. *The Times,* 26 Feb. 1966.
30. *The Times Educational Supplement,* 4 Mar. 1966, p. 655.
31. *The Times,* 7 Mar. 1966.
32. Magnus Turnstile, "B. Air," *New Statesman,* LXXI, 11 Mar. 1966, p. 326.

33. MacArthur, "An Interim History of the Open University," pp. 9–10.
34. Department of Education and Science, *The Open University: Report of the Planning Committee* (Venables Report) (London: H.M. Stationery Office, 1969).
35. Ibid., para. 119, p. 32.
36. Phoebe Hall et al., *Change, Choice and Conflict in Social Policy* (London: Heinemann, 1975), p. 275.
37. *House of Commons Debates*, Vol. 776, Col. 941.
38. Conservative Party Central Office, "Statement by Sir Edward Boyle," 27 Jan. 1969.
39. Venables Report, p. 2.
40. Ibid., p. 6.
41. Ibid., p. 13.
42. *The Times*, 22 July 1969, p. 9.
43. Perry, *Open University*, p. 55.
44. John Ferguson, *The Open University from Within* (London: University of London Press, 1975), pp. 31–32.
45. Naomi McIntosh, "Degrees of Achievement: How the Open University Obtained Its First in Perseverance" (Milton Keynes: Open University, 1979), mimeo, pp. 3–4.
46. Naomi McIntosh et al., *A Degree of Difference: A Study of the First Year's Intake of Students to the Open University* (University of Surrey: Society for Research into Higher Education, 1976), p. 27; and *Analysis of Applications for Undergraduate Study with the Open University in 1981* (Milton Keynes: Open University Information Services, 1980), p. 9.
47. For samples, see Tyrrell Burgess, "The Open University," *New Society*, XX (Apr. 1972), 176–78, and Ray Woolfe, "Social Equality as an Open University Objective," *Teaching at a Distance*, I (Nov. 1974), 41–44.
48. Woolfe, "Social Equality as an Open University Objective."
49. Open University, *Countdown to the OU*, videotape, n.d.
50. Ibid.
51. Perry, *Open University*, p. 24.
52. Naomi McIntosh, "The OU Student," in Tunstall, *The Open University Opens*, p. 59.
53. Ferguson, *Open University from Within*, p. 106.
54. Perry, *Open University*, p. 91.
55. Michael Drake, "The Curse of the Course Team," *Teaching at a Distance*, No. 16 (Winter, 1979), p. 50.
56. Andrew Blowers, "Carry on Course Teams," *Teaching at a Distance*, No. 16 (Winter, 1979), p. 55.
57. Open University Information Services, *An Introduction to the Open University* (Milton Keynes, 1978), p. 8.
58. Mairead Owen, "Fifth Column," *Sesame*, Mar./Apr. 1981, p. 11.
59. Ferguson, *Open University from Within*, p. 95.
60. Harold Wilson, "In the Beginning," *Sesame*, special edition (1979), p. 7.
61. MacArthur, "An Interim History of the Open University," p. 16.

62. Walter Perry, "Much Done, Much Won, Much Still to Come," *Outlook: A Magazine for Open University Graduates*, No. 6 (Autumn 1980), p. 4.

CHAPTER 7: THE DYNAMICS OF INNOVATION

1. John Wilson, *Introduction to Social Movements* (New York: Basic Books, 1973), p. 332.
2. Dankwart Rustow, *Philosophers and Kings: Studies in Leadership* (New York: George Braziller, 1970), p. 27.
3. Max Weber, *The Theory of Social and Economic Organization*, trans. A. M. Henderson and Talcott Parsons (Glencoe, IL: Free Press, 1947), pp. 358–59.

BIBLIOGRAPHY

CHAPTER 1: N. F. S. GRUNDTVIG

Albeck, Gustav, and William Michelsen. Papers presented at an international seminar, "A Century after Grundtvig," in *Grundtvig Studier* (Yearbook of the Grundtvig Society). Copenhagen, 1973. Vol IX. P. 214.

Allen, Edgar Leonard. *Bishop Grundtvig: Prophet of the North.* London: James Clarke, n.d.

Begtrup, Holger, Hans Lund, and Peter Manniche. *The Folk High Schools of Denmark and the Development of a Farming Community.* London: Oxford University Press, 1949.

Bresdorf, Elias. "Grundtvig in Cambridge," *Norseman,* X (1952), 2–12.

Campbell, Olive. *The Danish Folk High School: Its Influence in the Life of Denmark and the North.* New York: Macmillan, 1928.

Davies, Georgina Noëlle. *Education for Life: A Danish Pioneer.* London: Williams and Norgate, 1931.

Denmark, Central Co-operative Committee. *The Co-operative Movement in Denmark.* Copenhagen, 1966.

———, Ministry of Foreign Affairs. *Denmark: An Official Handbook.* Copenhagen, 1974.

Dixon, Cyril W. *Education in Denmark.* London: George Harrap, 1958.

———. *Society, Schools and Progress in Scandinavia.* Oxford: Pergamon Press, 1965.

Elvander, Nils. *Scandinavian Social Democracy.* Uppsala University, 1979.

Engberg, Paul. *The Northern Folk High School.* Odense: Northern Folk High School Council, 1955. 32 pp.

Forster, Frances M. *School for Life: A Study of the People's Colleges of Sweden.* London: Faber & Faber, 1974.

Georg, Anders, ed. *Denmark Today: The World of the Danes.* Copenhagen: Ministry of Foreign Affairs, 1979.

King, Edmund J. "Denmark," in his *Other Schools and Ours.* 4th ed. London: Holt Rinehart & Winston, 1973.

Knudsen, Johannes. *Selected Writings of N. F. S. Grundtvig.* Philadelphia: Fortress Press, 1976.

Koch, Hal. "The Education of Youth," in J. A. Lauwerys, ed., *Scandinavian Democracy.* Copenhagen: Danish Institute, 1958.

Kulich, Jindra. "N. F. S. Grundtvig and the Folk High Schools," *Dalhousie Review,* XLIII (1963), 67–75.

Lauwerys, J. A. *Scandinavian Democracy.* Copenhagen: Danish Institute, 1958.

Lindhardt, Paul Georg. *Grundtvig: An Introduction.* London: Society for the Preservation of Christian Knowledge, 1951.

Livingston, Richard. *On Education.* Cambridge: University Press, 1954.

Lund, Ragnar. *Scandinavian Adult Education.* Copenhagen: Danish Institute, 1952.

Manniche, Peter. *Rural Development and Changing Countries of the World.* London: Pergamon Press, 1969.

Marcussen, Ernst. *Social Welfare in Denmark.* 4th ed. Trans. Geoffrey French. Copenhagen: Danish Institute, 1980.

Novrup, Johannes. "Adult Education in Denmark," in Ragnar Lund, ed. *Scandinavian Adult Education.* Copenhagen: Danish Institute, 1952.

Pedersen, Clemens. *The Danish Co-operative Movement.* Trans. Patricia Hansen. Copenhagen: Danish Institute, 1977.

Ravnholt, Henning. *The Danish Co-operative Movement.* Copenhagen: Danish Institute, 1947.

Rørdam, Thomas. *The Danish Folk High Schools.* 2nd ed. Trans. Alison Borch-Johansen. Copenhagen: Danish Institute, 1980.

Skrubbeltrang, Fridlev. *The Danish Folk High Schools.* Trans. Reginald Spink. Copenhagen: Danish Institute, 1947. 85 pp.

Thaning, Kaj. *N. F. S. Grundtvig.* Trans. David Hohnen. Copenhagen: Danish Institute, 1972.

Thomsen, Ole B. *Some Aspects of Education in Denmark.* Toronto: University of Toronto Press, 1967.

Thrane, Eigil. *Education and Culture in Denmark.* Copenhagen: G. E. C. Gad, 1958.

CHAPTER 2: HORACE MANN

Carlton, Frank Tracy. *Economic Influences upon Educational Progress in the United States, 1820–1850.* Original edition published by University of Wisconsin, 1908. Reprint, New York: Teachers College Press, Columbia University, 1965.

Combe, George. *The Constitution of Mann.* Hartford, CT, 1844.

Cremin, Lawrence A. *The American Common School.* New York: Bureau of Publications, Teachers College Press, Columbia University, 1951.

———. ed. *The Republic and the School: Horace Mann and the Education of Free Men.* New York: Bureau of Publications, Teachers College Press, Columbia University, 1957.

Culver, Raymond B. *Horace Mann and Religion in the Massachusetts Public Schools.* New Haven: Yale University Press, 1929; reprint, Arno Press and The New York Times, 1969.

Curti, Merle. *The Social Ideas of American Educators.* New York: Charles Scribner's, 1935.

Davies, John D. *Phrenology: Fad and Science.* New Haven: Yale University Press, 1955.

Downs, Robert B. *Horace Mann: Champion of Public Schools.* New York: Twayne Publishers, 1974.

Harris, William Torrey. *Horace Mann.* Syracuse, NY, 1896.

Hinsdale, B. A. *Horace Mann and the Common School Revival.* Toronto: Copp Clark, 1902.

Jones, Howard Mumford. "Horace Mann's Crusade," in Daniel Aaron, ed., *America in Crisis.* New York: Alfred Knopf, 1952. Pp. 91–107.

Kaestle, Carl F., and Maris A. Vinovskis. *Education and Social Change in Nineteenth Century Massachusetts.* Cambridge, Eng.: Cambridge University Press, 1980.

Katz, Michael B. *The Irony of Early School Reform: Educational Innovation in Mid-Nineteenth Century Massachusetts.* Cambridge, MA: Harvard University Press, 1968.

McCluskey, Neil G. *Public Schools and Moral Education: The Influence of Horace Mann, William Torrey Harris and John Dewey.* New York: Columbia University Press, 1958.

Mann, Horace. *Lectures and Annual Reports on Education.* Cambridge, MA, 1867.

———. *Lectures on Education.* Boston, 1855. Reprint, New York: Arno Press and The New York Times, 1969.

———. *Slavery: Letters and Speeches.* Boston, 1851. Reprint, New York: Arno Press and The New York Times, 1969.

———. ed. *Common School Journal* Vols. 1–10, Nov. 1838–Dec. 1848. American Periodical Series, University Microfilms Library Services, Ann Arbor, MI, 1967.

Mann, Mary Peabody. *Life of Horace Mann.* Boston, 1888. Reprint, Miami: Mnemosyne Publishing Co., 1969.

Messerli, Jonathan. *Horace Mann: A Biography.* New York: Alfred Knopf, 1972.

Tharp, Louise Hall. *Until Victory: Horace Mann and Mary Peabody.* Boston: Little, Brown, 1953.

Tyack, David. *The One Best System: A History of American Urban Education.* Cambridge, MA: Harvard University Press, 1974.

Welter, Rush. *Popular Education and Democratic Thought in America.* New York: Columbia University Press, 1962.

Williams, E. I. F. *Horace Mann: Educational Statesman.* New York: Macmillan, 1937.

CHAPTER 3: MARY LYON

Baker, Liva. *I'm Radcliffe! Fly Me!: The Seven Sisters and the Failure of Women's Education.* New York: Macmillan, 1976.

Boas, Louise Schutz. *Women's Education Begins: The Rise of the Women's Colleges.* New York: Arno Press, 1971. Reprint of the 1935 edition.

Bradford, Gamaliel. "Mary Lyon," *Atlantic Monthly,* CXXII (December 1918), 785–96.

Burstyn, Joan N. "Catharine Beecher and the Education of American Women," *New England Quarterly,* 47 (1974), 386–403.

Cole, Arthur C. *A Hundred Years of Mount Holyoke College.* New Haven: Yale University Press, 1940.

Craven, Avery. "The Education of Women in the United States: The Northern Phase," in *Trends in Liberal Arts Education for Women.* New Orleans: Newcomb College, Tulane University, 1974. Pp. 7–19.

Cross, Barbara, ed. *The Educated Woman in America: Selected Writings of Catharine Beecher, Margaret Fuller, and M. Carey Thomas.* New York: Teachers College Press, Columbia University, 1965.

Fisk, Fidelia. *Recollections of Mary Lyon.* Boston: American Tract Society, 1866.

Frankfurt, Roberta. *Collegiate Women: Domesticity and Career in Turn-of-the-Century America.* New York: New York University Press, 1977.

Gilcrest, Beth Bradford. *The Life of Mary Lyon.* Boston: Houghton Mifflin, 1910.

Goodsell, Willystine, ed. *Pioneers of Women's Education in the United States.* New York: AMS Press, 1970. Reprint of 1931 edition.

Green, Elizabeth Alden. *Mary Lyon and Mount Holyoke: Opening the Gates.* Hanover, NH: University Press of New England, 1979.

Hitchcock, Edward. *The Power of Christian Benevolence Illustrated in the Life and Labors of Mary Lyon.* 3rd ed., Northampton, MA: Hopkins and Bridgman, 1852.

Kendal, Elaine. *Peculiar Institutions: An Informal History of the Seven Sisters Colleges.* New York: Putnam, 1976.

Langeman, Ellen. *A Generation of Women: Education in the Lives of Progressive Reformers.* Cambridge, MA: Harvard University Press, 1979.

Lansing, Marion, ed. *Mary Lyon through Her Letters.* Boston: Books Inc., 1937.

Lyon, Mary. ("Circular to Ladies"), n.d. (probably 1836), n.p.

———. *Female Education: Tendencies of the Principles Embraced, and the System Adopted in the Mount Holyoke Female Seminary.* South Hadley, MA, 1839.

———. "To the Friends and Patrons of Ipswich Female Seminary," 1834, n.p.

———. *General View of the Principles and Design of the Mount Holyoke Female Seminary.* Boston, MA, 1837.

———. *The Inception of Mount Holyoke College.* Portions of letters written by Mary Lyon between 1831 and 1837. Springfield, MA, n.d.

———. *Letters and Documents.* 2 vols. Mount Holyoke College Archives.

Mount Holyoke Alumnae Association. *One Hundred Year Biographical Directory, Mount Holyoke College, South Hadley, MA, 1837–1937,* ed. Mary C. F. Higley. South Hadley, MA, 1937.

———. *Mount Holyoke Female Seminary.* Boston: Old South Association, n.d. 16 pp.

———. *Mount Holyoke Female Seminary: Preparation for Admission.* South Hadley, MA, 1840.

Mount Holyoke College. *The Seventy-Fifth Anniversary.* South Hadley, MA: 1912.

———. *The Centenary of Mount Holyoke College.* South Hadley, MA.: 1937.

Mount Holyoke Seminary. *Memorial: Twenty-Fifth Anniversary of the Mount Holyoke Female Seminary.* South Hadley, MA, 1862.

Newcomer, Mabel. *A Century of Higher Education for American Women.* New York: Harper, 1959.

Notable American Women 1607–1950: A Biographical Dictionary. 3 vols. Cambridge, MA: Harvard University Press, 1971.

Rich, Adrienne. "Towards a Woman-Centered University," in Florence Howe, ed., *Women and the Power to Change.* New York: McGraw-Hill, 1975. Pp. 15–46.

Robinson, Mabel L. *The Curriculum of the Woman's College.* Bulletin No. 6, 1918, Department of the Interior, Bureau of Education. Washington: Government Printing Office, 1918.

Rudy, Willis. "The 'Revolution' in American Higher Education, 1865–1900," *Harvard Educational Review,* XXI, 3 (1951), 155–74.

Scott, Anne Firor. "What, Then, Is the American: This New Woman?" *Journal of American History* (Dec. 1978), 679–703.

Stow, Sarah D. *History of Mount Holyoke Seminary during Its First Half Century, 1837–1887.* 2nd ed. South Hadley, MA, 1887.

Women on Campus: The Unfinished Liberation. Selections from *Change* magazine, New Rochelle, NY, 1975.

Woody, Thomas. *A History of Women's Education in the United States.* 2 vols. New York: Octagon Books, 1966. Reprint of the 1929 edition.

Woolley, Mary. "Inaugural Address," *The Mount Holyoke,* inauguration number, 1901, pp. 8–15.

CHAPTER 4: JAMES TOMPKINS AND MOSES COADY

Antigonish Way, The: Nine Addresses by Professors of St. Francis Xavier University. Toronto: Mission Press, 1955.

Baum, Gregory. *Catholics and Canadian Socialism.* Toronto: James Lorimer & Co., 1980.

Boyle George. *Father Tompkins of Nova Scotia.* New York: P. J. Kennedy, 1953.

Coady, M. M. "Catholic Action," *Canadian Messenger* (July 1951).

———. "Indirect Action: Role of Adult Educator," *Canadian Messenger* (May 1950), 626–31.

———. *Masters of Their Own Destiny.* New York: Harper and Row, 1939.

Coady, M. M. (The addresses, articles, and briefs listed below were published by the Extension Department, St. Francis Xavier University.)

———. *Program of Catholic Social Action by St. Francis Xavier University.* Antigonish, 1933.

———. *The Antigonish Way: A Series of Broadcasts over CBC.* Antigonish, 1943.

———. *The Social Significance of the Co-operative Movement.* Antigonish, 1945. Reprinted 1949.

———. *Story and Philosophy of the Antigonish Movement in the Maritime Provinces: Hints to Speakers.* Antigonish, 1947.

———. *Educating the People for Democracy.* Antigonish, 1951.

———. *Socialism and Economic Co-operation.* Antigonish, 1951.

———. *Would You Be a Leader?* Antigonish, 1951.

———. *The Secret of Leadership in Adult Education.* Antigonish, 1953.

———. *My Story.* Antigonish, 1957.

Co-operatives Canada '81. Ottawa: Co-operative Union of Canada, 1981.

Corbett, E. A. "Dr. James Tompkins" and "Dr. M. M. Coady," in Harriet Rouillard, ed., *Pioneers in Adult Education.* Toronto: Thomas Nelson and Sons, n.d.

Extension Department, St. Francis Xavier University. *Annual Reports.*

Johnson, Harry G. *The Antigonish Movement: A Lecture to Students of Acadia University.* Antigonish: Extension Department, St. Francis Xavier University, 1944.

Laidlaw, Alexander F. *The Antigonish Movement: A Retrospective Analysis.* Address prepared for the 50th anniversary observance of the founding of the Extension Department, July 1978.

———. "The Antigonish Movement in Retrospect." Antigonish: Extension Department, St. Francis Xavier University, 1967. Mimeo.

———. *The Campus and the Community: The Global Impact of the Antigonish Movement.* Montreal: Harvest House, 1961.

———. *The Co-operative Alternative.* Saskatoon: Co-operative College of Canada, 1980.

———. *A Factual Outline of the Antigonish Movement.* Antigonish: Extension Department, St. Francis Xavier University, 1955.

———, ed. *The Man from Margaree: Writings and Speeches of M. M. Coady.* Toronto: McClelland and Stewart, 1971.

———, and Gregory Baum. "Report of Coady-Tompkins Seminar," Scarborough Foreign Mission Society, 1978. Mimeo.

MacDonald, A. A. "The Coady International Institute: Its Development, Program and Rationale." Antigonish: Coady International Institute, 1980. Mimeo.

———. "Extension Philosophy and Operation: The Antigonish Concept."

Antigonish: Extension Department, St. Francis Xavier University, 1969. Mimeo.

———, and F. J. Mifflen. "Some Considerations on the Transfer of a Social Movement: A Case Study of the Antigonish Movement." Antigonish: Coady International Institute, 1980. Mimeo.

MacDonald, D. J. *The Philosophy of the Antigonish Movement.* Antigonish: St. Francis Xavier University, 1942.

MacDonald, J. R. "Christian Principles Underlying the Antigonish Movement." Address delivered to Social Leadership Seminar, St. Francis Xavier University, 1948. Mimeo.

Macgillivray, Don, and Brian Tennyson, eds. *Cape Breton Historical Essays.* Sydney: College of Cape Breton Press, 1980.

MacInnes, Daniel W. "Clerics, Fishermen, Farmers and Workers: The Antigonish Movement and Identity in Eastern Nova Scotia, 1928–1939." Ph.D. dissertation, McMaster University, 1978.

MacKinnon, M. J. *A Program for Eastern Canada.* Extension Department, St. Francis Xavier University, 1937.

MacLellan, M. A. "Education for Social Needs." Address given at the Rural and Industrial Conference, 1938. Mimeo.

Mifflen, Francis J. "The Antigonish Movement. A Revitalization Movement in Eastern Nova Scotia." Ph.D. dissertation, Boston College, 1974.

Milner, Philip, ed. *Human Development through Social Change: Proceedings of St. Francis Xavier University's International Symposium.* Antigonish: Formac Publishing Co., 1979.

Tompkins, J. J. "Address to American Catholic Rural Life Conference." Rochester, New York, 1938. Mimeo.

———. "The Future of the Antigonish Movement." n.d. Mimeo.

———. *Knowledge for the People: A Call to St. Francis Xavier's College.* Privately printed, 1921.

Topshee, George E. "Philosophy, Programs, Accomplishments." Antigonish: Extension Department, St. Francis Xavier Universtiy, 1978. Mimeo.

CHAPTER 5: KURT HAHN

Annual Reports of Duke of Edinburgh's Award and Outward Bound Trust.

Arnold-Brown, Adam. *Unfolding Character: The Impact of Gordonstoun.* London: Routledge and Kegan Paul, 1962. Appendix 2 lists Kurt Hahn's speeches and other papers written between 1934 and 1960.

Blackburn, Robert. "The Atlantic College," in Richard E. Gross, ed., *British Secondary Education.* London: Oxford University Press, 1965.

Brereton, Henry. *Gordonstoun: Ancient Estate and Modern School.* London: W. & R. Chambers, 1968.

Byatt, D. A., ed. *Kurt Hahn: An Appreciation of His Life and Work.* Gordonstoun School, 1976.

Carpenter, Peter, ed. *Challenge: The Duke of Edinburgh's Award in Action.* London: Ward Lock, 1966.

———. "Kurt Hahn and the Salem Tradition," *New Era*, LV (Sept./Oct. 1974), 187–91.

Day, John H. "The Basic Conception of Education of Kurt Hahn and Its Translation into Practice." M.Ed. thesis, University of Queensland, 1980.

Fletcher, Basil. *The Challenge of Outward Bound*. London: Heinemann, 1971.

Hardcastle, Martin. *Report on Outward Bound*. London: Outward Bound Trust, 1969.

Hogan, James M. *Impelled into Experiences: The Story of the Outward Bound Schools*. London: Educational Publications, 1968.

Hunt, John. *Life Is Meeting*. London: Hodder and Stoughton, 1978.

James, David, ed. *Outward Bound*. London: Routledge and Kegan Paul, 1957.

Mann, Golo. "Kurt Hahn, Educator," *Encounter*, XLVI (March 1976), 84–86.

Prince Max of Baden. *Memoirs*. Trans. W. M. Calder and C. W. H. Sutton. London: Constable, 1928.

Roberts, Kenneth, Graham White, and Howard Parker. *The Character-Training Industry*. Newton Abbot: David and Charles, 1974.

Röhrs, Hermann and H. Tunstall-Behrens, eds. *Kurt Hahn*. London: Routledge and Kegan Paul, 1970. This work contains an excellent bibliography.

Schuster, George. *Private Work and Public Causes: A Personal Record, 1881–1978*. Cowbridge, Glamorgan: D. Brown and Sons, 1979.

Skidelsky, Robert. *English Progressive Schools*. Harmondsworth, Middlesex: Penguin Books, 1969.

———. "A Respectful Farewell," *Encounter*, XLVI (March 1976), 86–90.

Stewart, W. A. C. *Progressive Schools: 1881–1967*. Vol. II of *The Educational Innovators*. London: Macmillan, 1968.

Taylor, Alison. *For and Against: A Discussion of the Duke of Edinburgh's Award Scheme*. London: Pergamon Press, 1967.

Wainwright, David. *Youth in Action: The Duke of Edinburgh's Award Scheme 1956–1966*. London: Hutchinson, 1966.

Wilson, Renate. *Inside Outward Bound*. Charlotte, NC: East Woods Press, 1981.

CHAPTER 6: HAROLD WILSON, JENNIE LEE, PETER VENABLES, AND WALTER PERRY

British Broadcasting Corporation. *New Ventures in Broadcasting: A Study in Adult Education*. London: BBC, 1928.

Brosan, George, et al. *Patterns and Policies in Higher Education*. Harmondsworth, Middlesex: Penguin, 1971.

Department of Education and Science. *Adult Education: A Plan for Development*. London: H.M.S.O., 1973 (Russell Report).

———. *Education: A Framework for Expansion*. Cmnd. 5174. London: H.M.S.O., 1974.

Ferguson, John. *The Open University from Within*. London: University of London Press, 1975.

Foot, Michael. *Aneurin Bevan*. 2 vols. London: MacGibbon & Kee, 1962, 1974.

Glatter, Ronald, and Colin Morgan. "Universal Access to Post Secondary Education." Milton Keynes: Open University, Faculty of Educational Studies, 1978. Mimeo.

Hall, Phoebe, et al. *Change, Choice and Conflict in Social Policy.* London: Heinemann, 1975.

Lee, Jennie. *My Life with Nye.* London: Jonathan Cape, 1980.

———. *This Great Journey: A Volume of Autobiography 1904–45.* London: MacGibbon & Kee, 1963.

———. "A Warrior Can Fight Just So Many Battles," *Observer Magazine,* 10 Dec. 1972, 44–56.

McIntosh, Naomi E. "The Place of Summer Schools in the Open University," *Teaching at a Distance,* III (1975), 48–60.

McIntosh, Naomi E., Judith Calder, and Betty Swift. *A Degree of Difference: A Study of the First Year's Intake of Students to the Open University.* Guildford, Surrey: University of Surrey, 1976.

Ministry of Education. A Report to the Central Advisory Council for Education (England). *15–18*: Vol. I. London: H.M.S.O., 1959. (Crowther Report).

———. *A University of the Air.* Cmnd. 2922. London: H.M.S.O., 1966.

Noel, G. E. *Harold Wilson and the New Britain.* London: Victor Gollancz, 1964.

Open University. *Analysis of Applications for Undergraduate Study in 1981.* Milton Keynes: Open University Information Services, 1980.

———. *Report of the Committee on Continuing Education.* Milton Keynes: Open University, 1976.

Perry, Walter. *Higher Education for Adults: Where More Means Better.* Cambridge: University Press, the Rede Lecture, 1974.

———. "Lessons for Distance Education Derived from the Experience of the Open University." *Teaching at a Distance,* No. 4 (Nov. 1975).

———. "Much Done, Much Won, Much Still to Come," *Outlook: A Magazine for Open University Graduates,* No. 6 (Autumn, 1980), 4.

———. *Open University: A Personal Account by the First Vice-Chancellor.* Milton Keynes: Open University Press, 1976.

Perry, Walter. "The Open University," *Proceedings of the Royal Institution of Great Britain,* XLIV, No. 203 (Apr. 1971), 95–112.

———. *Annual Report of the Vice-Chancellor,* 1969–70 and later years. Milton Keynes: Open University Information Services.

Peterson, A. D. G. "A University of the Air?" *Universities Quarterly,* XVIII, No. 2 (Mar. 1964), 180–86.

Planning Committee of the Open University. *The Open University: Report of the Planning Committee to the Secretary of State for Education and Science.* London: H.M.S.O., 1969. (Venables Report).

Prime Minister's Committee on Higher Education. *Higher Education.* Cmnd. 2154. London: H.M.S.O., 1963. (Robbins Report).

Scupham, John. "The Original Brief for the Open University," *Teaching at a Distance,* No. 2 (Feb. 1975), 66–68.

Smith, Dudley, *Wilson: A Critical Biography.* London: Robert Hale, 1964.

Tunstall, Jeremy, ed. *The Open University Opens.* London: Routledge & Kegan Paul, 1974.

Wilson, Harold. *The Labour Government 1964–70.* London: Weidenfeld & Nicolson, 1971.

CHAPTER 7: THE DYNAMICS OF INNOVATION

Clark, Samuel D., et al. *Prophecy and Protest: Social Movements in Twentieth Century Canada.* Toronto: Gage, 1975.

Gibb, C. A., ed. *Leadership: Selected Readings.* Harmondsworth, Middlesex: Penguin Books, 1969.

MacDonald, A. A. "The Development of the Coady Institute," in *Human Development through Social Change.* Antigonish, Nova Scotia, Formac Publishing Co., 1979. Pp. 157–63.

McLaughlin, Barry, ed., *Studies in Social Movements.* New York: Free Press, 1969.

Rustow, Dankwart A. *Philosophers and Kings: Studies in Leadership.* New York: George Braziller, 1970.

Weber, Max. *The Theory of Social and Economic Organization.* Trans. A. M. Henderson and Talcott Parsons. Glencoe, IL: Free Press, 1973.

Wilson, John. *Introduction to Social Movements.* New York: Basic Books, 1973.